Lost Classroom, Lost Community

Lost Classroom, Lost Community

Catholic Schools' Importance in Urban America

MARGARET F. BRINIG
AND NICOLE STELLE GARNETT

The University of Chicago Press

CHICAGO AND LONDON

MARGARET F. BRINIG is the Fritz Duda Family Professor of Law at the University of Notre Dame and a fellow of Notre Dame's Institute for Educational Initiatives. She is the author of several books, including, most recently, *From Contract to Covenant: Beyond the Law and Economics of the Family*.

NICOLE STELLE GARNETT is professor of law at the University of Notre Dame and a fellow of Notre Dame's Institute for Educational Initiatives. She writes extensively about both urban policy and education policy and is the author of *Ordering the City: Land Use, Policing, and the Restoration of Urban America*.

The University of Chicago Press, Chicago 60637
The University of Chicago Press, Ltd., London
© 2014 by The University of Chicago
All rights reserved. Published 2014.
Printed in the United States of America

23 22 21 20 19 18 17 16 15 14   1 2 3 4 5

ISBN-13: 978-0-226-12200-7 (cloth)
ISBN-13: 978-0-226-12214-4 (e-book)
DOI: 10.7208/chicago/9780226122144.001.0001

Library of Congress Cataloging-in-Publication Data

Brinig, Margaret F., author.
  Lost classroom, lost community : Catholic schools' importance in urban America / Margaret F. Brinig and Nicole Stelle Garnett.
    pages ; cm
  Includes index.
  ISBN 978-0-226-12200-7 (cloth : alkaline paper) — ISBN 978-0-226-12214-4 (e-book) 1. Catholic schools—Social aspects—United States.   2. School closings—Social aspects—United States.   3. Community schools—United States.   4. Charter schools—United States.   5. School choice—United States.   I. Garnett, Nicole Stelle, author.   II. Title.
  LC501.B585 2014
  371.071'2—dc23

                                                            2013036575

♾ This paper meets the requirements of ANSI/NISO Z39.48-1992 (Permanence of Paper).

Contents

WITHDRAWN

For our Catholic school kids, present, past, and future
Mary, Wendy, Katie, Jill, and Brian
— mfb
Maggie, Tommy, Libby, and Johnny
— nsg

Preface

In January 2012, the new archbishop of Philadelphia, Charles Chaput, announced that he would close forty-eight Catholic schools at the end of the school year. The closures, of forty-four elementary schools and four high schools, displaced nearly 24,000 students. While heartbreaking for the students, parents, and teachers at the schools targeted for closure, Chaput's decision came as no surprise to those familiar with the current landscape of Catholic education. Nationwide, over 1,600 Catholic schools have closed in the past two decades, displacing more than 300,000 students. The Archdiocese of Philadelphia itself had closed thirty schools in the previous five years, as enrollments plummeted (falling by 35 percent since 2001) and costs skyrocketed.[1] The 68,000 students enrolled in the archdiocesan schools in 2011 were the same number that the Archdiocese served in 1911. At its peak in 1961, enrollment in Catholic schools in the Archdiocese of Philadelphia exceeded 250,000 children.[2] Total enrollment in U.S. Catholic schools fell from 5.2 million to 2.1 million during the same period.[3]

The reasons for the Catholic school crisis are complex, and, since we discuss them in detail later, we do not rehearse them. For now it suffices to simply observe that the persistence of the economic and demographic realities underlying Catholic school closures suggests that the trend likely will continue or even accelerate in future years, at least absent a shift in education policy favoring a dramatic expansion in school choice. This book represents our effort, the first of its kind, to measure the effects of the school closure trend on the urban neighborhoods where Catholic schools have served for decades, and in some cases, for over a century.

The seeds of the book were planted at a 2008 gathering of community and education policy leaders in Washington, D.C. The primary purpose of the meeting was to consider the educational implications of the disappearance of Catholic schools from inner-city neighborhoods. One of us attended this event and was intrigued to hear, during breaks in the formal program, snippets of discussions about different, noneducational effects of Catholic school closures—namely, their consequences for urban neighborhoods: "When the school closes, the neighborhood just isn't the same." "The whole neighborhood suffers when a school disappears."

These comments led the two of us to ask whether we might find a way to test empirically whether Catholic school closures hurt urban neighborhoods. This book emerges from our effort to do so. Our answer is sobering. We conclude that Catholic elementary schools are important generators of social capital in urban neighborhoods. Relying primarily on data from Chicago, we find that Catholic school closures precede elevated levels of crime and disorder and suppressed levels of social cohesion. Conversely, we link the presence of an open Catholic school in a neighborhood with lower levels of serious crime. Moreover, our preliminary analysis suggests that, at least in Chicago, charter schools—which are filling both the physical and educational void left by Catholic school closures—do not yet appear to generate the same positive community benefits. We replicate these results for urban Philadelphia, although, interestingly, we are unable to do so for the greater Los Angeles area. Our bottom-line conclusion is that the community leaders gathered in Washington were right. Catholic schools matter to urban neighborhoods not only as educational institutions—although, to be sure, they matter a great deal educationally—but also as community institutions. Our results therefore lend support for school-choice devices, such as tuition vouchers or tax credits, which might help stem the tide of Catholic school closures by making them accessible to low-income urban children.

This book would have been impossible without the assistance and insights of a number of people. At the beginning of our research, Sister Mary Paul McCaughey, the superintendent of Catholic schools in the Archdiocese of Chicago, generously agreed to meet with us to help us better understand the landscape of Chicago's Catholic schools. Sister McCaughey not only provided data on Catholic schools in the city (closed and open) but, along with her staff, spent several hours discussing the Archdiocese's school closure process with us. These discussions led us to identify variables (specifically the parish leadership characteristics employed in chapters 3, 4, and 6) that enable us to show causation by decoupling school closure decisions from neighborhood demographics. Kevin Baxter, superintendent of elementary schools in the Archdiocese of Los Angeles, provided similar assistance for Los Angeles schools.

We received invaluable statistical support from Michael Clark and Melissa Petrelius of the Center for Social Science Research at the University of Notre Dame. We are also grateful to Christopher Maxwell and Cedrick Heraux of the Inter-University Consortium for Political and Social Research at the University of Michigan for matching our Chicago school data to the Project on Human Development in Chicago Neighborhoods (PHDCN) neighborhood clusters, thus enabling us to use the rich PHDCN data sets to analyze the effects of closed and open Catholic schools on perceived disorder and social cohesion. A number of individuals provided or helped us to obtain access to critical data, including Michael Pollard of the Rand Corporation, Timothy McOsker of Mayer, Brown in Los Angeles, and Lieutenant Michael Dwyer of the Philadelphia Police Department. Our dean at Notre Dame Law School, Nell Jessup Newton, generously supported our efforts financially and granted us a research leave to complete this manuscript. Notre Dame Law School research librarian Patti Ogden carefully reconstructed this history of Catholic schools in Philadelphia, and Notre Dame Law School students Kathleen Brogan, Alison Curran, Brian Mahoney, Jason O'Brien, Thomas Porrazzo, Peter Reed, Carolyn Sweeney, and Michael Wilde provided excellent research assistance. We are also indebted to Sharon Loftus, Nicole Bourbon, and Leslie Berg for superb administrative support.

We are grateful to our editors at the University of Chicago Press for their helpful advice and suggestions about the book at all of its stages. We also appreciate the suggestions and insights of several anonymous reviewers and of a number of friends and colleagues, especially David Campbell, Lou DelFra, C.S.C., Bob Ellickson, Bill Evans, Jeffery Fagan, Lee Anne Fennell, William Fischel, Rick Garnett, Michael Heise, Rick Hills, Daniel Kelly, Mark McKenna, Tracey Meares, Christian Smith, and Timothy Scully, C.S.C. The book was strengthened immensely by input we received during presentations at the annual meetings of the American Law and Economics Association, the Midwest Law and Economics Association, and the Canadian Law and Economics Association; at the 2010 Conference on Empirical Legal Studies; and at the University of Chicago Law School, the Notre Dame Law School, the Notre Dame Institute for Educational Initiatives, the Notre Dame Center for Research on Educational Opportunity, and the Notre Dame Department of Economics.

This book includes, in substantially revised and reordered forms, portions of several previously published articles. These include "Catholic Schools and Broken Windows," *Journal of Empirical Legal Studies* 9, no.2 (2012): 347; "Catholic Schools, Charter Schools, and Urban Neighborhoods," *University of Chicago Law Review* 79, no. 1 (2012): 31; "Catholic Schools, Urban Neighborhoods, and Education Reform," *Notre Dame Law Review* 85, no. 3 (2010): 887; and "Affordable Private Education and the Middle Class City," *University of Chicago Law Review* 77, no. 1 (2010): 202. All are reprinted with permission.

Introduction

Our Lady of Hungary Catholic School in South Bend, Indiana, in many ways typifies the Catholic schools we study here. The school opened its doors in 1927, about a decade after the local diocese established Our Lady of Hungary Parish to minister to the city's ethnic Hungarian population. Throughout the first half of the twentieth century, the school's mission was to educate working-class, white, Catholic children—a mission that was primarily carried out by religious sisters from the Daughters of Divine Charity, an Austrian religious order. By 1950, enrollment at Our Lady of Hungary had grown to over seven hundred students in kindergarten through eighth grade, and the school was staffed by fourteen nuns and four lay teachers.

Like most urban Catholic schools, Our Lady of Hungary underwent a profound transformation in the second half of the twentieth century. While Mass is no longer offered in Hungarian at Our Lady of Hungary Catholic Church, it is offered in Spanish. The students are no longer taught by nuns—the Daughters of Charity withdrew from the school in 1993—but exclusively by lay teachers. The student body is no longer predominantly white and working class but rather racially diverse and poor. During the 2011–12 school year, over 50 percent of the students at Our Lady of Hungary were racial minorities and over 60 percent qualified for the federal free and reduced-price lunch program. The former convent is now a Title I tutoring site. By 2009, enrollment at Our Lady of Hungary had dropped to fewer than ninety students, and the local bishop announced plans to close the school. In response, the school and parish communities rallied to raise enough money to scrape by for another year. But the writing appeared to

1

be on the wall. Eventually, in one year or five, it seemed inevitable that Our Lady of Hungary would meet the same fate as thousands of other urban Catholic schools, including the hundreds of schools we study here. It would vanish from the urban landscape forever.

Everything changed for Our Lady of Hungary in 2011, when Indiana adopted an ambitious new school-choice program that enables low- and moderate-income students to transfer from public to private schools. In the first year of the program, over 4,500 Indiana students took advantage of the opportunity and exited public schools for private ones; in the second, nearly 9,500 students were attending private schools through the program. About half of these students enrolled in Catholic schools, many of them in fragile urban schools, including Our Lady of Hungary. In 2011, sixty-seven students enrolled in Our Lady of Hungary through the program. In August 2012, 108 of the 210 students enrolled in the school were receiving publicly funded scholarships. Most of these students were Latino, and all of them were poor. Our Lady of Hungary's hallways are bustling again, and its teachers and administrators are struggling with the real, but happier, problem of adjusting to a massive influx of new students and financial resources. Versions of this story are repeating themselves hundreds of times across the State of Indiana. As a pastor of another struggling Catholic school remarked to one of us in an email, "[T]he voucher law has quite literally saved our school. It was like manna from heaven."

This book presents new evidence relevant to the question of whether—and why—it matters if a school like Our Lady of Hungary closes its doors. The seeming inevitability of urban Catholic school closures gives rise to the temptation for policy makers and Catholic leaders alike to discount the consequences of their disappearance. It is easy enough to conclude that urban Catholic schools simply do not make sense anymore. They have, after all, long outlived their original purpose—to provide a religion-infused education for working-class ethnic Catholics, most of whom migrated to the suburbs four or five decades ago. The Catholic school financial model—which depended upon the generosity of parishioners in pews that are now empty and the free labor of nuns who are now retired—cannot be sustained, and Catholic leaders frequently appear unwilling or unable to develop new, sustainable, models to replace it. Meanwhile, charter schools have exploded onto the educational scene and are replacing Catholic schools as the dominant alternative to public schools in urban communities. Catholic school enrollments are dwindling for a host of reasons, including competition from charter schools, the rising cost of tuition, and the fact that most Catholics, including the vast majority of the Latino Catholics who might fill the empty seats in urban Catholic schools, currently send their children to public (and increasingly charter) schools.

Our bottom-line conclusion is that it *does* matter if the Our Lady of Hungarys disappear from our cities. Catholic school closures have serious consequences for cities, especially for the residents of urban neighborhoods. We believe that education policy makers in both the Church and the state should come to terms with these consequences—to pause to imagine cities without Catholic schools, and to ask themselves whether something should be done to reverse the current course, lest we lose them to civil society forever. As we review in the final chapter of this book, many of the consequences of Catholic school closures are already evident from previous scholarship. Importantly, Catholic school closures likely will have profound educational consequences for poor urban and minority students, who— the available evidence suggests—tend to benefit the most from Catholic education in terms of educational outcomes. Catholic school closures may also affect urban development prospects by reducing the number of high-quality educational options available to would-be urban dwellers of modest means.

This book, however, identifies and explores consequences of urban Catholic schools' disappearance that are not directly related to their educational mission. In contrast to previous scholarship on Catholic schools, which focused on Catholic schools as educational institutions—that is, on their effects on students, teachers, and parents—we seek here to understand Catholic schools as community institutions—that is, to focus on their effects in the neighborhoods where they are (or were) situated. The research that we present here is the first of its kind. We empirically demonstrate that Catholic school closures have negative effects on urban neighborhood health. Relying primarily on survey data collected for the Project on Human Development in Chicago Neighborhoods (PHDCN) and on crime data provided, at the police-beat level, by the Chicago Police Department, we find that Catholic schools in Chicago appear to bolster neighborhood social cohesion and suppress neighborhood disorder and crime—findings that, we hypothesize, stem from the fact that these schools generate neighborhood-level social capital. As a result, it is reasonable to assume that neighborhoods that lose their Catholic schools also lose the benefits of the social capital they generate: they become less socially cohesive, more disorderly, and, ultimately, more dangerous. Moreover, our initial analysis suggests that the charter schools that are filling the educational void left by Catholic school closures may not be, at least not yet, replicating Catholic schools' benefits as community institutions.

The book proceeds as follows: chapters 1 and 2 chronicle, respectively, the precipitous decline in the number of Catholic schools and the remarkable rise in charter schools over the past few decades. We review these developments in order to situate our empirical findings in historical context, as well as to provide a sense of the magnitude of this shift in the urban educational landscape. These trends also are important to our empirical analysis, since understanding the reasons for Catholic school closures is a critical component of demonstrating a causal link between their disappearance and the neighborhood effects that we seek to measure.

Chapters 3–5 report our core empirical findings. In these chapters, we employ a variety of statistical methods, as appropriate for the available data, to measure the effects of Catholic schools on Chicago neighborhoods. In chapter 3, we rely upon survey data collected by researchers from the PHDCN in 1994 and 1995 to measure the effects of Catholic school closures on social cohesion and disorder in Chicago neighborhoods. In order to do so, we employ a two-step regression analysis, a method that enables us both to control for demographic variables that might predict neighborhood distress and to consider instrumental variables, that is, variables predicting school closures that are entirely unrelated to neighborhood demographics—irregularities in the leadership structure of the parish running a Catholic school. This method addresses the endogeneity problem endemic to our project—specifically, that variations in crime, disorder, and social cohesion might both cause and be caused by Catholic school closures. We find, controlling for neighborhood demographics, that Catholic school closures between 1984 and 1994 predicted a substantial between-neighborhood variance in the levels of social cohesion and disorder in 1995: neighborhoods experiencing a Catholic school closure during the relevant time period were more disorderly, and less socially cohesive, than those that did not.

Admittedly, the data employed in chapter 3 has limitations, the most significant of which is the fact that the PHDCN survey data was collected only once, preventing us from measuring the effects of Catholic school closures over time, as we do with respect to crime in chapter 4. Unfortunately, this limitation is unavoidable. The PHDCN did collect longitudinal survey data, but the response rates were too low, and the neighborhoods with Catholic schools too few, to produce reliable statistical results. We cannot retrospectively change the rich data collection of the PHCDN project to obtain longitudinal survey data from more neighborhoods where there were or are Catholic schools. A different longitudinal survey of Chicago neighbor-hoods, perhaps one that asked specific questions about Catholic schools as community institutions, is theoretically possible but would postpone the completion of this project by years. While we certainly would welcome such an undertaking by other scholars, we do not think it critical to our project here, especially since our analysis of crime data is longitudinal.[1]

In chapter 4, we turn to the question of whether, and how, Catholic school closures affect the rate of serious crime in urban neighborhoods. Specifically, we seek to measure the effects of Catholic school closures on serious crime. Since many scholars have postulated that both neighborhood social cohesion and disorder affect crime rates, our findings in chapter 3 led us to suspect that police beats where Catholic schools have closed might have higher rates of serious crime. In order to test this hypothesis, we con-duct a boosted logistic regression of the effects of Catholic school closures between 1990 and 1996 on the total rate of serious crime in Chicago police beats between 1999 and 2005. We find, as we suspected, that school clo-sures appear to affect serious crime rates over time. Specifically, although crime declined significantly during the period that we study across the City of Chicago (in keeping with national trends), Catholic school closures af-fected the rate of decline in a police beat. That is, crime declined more slowly in police beats experiencing a Catholic school closure than in those beats that did not. Our analysis, as above, incorporates variables predicting school closures unrelated to neighborhood demographics (the instrumental variables), thereby enabling us to demonstrate a causal link between school closures and crime rates. These findings are perhaps more significant than those reported in chapter 3, both because crime data, while not perfect, is less subjective than survey data and because they demonstrate that the ef-fects of Catholic school closures persist over time.

Chapter 5 expands our analysis to compare the effects of open Catholic and charter schools on rates of serious crime in police beats between 1999 and 2005. We incorporate charter schools into our analysis for a number of interrelated reasons. As a matter of education policy, charter schools are not only filling the educational void left when Catholic schools close but also are influencing Catholic school closure trends by offering a free alternative to struggling urban public schools. Moreover, charter schools frequently are offered as a less controversial alternative to school-choice programs that enable students to spend public funds to attend private schools. Expanding school choice to include private schools likely would stem the tide of Catho-lic school closures by increasing their affordability. Our analysis of charter schools also enables us to partially answer whether other kinds of educational institutions might also have positive effects on urban neighborhoods, as well as to measure the neighborhood effects of *open* Catholic schools. Our findings are tentative but concerning. They are tentative because, unlike our analyses in chapters 3 and 4 for Catholic schools, we cannot disentangle the location of charter schools from neighborhood demographics. While we control for demographic variables, we cannot definitively say that these factors do not influence charter schools' decisions about where to locate (and, in some cases, we know that they do). We therefore are unable to demonstrate causation. They are concerning because we find that, while open Catholic schools are associated with lower rates of crime throughout the study period, charter schools appear to have no statistically significant effect on crime rates. Thus, we are left wondering what the transition from Catholic to charter schools as schools of choice will mean for long-term urban neighborhood health.

We replicate, in a truncated fashion, our analysis for the City of Philadelphia and for Los Angeles County in chapter 6. Interestingly, we find that Catholic schools appear to have similarly positive effects in Philadelphia but not in Los Angeles. We explore several possible reasons for this curious divergence, ranging from immigration to land use patterns, which suggest fruitful areas of further research.

The remainder of the book shifts from the empirical to the normative. In chapter 7, we explore a number of possible explanations for Catholic schools' positive neighborhood effects. Ultimately, we conclude that Catholic schools benefit urban neighborhoods because they generate social capital. In making this claim, we stand on the broad shoulders of previous scholars, especially James Coleman, who argued that the social capital generated in a Catholic school community explained the positive academic effects of Catholic education on poor and minority students, and Anthony Bryk, who tested and refined Coleman's hypothesis. These and other scholars' work on social capital and Catholic schools, however, has focused on the effects of social capital inside Catholic schools—that is, on the role that social capital plays in making Catholic schools particularly successful educational institutions. Our focus on Catholic schools as community institutions enables us to make a distinct and novel claim—that is, that Catholic schools generate social capital beyond classroom walls in the communities that surround them. We admittedly do not know why this is so. Perhaps because of its positive effects on members of the school community, the social capital generated inside Catholic school classrooms and documented by previous scholars may produce positive externalities outside of them. Or perhaps Catholic schools generate neighborhood-level social capital for reasons not directly related to their educational missions.

In chapter 8, we turn to what our findings mean for questions of education policy—and specifically the hot-button issue of school choice. Evidence of the effects of Catholic school closures on urban neighborhoods, in our view, supports the case for expanding school choice beyond public and charter schools to enable students to spend public resources in private schools. Voucher or tax credits programs might well help stem the tide of Catholic school closures by making Catholic schools more affordable to students of modest means. While evidence that Catholic school closures harm urban neighborhoods certainly will not be enough to convince every reader of the wisdom of expanding school choice, we hope to convince even school-choice skeptics that the evidence we present here should be a part of the heated education reform debates that currently rage in legislatures throughout the country.

Catholic schools, of course, do not primarily function as community institutions. They are, first and foremost, educational institutions. In order to fully understand the effects of their gradual disappearance from the urban landscape, therefore, it is important to consider their educational benefits along with the community benefits that we explore in this book. Thus, the book's final chapter closes by discussing the consequences for cities and their residents of losing Catholic schools as educational institutions. These consequences are not unrelated to those that are the focus of our research on Catholic schools as community institutions. When Catholic schools disappear, their loss is felt most acutely in the same poor urban neighborhoods likely to suffer most from a decline in social capital, neighborhoods where they have long represented a high-quality alternative to struggling urban public schools. Moreover, since a lack of high-quality, affordable educational options represents a primary impediment to urban development prospects, Catholic schools' departure from cities also may indirectly trigger a decline in social capital by discouraging families of modest means from living and raising families in urban neighborhoods.

After years of decline, urban centers experienced an unexpected renaissance beginning in the early 1990s. Today, however, cities' long-term prospects are beginning to appear bleak once again. New development in urban centers has slowed to a trickle, and many projects completed during the real estate boom sit empty. Many American cities labor under the burden of crushing debt; increasing numbers are declaring bankruptcy. Faced with unprecedented fiscal woes, urban leaders have been forced to scale back city services, including police services, leading to concerns about rising crime. Despite the hopeful picture of urban health painted by demographic and crime statistics in the early years of the current century, the current fiscal crisis has unearthed deep structural impediments to long-term urban renewal that require pervasive, multifaceted reform. We are certainly not prepared to make the case that Catholic schools can save our cities. Our claim here is a far more modest one—that urban neighborhoods are better off with their Catholic schools than without them. Catholic schools have, for decades, helped generate the social capital needed to make urban neighborhoods work, and their disappearance raises serious concerns. Thus, in good times and perhaps especially in bad, policy makers and Catholic Church leaders alike should confront these concerns and, when possible, take steps to preserve the schools for their students and their neighborhoods.

We emphasize that, in making this claim, we do not intend to suggest that only Catholic schools serve as effective neighborhood institutions. We focus on Catholic schools for a number of reasons, which we detail throughout the book. Most importantly, the phenomena that we study here—the disappearance of Catholic schools and their gradual replacement by charter schools as the dominant alternative to struggling urban public schools— represent seismic shifts in the urban educational landscape. The effects of these shifts on the communities that have long been anchored by Catholic schools are not well understood, and we seek to begin to fill that important gap here. Catholic schools, however, are not the only educational institutions that are disappearing from urban neighborhoods. In 2013, the Chicago Public Schools and the School Commission of Philadelphia announced plans to shutter, respectively, 50 buildings and 23 schools (the equivalent of 10 percent of each district's total). These announcements were in keeping with trends in public education, where urban school districts struggling with enrollment and budget deficits are increasingly making the difficult decision to close or consolidate schools. Debates about public school closures are characterized by the same claims about neighborhood effects that piqued our interest in Catholic school closure effects. In conducting our research for this book, we were struck by how little is understood about how schools of any type function as community institutions, and we hope that this book will prompt other scholars to engage the questions we confront in other educational sectors.

CHAPTER ONE

The Vanishing Urban Catholic School

Before turning to our empirical findings and their legal policy implications, we provide a brief snapshot of the schools that we study in this chapter and the next. This chapter situates the urban Catholic schools that we study in historical perspective, with a particular focus on the experience of Catholic schools in two of the cities that we study here—Chicago and Philadelphia. (In chapter 6, we briefly discuss the much later development of the Catholic school system in the third city, Los Angeles.) We provide this abbreviated historical overview in order to explain what urban Catholic schools are (and were), to shed light on the reasons why they are closing, and to begin to understand why they may be important social anchors in urban neighborhoods. In chapter 2, we provide a similar overview of charter schools.

A WORLD SET APART

For Roman Catholics living in northern and midwestern cities prior to the Second Vatican Council,[1] parishes were more than church buildings. They were the building blocks of community life. In canon law, the term "parish" refers not simply to a particular church but rather to social and religious communities bound to a particular church. As John McGreevy has observed, these communities were all important to parish members: "Catholics used the parish to map out—both physically and culturally—space within all of the northern cities."[2] Most parishes were (and technically still are) territorial. That is, they have geographic boundaries and are spiritually responsible for all Catholics residing within those boundaries. A smaller number of "personal parishes" are charged by Church authorities with ministering to a distinct group, frequently a non-English-speaking ethnic group (in which case they are usually called "national" parishes). Until the second half of the twentieth century, territorial parish churches (which tended until the second half of the twentieth century to be de facto Irish American and, in some cities, Italian American) were ideally placed so as to guarantee that a church was within walking distance of every home in the city. Other national parishes frequently were located within the boundaries of territorial parishes. For example, in Chicago's Back of the Yards neighborhood, which gained international notoriety in Upton Sinclair's 1920 classic, *The Jungle*, there were eleven Catholic churches in the space of little more than one square mile—two territorial/Irish parishes, two Polish, one Lithuanian, one Italian, two German, one Slovak, one Croatian, and one Bohemian.[3] Until relatively recently, Catholics were obligated to attend their territorial parish, unless dispensed to attend another church.[4]

Parish life was, in McGreevy's words, "disciplined and local"—"each parish was a small planet, whirling through its orbit, oblivious to the rest of the ecclesiastical solar system."[5] Parishes were massive operations: Almost all included a church, a parochial school (and often a convent to house the nuns who taught in the school), and dozens of formal social organizations. Parishioners were expected to attend Mass each week, to send their children to the parish school, and to contribute socially and financially to parish life. Priests encouraged—even commanded—parishioners to purchase homes within the parish boundaries, reasoning that homeownership would promote stability and intensify commitment to, and rootedness in, the parish community. An obituary of a Philadelphia pastor read, for example, "the priest advised his parishioners, almost entirely of the working class, to strive sacrificially to buy their homes as their greatest step toward security." There is significant evidence that the strategy worked. Homeownership rates among Catholics, including poor immigrants, were remarkably high. The presence of an ethnic parish in a neighborhood tended to lead to the creation of geographic ethnic enclaves that further reinforced the connection between religious life and community.[6] But territorial parishes commanded intense loyalty as well. Identity with a parish was so complete that, in many cities, most Catholics (and some non-Catholics) would respond to the question "Where are you from?" with their parish name rather than their street address or the name of their neighborhood.[7] As one Chicago resident observed, "There was no reason to stretch out to any other place . . . because you had that wide territory of your own people."[8]

THE RISE OF THE PAROCHIAL SCHOOL SYSTEM

The importance of the parish school within this insular and intensely Catholic world can hardly be overstated. Beginning in the mid-nineteenth century, fueled by Irish immigration, Catholic populations in northern cities grew exponentially. For example, when the Diocese of Philadelphia was carved out of the Archdiocese of Baltimore in 1808, it encompassed the states of Pennsylvania and Delaware, as well as the western and southern portions of New Jersey. The new diocese included about 30,000 Catholics, served by eleven priests.[9] The city of Philadelphia proper was home to 10,000 Catholics (out of a total population of 47,486) and four Catholic churches.[10] This was an unusually high Catholic density by American standards at the time, generated in large part because many Catholics were drawn to Pennsylvania's practice of religious toleration. This number also represented a remarkable increase over the approximately 1,000 Catholic citizens present in Philadelphia in 1750.[11] By 1851, the number of Catholics in the City of Philadelphia had grown to 170,000, served by ninety-three priests.[12]

This period of rapid expansion for the Catholic Church in the United States also corresponded to the rise of the fledgling public, or "common," school system. At least initially, many American Catholics welcomed, and participated in, efforts to develop public schools. Until the second half of the nineteenth century, very few Catholic schools existed in the United States, and most that did tended to educate either the very rich or the very poor. For example, the Ursuline Sisters had operated a school for upper-class Protestant and Unitarian families in Boston since their arrival in 1818.[13] (In 1834, a nativist mob burned the convent and school.[14]) Religious orders also operated poorhouses and orphanages in major cities throughout the United States. During the early years of the nineteenth century, American bishops had, on several occasions, issued letters exhorting the faithful to establish more schools. But they did not assign anyone in particular the responsibility for carrying out the task, and, as a result, progress on the development of Catholic schools in the nineteenth century proceeded in fits and starts.[15]

Catholics accordingly welcomed free schools for their children and assumed, perhaps naively, that their religious beliefs would be accommodated. Indeed, in the nineteenth century, efforts to cooperate in the formation of quasi-Catholic public schools were undertaken in a number of cities. Catholics lost patience with this strategy, however, when it became apparent that a Protestant ethos dominated—pervasively and intentionally—the fledgling public schools. Early common school leaders, including Horace Mann, who is widely regarded as the father of American public schools, endorsed the view that "nonsectarian" Protestant religious instruction ought to be a cornerstone of the common school curriculum. Most early school reformers, including Mann, also held a deep suspicion of Catholicism. Mann, in fact, once observed that the sight of Catholics worshipping moved him to concern about the "baneful influence of the Catholic religion on the human mind."[16] Mann's views were, for the time, relatively moderate; he at one point nodded approvingly to the formation of Catholic common schools in his native Lowell, Massachusetts.[17] Protestant clergymen dominated the common school movement. In fact, all but one of the first eleven state superintendents of public education was a Protestant minister. Some of these leaders were virulently anti-Catholic. For example, in 1835, the General Presbyterian Assemblies commissioned Reverend Robert J. Breckenridge—who enjoys the title "Father of public education in Kentucky"—to study "the Prevalence of Popery in the West."[18] In his final report, Breckenridge denounced the Pope as the "Anti-Christ, a man of sin and son of Pestilence" and "an apostate from God," who was corrupted by "profane exorcisms, idolatrous incantations, and unauthorized additions, mutilations and ceremonies."[19]

Many early conflicts between Catholics and Protestants were sparked by the pervasive inclusion of mandatory Protestant devotional exercises in early public school curricula. A particularly sensational example occurred in Boston in 1859, when a public school principal was charged with assault for beating a student who refused to recite the Ten Commandments from the Protestant King James Bible. The student, Thomas Whall, was a Catholic—like three-quarters of the students in the school—and informed his teacher that his father had forbidden him to read from the Protestant Bible. Whall's pastor, Father Bernardine Wiget, had also ordered him and several hundred other boys in the Saint Mary's parish Sunday school, not to recite Protestant prayers in school. Wiget told the boys that doing so would be heresy and threatened to read the names of any boys who disobeyed him from the pulpit. A week after Whall first refused to read the required passage, the assistant principal announced that she would "whip him until he yields." Whall withstood thirty minutes until, with his hands beaten to shreds by with a rattan cane, he relented. The mayor of Boston subsequently ordered the expulsion of all students who refused to conform to the school curriculum, including the recitation of the Protestant Bible. Over the next several weeks, hundreds of Catholic schoolchildren were expelled when, on orders from the local bishop, they attempted to read the Ten Commandments from the Catholic Bible.[20]

When the assault case reached the Boston police court, the defendant's attorney argued that the real criminals were Whall and Wiget, complaining, "Who is this priest who comes here from a foreign land to instruct us in our laws? . . . [T]he real objection is to the Bible itself, for, while that is read daily in our schools, America can never be Catholic." Following a trial, the judge—who was a member of the nativist Know-Nothing Party—ruled that the school official had not committed a criminal act but had instead correctly reprimanded an insubordinate child for refusing to comply with the mandatory curricular requirements of the Boston public schools.[21] Whall's refusal to recite the Protestant version of the Ten Commandments threatened, in his view, the "granite foundation on which our republican form of government rests."[22]

Catholic parents seeking recourse in civil courts met a similarly cold response. For example, in 1854, the Maine Supreme Court rejected a claim that a Catholic student's expulsion from a public school for refusing to read from the King James Bible violated her religious liberty. Although the student expressed a willingness to read the Catholic Douay-Rheims Bible aloud, the court stressed the importance of a uniform public education and the need to adhere to the established curriculum. That anti-Catholic (and anti-immigrant) sentiment influenced the decision was made crystal clear in the opinion's concluding paragraph:

> Large masses of foreign population are among us, weak in the midst of our strength. Mere citizenship is of no avail, unless they imbibe the liberal spirit of our laws and institutions, unless they become citizens in fact as well as in name. In no other way can the process of assimilation be so readily and thoroughly accomplished as through the medium of the public schools. . . . It is the duty of those to whom this sacred trust is confided, to discharge it with magnanimous liberality and Christian kindness.[23]

The import of the court's words was clear. Mandatory Protestant devotions in public schools were necessary to assimilate and Americanize the Catholic immigrant masses. Such devotions exposed Catholic children to "the liberal spirit of our laws and institutions," which, the court implied, stood in sharp contrast to the Catholic Church's presumed deep suspicion of liberalism and democracy.

Elsewhere, the Catholic objection to the inclusion of the King James Bible in public school curricula provoked mob violence. The most spectacular of these incidents was the 1844 Philadelphia Bible Riots. In 1838, Pennsylvania—like many states—had enacted a law making the King James Bible a mandatory textbook in all public schools. Philadelphia Bishop Francis Kenrick, in response, repeatedly asked that schools permit Catholic children to read the Catholic version of the Bible in school and urged Catholic parents to remove their children from public schools that insisted on using the King James Bible. In 1843, the Philadelphia Board of School Commissioners passed a resolution allowing children to opt out of religious exercises upon the request of their parents and further permitting them to read any version of the Bible that they pleased, provided that it was "without note or comment."[24] Those final words prevented Catholic children from reading the heavily annotated Catholic Douay-Rheims Bible, and there was no unannotated English version of the Catholic Bible available at the time. Still, Kenrick welcomed the resolution as a compromise. Nativist Protestants did not. There ensued a flurry of anti-Catholic polemics in local papers arguing that Catholics were attempting to convert public schools into "infidel" institutions. "The Bible in the public schools" quickly became a nativist rallying cry.

On May 3, 1844, Catholics clashed with a nativist mob in the city's Kensington neighborhood. After shots were fired and a young Protestant boy was killed, a riot ensued. Over the next three days, Philadelphia was a city under siege. Entire blocks of Catholic homes were burned, as were the Saint Michael and Saint Augustine churches and schools. The city's oldest church—Saint Mary's—was fortunately spared but only because the nativist mob arriving to burn it down was dispersed by military troops. After three days, the violence subsided, although the governor was forced to dispatch troops to guard all Catholic churches for the next two weeks. Violence ensued on a smaller scale in July 1844 and culminated with nativists dragging a cannon to the door of Saint Philip Neri church. The mob dispersed only after the governor dispatched several thousand soldiers to the city. Saint Michael and Saint Augustine later secured damage verdicts against the County of Philadelphia—Saint Michael was awarded $27,090, and Saint Augustine $47,433—although historians agree that the property damage resulting from the riots likely was several million dollars. A grand jury subsequently issued a statement laying the blame for the riots at the feet of the Catholics, concluding that the riots had been caused "by the efforts of a portion of the community to exclude the Bible from our public schools."[25]

The Philadelphia Bible Riots left Bishop Kenrick convinced of the futility of compromise with public school officials and of the need to establish a comprehensive system of Catholic schools. He was not alone. Catholic efforts to secure accommodation in the public schools were almost universally unsuccessful and, more often than not, provoked a virulent anti-Catholic reaction. Moreover, the violence in Philadelphia departed in scale but not in kind from other anti-Catholic attacks. As Philip Hamburger has observed, "[I]n the 1830s, Protestants initiated the practice of burning down Catholic churches. . . . For decades afterwards, Protestant mobs sporadically indulged in open conflict, often stimulated by both settled ministers and less respectable but gifted street preachers . . . who incited Protestants to attack Catholics and torch their houses and churches."[26]

By 1852, when the Catholic bishops in the United States met for the first time as a "Plenary Council," they had grown weary of attempts to compromise on the school question, especially in the face of escalating ant-Catholic sentiment. At the council, Bishop Kenrick, who had been named the Archbishop of Baltimore in 1851, and the fiery Bishop "Dagger John" Hughes, who had clashed with school officials in New York City and had been forced to save his churches by arming priests and congregants,[27] led the charge for the formation of an independent school system large enough to educate all Catholic children. Thus, Joseph Viteritti has observed, Catholic schools began "in a spirit of protest."[28] As Bishop Hughes explained, the public school practice of putting Protestant material "in the hands of *our own* children, and that in part at our expense, was . . . unjust, unnatural, and at all events to us intolerable. Accordingly, through very great additional sacrifices, we have been obliged to provide schools . . . in which to educate our children as our conscientious duty required."[29]

In its final decrees, the First Plenary Council of Baltimore mandated that all parishes establish schools, declaring, "We exhort the bishops . . . to see that schools be established in connection with all the churches of their diocese; and, if it be necessary and circumstances permit, to provide, from the revenues of the church to which the school is attached, for the support of competent teachers.[30] In 1866, the U.S. bishops reiterated that every church should operate a school. The Third Plenary Council, which met in 1884, ordered all parish priests to establish parochial schools within two years and provided that they would be removed from their posts for failure to do so. The bishops also informed the lay faithful that they would suffer "spiritual punishment" for failing to support their pastor's efforts to erect a school, and decreed that "all Catholic parents are bound to send their children to parochial schools unless at home or in other Catholic schools, they provide sufficiently and fully for their Christian education."[31]

THE FUNDING QUESTION

Three details about the structure of the system of schools suggested by the bishops' decrees deserve particular attention. The first is the fact that the bishops exhorted priests serving as pastors to establish parochial schools —

that is, they envisioned, and indeed mandated, a highly decentralized system of schools operated by individual parishes. The second is that they vested financial responsibility for these schools with parishes and their pastors, rather than with dioceses and bishops. The third was the suggestion by the First Plenary Council of Baltimore that parishes must finance these schools only "if it becomes necessary." Each of these three elements would lead, for reasons that the bishops struggling to shepherd a fledgling immigrant church in the nineteenth century could not have anticipated, to a different school crisis facing a different set of bishops in the late twentieth and early twenty-first centuries.

For example, the bishops' directive that parishes should support parochial schools financially "if it becomes necessary" clearly reflects optimism that Catholic schools might eventually secure access to public funding. This was not an irrational pipe dream at the time. Not only was public funding of education a relative novelty but public schools were, for all practical purposes, Protestant schools. Moreover, Catholics were, in some cities, a near majority by the end of the Civil War. In the decades following the bishops' mandate, some dioceses experimented—where they could muster the political will—with establishing public Catholic schools. These schools were lodged on parish properties, and parishes exercised some control over teacher selection, but they were publicly funded with secular instructional programs. These experiments tended to be short-lived—neither popular nor conservative Catholic opinion favored the arrangement, and the schools had largely disappeared by the turn of the twentieth century.[32]

As early as 1840, Hughes had clashed with New York school officials over a different model of public funding—one that would today be called "school choice" or "vouchers." He demanded that Catholic schools be awarded a proportional, per-pupil share of public education funds for the students that they enrolled. In making his case, Hughes cited both New York City's historical practice of distributing public funds to quasi-denominational Protestant schools and the dominant Protestant character pervading the public schools. The state legislature responded in 1842 by explicitly prohibiting public funds from flowing to sectarian schools; two years later, the legislature passed additional legislation making the King James Bible mandatory reading in all public schools.[33] Neither Hughes's demands nor the government's response to them were unique. In the years following the Civil War, Catholic demands for public funding of their schools on equality grounds increased. The call for public funding, however, universally backfired—fueling new waves of nativism and conspiracy theories that Catholics were engaged in a concerted effort to destroy American democracy. In fact, Catholic demands for equality of school funding, and the nativist reaction to them, prompted an effort to amend the federal Constitution to prohibit forever the funding of parochial schools. In 1875, James G. Blaine, then Speaker of the U.S. House of Representatives, proposed an amendment to the U.S. Constitution prohibiting any public funds from flowing to "sectarian" (i.e., Catholic) schools.[34] That anti-Catholic animus fueled this effort is not disputed. Expressing support for the Blaine Amendment, President Grant referred to the "Romish Church" as a source of "superstition, ambition and ignorance" and charged that it was seeking to overthrow the American public school system.[35] His views were widely shared. In the debate over the amendment, for example, one senator quoted Pope Pius IX to prove that Americans Catholics—instigated by their "universal, ubiquitous, aggressive, ambitious, restless and untiring" Church—were seeking to destroy the common school system.[36]

While the federal Blaine Amendment narrowly failed to secure approval in Congress—passing overwhelmingly (180-7) in the House, but failing by four votes in the Senate—its defeat hardly spelled the end to efforts to enshrine the no-funding principle in American law. Congress thereafter required new states to include similar language in their state constitutions as a condition of statehood. Other states voluntarily amended their own constitutions to prohibit the public funding of sectarian schools. Eventually, thirty-seven states' constitutions would include "Baby Blaine" amendments that prohibited the funding of sectarian schools, provisions that continue to represent perhaps the most significant legal impediments to state education reforms extending public financial assistance to students attending religious schools.[37] Nor did the debate over public assistance to Catholic schools and their students end in the late nineteenth century. On the contrary, hostility to Catholic schools generally, and to the public funding of Catholic schools in particular, influenced the course of Constitutional law throughout the twentieth century and, arguably, continues in education reform debates to this day.

The failure of Catholics to secure access to public funds for their schools in the nineteenth century, however, solidified the course set by the First Plenary Council of Baltimore in 1852. Faced with a burgeoning immigrant Catholic population, the Catholic Church in the United States set about creating the largest private school system in the world entirely on its own. This system was to be built, as the bishops anticipated and commanded, one school at a time—most of them financed and operated by individual parishes dependent on the support of a largely working-class religious minority.[38]

Despite the obstacles facing the Catholic Church in the United States—including widespread religious discrimination and the crushing poverty of the immigrant Catholic masses—the parochial school system grew exponentially in the late nineteenth and early twentieth centuries. In 1853, for example, Bishop John Neumann told his father that the number of students enrolled in Philadelphia's Catholic schools had increased from five hundred to almost five thousand between 1842 and 1843; one year later, he reported to the Vatican that enrollment had increased to nine thousand.[39] (Although Neumann was canonized in 1976 in part for his commitment to the cause of building Catholic schools, these numbers sound a bit fantastic.) Nationwide, the number of parish schools in the United States had grown to 1,400 by 1875 and 2,500 by 1885.[40] By 1900, an estimated 3,500 parochial schools existed in the United States; twenty years later, the number of elementary schools had reached 6,551, enrolling over 1.7 million students. By the mid-1960s, Catholic school enrollment exceeded 5 million.[41]

During the last decades of the nineteenth century and first decades of the twentieth, a dense system of parochial schools became part of the fabric of urban neighborhoods in all major northern and midwestern cities. By the late nineteenth century, parish schools emerged as the prototype for an entirely independent educational system, and Catholic bishops began to take a particular interest, and pride, in establishing new schools and parishes. As parish membership rolls grew and Catholics migrated farther from the city centers, bishops carved new parishes from old. For example, Philadelphia archbishop Dennis Dougherty, who served from 1918 to 1951, called himself "God's Bricklayer." During his thirty-three years as Archbishop of Philadelphia, he established 112 parishes, 145 parochial schools, and four Catholic colleges and ordained over two thousand priests to serve in them.[42] Within this parochial school system, two types of parish schools emerged. A majority of parish schools were operated by territorial parishes—that is, English-speaking parishes with primarily Irish American members. These parish schools were, in some ways, modeled on geographic public schools, and Church officials were determined to be fully competitive with, if not superior to, their public counterparts. In an effort to rebut claims that Catholic schools were "un-American," parochial schools' curricula included heavy doses of patriotism along with Catholic religious formation. A sizable minority of Catholic schools, however, operated on the opposite impulse— that is, from a desire to maintain ethnic identities and language and to avoid the full "Americanization" of immigrants' children. Throughout the North and Midwest, thousands of ethnic parishes with parochial schools educating dozens of different ethnic groups were established during the late nineteenth and early twentieth centuries. The curricula in ethnic Catholic schools emphasized ethnic culture and native-language instruction as part of an effort to sustain the culture of the students' immigrant ancestors. Some immigrant groups, including notably Italian Americans, rejected this model in favor of relatively rapid assimilation into the territorial parish system (and mainstream American society). Others enthusiastically embraced it. For example, although Poles did not begin to enter the United States in large number until 1890, by 1910, there were more than 350 Polish Catholic schools in more than a dozen states.

The ethnic Catholic footprint in Chicago was particularly distinct. As a recent history of the Archdiocese observes, "no Catholic ethnic group was too small to build its own community." For example, in 1903, although there were only a few thousand Belgians scattered to the far corners of Chicago, Archbishop James Quigley, whose tenure has been described as "one long peace treaty" among ethnic groups, helped locate a Flemish-speaking priest and permitted him to organize Saint John Berchmans Parish. Saint John Berchmans school, which opened in 1907, now enrolls primarily Latino children.[43] In 2005, the Archdiocese announced that it would no longer subsidize the school, making continued operation untenable in light of outstanding debt. The parish and school subsequently launched a successful "save our school" campaign and survived, although low enrollments call its continued viability into question.

Although ethnic parish schools thrived before the First World War, they eventually faced pressure to "Americanize" from both inside and outside the Catholic Church. Two states' efforts to force the Americanization of immigrant children—Nebraska's law mandating that instruction in all schools, public and private, be conducted in English and Oregon's mandate that all children attend public schools—were invalidated in landmark U.S. Supreme Court decisions that establish the right of parents to direct the upbringing and education of their children.[44] Despite these legal victories, however, many of the intentionally ethnic elements of the curricula in ethnic parish schools disappeared by the 1920s as the result of internal reforms implemented by Catholic leaders eager to minimize the divisions among

American Catholics.[45] By the 1930s, students from all ethnic backgrounds (except, as discussed below, African Americans) were routinely accepted at Catholic schools.[46] The neighborhood ethnic footprint resulting from ethnic parishes and schools, however, remained firmly in place until the latter half of the century—as did the density of urban parishes, which, in time, would come to haunt church leaders struggling to accommodate suburbanizing Catholics while continuing to maintain a foothold in urban centers.[47] For example, when Archbishop Quigley died in 1915, if the City of Chicago had been divided into one-mile squares, fifty-five out of two hundred squares would have had more than one Catholic parish. All told, in 1916, Chicago consisted of ninety-three territorial/Irish parishes, thirty-five German parishes, thirty-four Polish parishes, and fifty-three additional parishes serving various and sundry ethnic groups. These parishes enrolled approximately 650,000 members, or about 30 percent of the city's population. Quigley's successor, Archbishop George William Mundelein, was a "confirmed Americanizer" who would never have permitted this level of balkanization, but, in the end, he and his successors were stuck with it.[48]

Establishing schools on this scale required a large supply of teachers, and, in both American and ethnic parishes, most students were taught by religious sisters—that is, nuns—who had taken vows of poverty and therefore could work for a nominal wage. In 1809, Elizabeth Ann Seton—a widow, Catholic convert, and mother of five—established the first American teaching order, known as the Sisters of Charity. Close to 1,600 women belonged to this community by 1900, most of them teaching in parish schools throughout the United States. Throughout the nineteenth century, European and Canadian religious congregations also established a presence in the United States, often in response to the explicit invitation of a bishop eager to establish new schools. At the turn of the twentieth century, there were 119 women's religious orders sending tens of thousands of nuns to teach in parochial schools.[49] When new waves of Catholic immigrants arrived from Eastern and Southern Europe in the early twentieth century, new orders of nuns arrived with them to staff ethnic parish schools. Well into the twentieth century, many of the sisters staffing Catholic schools were as poor as their immigrant pupils, and most lacked any formal training besides that provided by experienced mentor teachers on the job—indeed the poor preparation of teachers was a perennial complaint of Catholic school critics—but the exponential growth of parochial schools could not have occurred without them.[50]

During this period of exponential growth, the question of public funding of Catholic schools resurfaced in some regions—although quietly and, at least initially, without controversy. As Sarah Barringer Gordon has documented, between 1925 and 1950, pressure by state and federal officials to make public education universally available led to a reemergence of a new, more religious version of the "Catholic-public" school arrangements discussed previously. Public officials essentially created "public" schools, whole cloth, out of Catholic ones, leasing existing parochial school buildings but leaving the day-to-day operation of the schools unchanged. In these schools, the pastor of the parish remained in charge of the school, nuns continued to occupy classrooms, and, in most cases, Catholicism continued to pervade the curriculum. A survey conducted by a Catholic organization in 1948 indicated that there were at least 340 of these "Catholic-public schools" in the United States. Most of them were located either in rural areas or in midwestern cities with heavily (or, in some neighborhoods, exclusively) Catholic populations. The Supreme Court's 1947 *Everson* decision, which made clear both that the First Amendment's Establishment Clause applied to the states and that it required that public assistance to religious schools be secular in nature, signaled the death knell of this arrangement. In the years following *Everson*, Catholic school opponents launched a successful litigation campaign to eliminate this "captive schools" practice. This litigation presaged a host of Supreme Court decisions invalidating on Establishment Clause grounds a wide range of programs extending government aid to Catholic schools and their students—many of which programs were enacted in response to the first "Catholic school crisis" described below. These decisions, which reaffirmed earlier political ones demanding the private financing of Catholic schools, have been significantly eroded in recent decades, opening the constitutional door to school-choice programs that enable students to use public funds at religious schools.

RACE, SUBURBANIZATION, AND A CHANGING CHURCH

The insular urban Catholic world described above—a world that supported and relied upon parochial schools—began to unravel in the second half of the twentieth century, as Catholics became wealthier and entered the American mainstream and African Americans began to move into ethnic Catholic neighborhoods. The combined result of these trends, which was the suburbanization of urban Catholics, had devastating consequences for urban parochial schools.

During most of the twentieth century, the white residents of most northern cities sought to "contain" African Americans by preventing them—economically, legally, and even violently—from moving into white neighborhoods. Housing shortages were a perennial problem, as continued migration north increased the number of residents vying for the limited supply of residential units within the "Black Belt," and pervasive discrimination prevented exit from it. By the end of the Second World War, however, African Americans' economic situation began to improve at a time that increasing numbers of whites suburbanized, creating housing vacancies in white neighborhoods. As a result, African Americans began to seek housing in areas previously closed off to them. White residents, especially the white residents of ethnic Catholic neighborhoods, responded to the threatened "invasion" in various ways. Some organized neighborhood preservation committees that sought to use legal means—such as the enforcement of racially restrictive covenants and housing codes—to drive away new black neighbors; others turned to violence—including arson and physical assault.[51] In Chicago, it is widely accepted that Mayor Richard J. Daley, who was a Chicago Irish Catholic raised in a neighborhood that was facing integration pressures by the mid-1950s, gerrymandered the path of the Dan Ryan expressway to protect South Side Catholic neighborhoods from the city's expanding Black Belt. He also insisted on locating almost all the city's massive public housing projects in African American neighborhoods—a containment strategy with terrible consequences for the social fabric of the city.[52]

Scholars dispute the extent to which race provided the catalyst for the destabilization and decline of previously healthy urban residential enclaves like Mayor Daley's Bridgeport neighborhood. John McGreevy, Arnold Hirsch, and Thomas Sugrue provide the conventional account—that the ultimate nail in the urban coffin was postwar white flight from integration in city neighborhoods.[53] Others, including Gerald Gamm and, more recently, Robert Bruegmann, argue that postwar exiters were really the last strands of a well-frayed urban fabric.[54] Gamm argues that flight from American cities was well underway by the 1920s and that urban Catholics' attachments to their parishes and schools fostered a strong geographic rootedness that caused them to suburbanize later, and to resist racial integration more strenuously, than other white urban residents.[55] According to Gamm, the last massive wave of postwar suburbanization occurred when the urban Catholics' attachments to their neighborhoods and, importantly, parishes finally gave way.[56] Whatever the cause, most white Catholics eventually suburbanized.[57] And while race was not the only factor—or even the dominant factor—that pushed them to the suburbs, it was certainly a significant one.[58]

The demographic shifts experienced in urban neighborhoods during the second half of the twentieth century had profound implications for the Catholic Church in the United States, and for urban Catholic schools in particular. Prior to the Second World War, most African American Catholics worshipped in separate African American parishes, and their children attended African American parish schools if they attended Catholic school at all.[59] Although a handful of Catholic liberals (both white and black) condemned segregation in Catholic parishes and schools as contrary to Catholic teaching, it remained firmly entrenched until well into the twentieth century. In the postwar period, however, as African Americans began to move into white neighborhoods, pressure to accept black Catholic children in white parish schools intensified. Gradually, beginning with Cardinal Francis Spellman's decision to desegregate New York City's Catholic Schools in 1939, Catholic leaders demanded school integration. In 1958, the American bishops issued a pastoral letter condemning race discrimination. Although many individual parishes resisted the import of these directives, African American students—first Catholic and then non-Catholic—gradually began to enroll in previously all-white schools. And, as the schools changed, the parishes and neighborhoods changed along with them.[60]

Consider, for example, the story of Saint Sabina on Chicago's South Side. When founded to serve Chicago Irish Catholics in 1916, Saint Sabina was essentially a suburban parish: the parish's first Mass was celebrated in a storefront on a muddy field, and the altar had made its way by horse and wagon along unpaved roads. Soon, however, streetcar line extensions made the Auburn-Gresham community more attractive to working-class Irish residents migrating south from tougher "city" neighborhoods like Back of the Yards.[61] In 1934, the surrounding Auburn-Gresham neighborhood was home to approximately 60,000 people; about 45 percent of them attended one of the five parishes in the neighborhood. Saint Sabina had a membership of 7,000, almost exclusively Irish American or native-born Irish. That same year, the Dominican Sisters staffing Saint Sabina school taught 1,232 children.[62] In the postwar years, Auburn-Gresham, like all South Side neighborhoods, faced integration pressure. In contrast to those parishes that violently resisted integration in the postwar years, however, the leadership of Saint Sabina refused to embrace the fear that the entry of a few black families would immediately lead to the exit of all white families. The pastor of the church made a point of visiting new black neighbors and of welcoming black children into the parish school.[63]

During the 1960s, racial tensions increased, the crime rate in the community crept up, and parishioners moved away. Saint Sabina's membership aged and declined. The parish school enrollment declined as well. In 1967, the school enrolled 930 students, one hundred of them African American. Parish members began to debate whether to admit non-Catholic children to fill the empty seats and, if so, whether conversion to Catholicism should be required as a condition of admission. African American parish members, who gradually began to assume leadership roles, objected to these practices as outdated, unrealistic, and unreasonable—and they eventually won out.[64] By the end of the 1960s, the racial transformation of Auburn-Gresham in general, and Saint Sabina in particular, was nearly complete. Thanks in part to the work of Saint Sabina's priests and sisters, however, the transition at the parish had been free of violence and, by and large, racial hostility. These efforts to be welcoming paid off in the long term as well. Saint Sabina today remains a vibrant parish—perhaps the preeminent African American parish in Chicago—with a thriving school, albeit one that looks very different from the Saint Sabina of the 1950s.[65]

The parishioners who left parishes like Saint Sabina's were lost to their parishes but not their Church. On the contrary, the Catholic Church in the United States during the postwar years was a remarkable institutional success story—more vibrant and institutionally thick than ever. Suburbanizing Catholics required new parishes and schools to serve them. Thanks in large part to the Catholic baby boom, the Catholic population in the United States nearly doubled from 24 million to 42 million between 1940 and 1960, and the number of children enrolled in Catholic schools during this time doubled as well, from 2 million to 4.2 million. Thus, a new generation of "bricklayers" dominated the hierarchy during the postwar years. During the 1950s, New York's Cardinal Spellman built more than two hundred elementary schools, and, by 1960, there was one child in Catholic school for every two in public schools. Philadelphia's Cardinal O'Hara built 133 elementary schools, and Chicago's Cardinal Stritch seventy-five. Still, church leaders found it impossible to keep up with demand. Spellman expressed frustration that "in spite of the great progress made in expanding the Catholic school system in New York," a majority of Catholic children did not attend Catholic schools. Stritch complained to a colleague, "We need more classrooms, more teachers, and more money."

In 1954, a survey of twenty-eight dioceses suggested that every one of them found their schools strained beyond capacity. Moreover, as Catholic enrollments grew, the traditional model of relying almost exclusively on nuns as teachers became unsustainable, and Catholic classrooms increasingly were staffed by laypeople.[66] Many diocesan systems began to crack under the strain. In 1962, Cardinal Joseph Ritter of Saint Louis called for a halt to new school construction until his pastors could organize schools with fewer than forty-nine (!) students per classroom and a ratio of three religious to every lay teacher. Saint Louis was not an isolated case. By the early 1960s, high costs, unsafe classrooms, and a scarcity of teachers forced many dioceses to close schools.[67]

THE ROOTS OF THE SCHOOL CLOSURE CRISIS

The demographic shifts that preceded this initial crisis in Catholic education go a long way toward explaining the origins of the current school closure crisis. As Gamm observes, unlike Protestant and Jewish congregations, Catholic parishes cannot move: "Rules dictated that a geographic parish could not relinquish responsibility for its geographical area, and no church could close except on the authority of the [local bishop]."[68] Parishes depend upon their parishioners for support, and "parishioners who moved to the suburbs were lost to the parish."[69] As anticipated by the nineteenth-century American bishops, almost all Catholic elementary schools, and many high schools, were operated and funded by parishes. Parish schools were essentially tuition free for parish members,[70] thanks to the generosity of parishioners who funded them by tithing and the labor of religious sisters who staffed the schools as teachers and principals. Most parishes also were served by multiple priests, with a senior pastor having final authority in all matters of parish administration—including school administration.[71] The suburbanization of Catholics was devastating for a church that was as institutionally dense as the Catholic Church in the urban North, where it was not unusual to have several parishes, each complete with a church, rectory, convent, and school, in a single neighborhood or even on a single block. Without parishioners, the funds that traditionally financed these schools disappeared. As urban parish membership roles declined, dioceses were forced to take on more of the financial burden of operating urban parish schools at the same time that they were obligated to build new schools to serve suburbanizing Catholics.

Suburbanization, of course, was not the only cause of the school closure crisis. With Vatican II, the Catholic Church underwent a radical transformation, and the Catholic lay faithful were transformed with it. To be sure, theological evolution was not the only or even most significant reason for the increasing secularization of Catholic culture—just as race was not the only, or even most significant, reason for Catholic suburbanization. Catholics in the postwar world were able to assimilate, both economically and socially, into mainstream American culture.[72] Suburbanization, along with the educational and economic advantages that it represented and enabled, likely was both a cause of and a symptom of this assimilation. But the dramatic shift in Catholic culture that began during the 1960s had, and continues to have, profound effects on Catholic schools. Vocations to the priesthood and religious life began to decline dramatically at approximately the same time. As a result, parish schools experienced dramatic increases in labor costs just as revenues declined precipitously.[73] In 1950, 90 percent of the teachers in Catholic schools were religious sisters; today, less than 5 percent are.[74]

Moreover, in urban schools, seats formerly filled with white Catholic pupils slowly were taken by African American Protestant ones, leading some conservative voices to question the point of continuing to operate Catholic schools without Catholics. At a retail level, some pastors—many of whom now labored without the help of younger priests—began to view their schools as an unnecessary burden, especially as enrollments declined and the non-Catholic population increased. New waves of Catholic immigrants arrived from countries, especially in Latin America, without a history of Catholic education. Moreover, progressive voices in the Catholic Church began to argue that the parochial education was anachronistic, interfered with public school desegregation efforts, and propped up segregated housing patterns. These Catholic activists, including even some bishops and nuns who formerly staffed Catholic schools, asserted that the Church should prioritize social services for the poor and depend upon religious education classes for public school students to replace Catholic schools' traditional catechetical function.[75]

The first waves of Catholic school closures began—as suggested by the story of Philadelphia's Saint Augustine—in the late 1960s. Founded in 1796 by the Augustinian Friars, Saint Augustine Church is the third oldest Catholic church in Philadelphia.[76] In 1811, Saint Augustine's Academy, a boarding school for Catholic boys, was established at the church. The enterprise did not thrive—at its peak, only thirty-nine students were enrolled—and the Academy closed in 1815.[77] The second pastor at Saint Augustine helped established a school and orphanage for destitute Catholic children, Saint Joseph's Orphan Asylum, around the same time. (The latter was staffed by three of Saint Elizabeth Ann Seton's Sisters of Charity.) It is difficult to discern exactly when Saint Augustine opened an elementary school again, although the church records indicated that the basement was outfitted as a school at the time of the 1844 riots. In 1853, when the school reopened again following postriot reconstruction, *The Official Catholic Directory* for the diocese indicated that "Saint Augustine's parish had flourishing male and female schools before the incendiary destruction of 1844." One year later, *The Official Catholic Directory* reported that Saint Augustine "has two schools attended by 400 children." A separate account, however, indicates that Saint Augustine's school opened for the first time in 1853 and enrolled only two hundred students. In 1899, the Annual Report of the Parish Schools in the Archdiocese of Philadelphia indicated that there were 418 students enrolled in Saint Augustine's school.[78]

By 1940, enrollment in Saint Augustine's school had declined to 120, likely as a result of the early suburbanization of Philadelphia—that is, the migration of Catholic families to surrounding residential neighborhoods. For example, in the same year, Saint Columba school in North Philadelphia enrolled 1,400 children.[79] During the postwar years, the neighborhood surrounding Saint Augustine experienced further depopulation as a result of urban renewal and expressway construction—the church sits at the foot of the Ben Franklin Bridge and just to the north of the submerged, multilane Vine Street Expressway (I-676). In 1968, the Archdiocese of Philadelphia closed Saint Augustine's school and consolidated it with six other parish schools to form the nation's first interparochial school at nearby Old Saint Mary's parish. (Founded in 1783, Saint Mary's school also claims to be the first parochial school in the United States.) Today, Saint Mary's Interparochial School enrolls approximately 250 students of diverse racial backgrounds, and the area surrounding Saint Augustine and Saint Mary's parishes has repopulated, thanks to gentrification. The Saint Augustine's story is not an outlier. In 1968 alone, 637 Catholic elementary schools closed. Some dioceses closed nearly all of their urban schools before 1970. For example, in Detroit, 137 of the archdiocese's 360 schools had closed before 1973.[80]

Despite these obstacles, many urban schools adapted to a new role of educating poor, predominantly minority, students. Indeed, threats of early school closures frequently prompted (and indeed continues to prompt) groups of parents to rally and save them.[81] Over the past five decades, many hundreds of inner-city Catholic schools have—in our view, heroically—provided a high-quality education for the most vulnerable students. Parents, Catholic and not, cite a number of reasons for choosing these schools for their children, including a desire for systematic religious instruction, for the inculcation of "values," for a "traditional" curriculum, and for a more structured, disciplined, learning environment.[82] These schools remained open thanks to the sweat equity of pastors, administrators, teachers, and parents and financial support from dioceses and, increasingly, private philanthropy. It was these schools that were the backdrop of Andrew Greeley's and James Coleman's important studies of the effects of Catholic education on minority students. Both of these studies—and many others—demonstrate the critical role that urban Catholic schools have played in educating disadvantaged children. Numerous studies suggest, as discussed previously, that minority students in Catholic schools score higher on standardized achievement tests and are more likely to attend and graduate from college than their public school counterparts, regardless of their family's educational or financial background. Many of these schools performed miracles in the midst of urban chaos. As Nicholas Lemann observed in a 1986 *Atlantic Monthly* article, "In the . . . ghetto today, the only institutions with a record of consistently getting people out of the underclass are the parochial schools."[83]

Recognizing these benefits, and identifying inner-city Catholic schools' importance to the poor, some bishops simply committed to keeping them open no matter how desperate their financial situation. Cardinal John O'Connor, for example, refused to close any Catholic schools in the Archdiocese of New York between 1994 and his death in 2000.[84] O'Connor also repeatedly offered to absorb the lowest performing 5 percent of New York City's public school children and pledged that, in Catholic schools, they would quickly be performing at grade level.[85] Catholic schools like the ones that O'Connor offered to open to New York City's struggling students—which seemed able to perform miracles for comparatively little cost—have long taken center stage in the debates about the wisdom and efficacy of school-choice programs.[86] In New York, for example, Mayor Rudolph Giuliani publicly took Cardinal O'Connor up on his offer to educate some of the most disadvantaged students, although he was unable to use public resources to finance scholarships for the students who transferred.[87]

Both O'Connor's refusal to close additional schools in New York and his public challenge to the quality of instruction in urban public schools are emblematic of a post-1960s commitment by the Catholic Church to maintain schools in the inner city for poor minority students. For some Catholic leaders, like O'Connor, this commitment flowed from an unwavering belief that inner-city Catholic schools were an important act of social justice—a way that the Catholic Church could serve the poor effectively, by literally saving poor children from the urban public schools that were failing them. In fact, at least until the rise of charter schools in the mid-1990s, Catholic schools were, in many urban communities, among the only quality educational options available to poor families. The Catholic Church's continued support of urban Catholic schools also represented in some dioceses a sort of compromise between Catholic leaders and African American parents in the wake of the racial transformation of formerly Catholic urban neighborhoods and perhaps, at least initially, as reparation for the unseemly and racist behavior of some Catholics as that transformation occurred.

Chicago's Holy Angels school is emblematic of the Catholic Church's late twentieth-century commitment to maintaining high-performing Catholic schools in urban neighborhoods. Dedicated in 1892, Holy Angels parish served a primarily working-class, Irish American population until the postwar period. Located on the city's South Side, Holy Angels experienced desegregation pressure relatively early—that is, by the 1950s. The pastor during the period of initial racial transition was decidedly unwelcoming—one parishioner wrote Cardinal Stritch to complain that black Catholics were asked to sit in the back pews "and let the white people who built this church sit in the center." The pastor also refused to admit black Catholic children to the school, even as classrooms slowly emptied and the African American parochial school nearby was bursting at its seams. When a new pastor was installed in the mid-1950s, he gradually began to admit black students—on condition that their parents converted to Catholicism. In 1969, Cardinal Cody appointed, somewhat under duress, an African American pastor, Father George Clements, at Holy Angels. (Privately, Cody complained that Clements—an outspoken civil rights activist—was "a black priest" and "blatant, arrogant and one of little knowledge" who had "turned off completely" many clergy who were "well disposed toward the black cause.")[88] After Clements's appointment, however, Stritch went to great lengths to ensure the success of Holy Angels, granting the school generous subsidies and working to ensure that the school was staffed by religious sisters.[89]

By the early 1970s, Holy Angels was the largest African American Catholic school in the United States, with nearly 1,300 students. Since then, the school has earned national attention for its remarkable success educating students who live in one of the poorest, most segregated, and most dangerous communities in the United States. For decades, Holy Angels sat literally in the shadow of the notorious Robert Taylor Homes, which had become by the late 1990s a symbol of urban chaos and despair.[90] As a 1989 profile of the school described, the neighborhood surrounding Holy Angels had the highest crime rate and the highest concentration of public housing tenants in Chicago. Two-thirds of the residents in the neighborhood were on welfare. Holy Angels' own heartbreaking encounters with urban violence illustrate the desperate situation in the surrounding community. In

1993, a recent Holy Angels graduate, fourteen-year-old Shaun Carey, was gunned down by gang members in broad daylight as he was leaving a Halloween party near the school; his mother had enrolled him at Holy Angels because it provided a safer environment than the local public schools. And, in 1996, the long-time principal—Father Paul Smith—was murdered in a home invasion. The thieves stole $200, a watch, a cell phone, and the priest's car, which they later rented to a drug dealer in exchange for crack cocaine.

Father Clements, who once served as an advisor to the Black Panthers, had a very clear formula for success at Holy Angels. He explained that, when he hired Father Smith in 1970, they decided that "far from going the liberal route with the creativity and do-your-own-thing and all that, we were going to make this place a bastion of strict, conservative rules and regulations." Clements insisted that every family pay tuition, reasoning that "what one pays for, one values more," although tuition rates were kept artificially low to increase affordability and parents were required to volunteer to keep costs down. Fighting, bullying, vandalism, and even excessive tardiness led to suspension. (Today, the list of prohibited infractions has been expanded to include cyberbullying.) Parents were, and are, required to participate fully in the academic and religious life of the community, by monitoring their children's homework and use of technology and attending Mass weekly even when they are not Catholic. Clements once suspended two hundred students when their parents failed to bring them to Sunday Mass. The strategy worked, both as a marketing device and as educational policy. Clements explained, "We found that every time we put in another rule, the line to get into the school got longer. The people around here were thirsting . . . they had seen enough chaos in the public schools." And, in the 1980s, Clements could boast that 99 percent of Holy Angels students, most of whom were desperately poor and all of whom were African American, went on to graduate from college.

Despite their educational benefits, by the mid-1990s, the continued viability of urban Catholic schools like Holy Angels was called into question as enrollments declined and dioceses faced new financial pressures, including, unfortunately, the need to settle clergy abuse lawsuits. For example, Holy Angels remains open today, although enrollment had fallen in 2000 to under eight hundred and today hovers just above the "danger" level of two hundred. The last community of religious sisters left the school in 1999. Tuition has risen from $300 in 1986 to $3,200 for parish members and $4,200 for nonparishioners.[91]

That is not to say that there are no signs of hope for inner-city Catholic schools. Many dioceses continue to struggle valiantly to strengthen and sustain urban schools. For example, in 1999, the Diocese of Memphis began to reopen previously shuttered urban schools. The diocese now operates eight reopened and two new "Jubilee" elementary schools, all of which serve poor children. Ninety-nine percent of students who attend a Jubilee elementary school go on to graduate from high school.[92] Private philanthropic efforts, such as Chicago's Big Shoulders Fund, provide financial assistance to poor schools in many dioceses.[93] Some dioceses are experimenting with new administrative structures that enable parish schools to pool resources to access a range of goods and services centrally. Others have gone so far as to centralize the administration of schools themselves—essentially putting an end to the parochial structure of schools established by the bishops in 1854. The Diocese of Brooklyn, for example, has eliminated parochial schools altogether, wresting control over schools from parishes and vesting it with lay boards.[94] New, independent Catholic school models have developed, including some, such as the Cristo Rey and Nativity Miguel schools, that serve poor minority students in urban centers. Catholic schools continue to open in the suburbs, and nationwide, over 2,500 Catholic schools (most, but not all, of them in suburbs) have waiting lists. Eighteen states and the District of Columbia now provide some form of public assistance to students attending private schools, including Catholic schools, and school-choice advocates are optimistic that the number will increase. Where public funds have become available to Catholic school students, the tide of school closures generally has reversed or at least slowed.

Still, the mood in Catholic education circles is somber at best. The number of Catholic schools in the United States fell from 13,000 schools in 1960 to 7,000 in 2010. The percentage of students being educated by Catholic schools in the United States has fallen by more than half—from 12 percent in 1965 to 5 percent during the same period. And student attrition rates in Catholic schools outpace school closure rates. Between 2000 and 2006, six hundred Catholic schools closed (nearly 7 percent), but 290,000 students left the Catholic school system (nearly 11 percent). Elementary schools in the largest urban dioceses experienced the most dramatic rates of attrition, losing nearly 20 percent of their students.[95] The vast majority of school-aged Catholic children are enrolled in public schools today,[96] making it difficult for pastors and church leaders to prioritize Catholic schools over religious education programs for public school students. And, tellingly, only 3 percent of Latino students—the group most likely to fill empty seats in urban schools — attend Catholic schools. Some dioceses make the difficult and controversial decision to convert Catholic parochial schools to secular charter schools — a phenomenon discussed in greater detail in the next chapter.

Cardinal Timothy Dolan, the Archbishop of New York, recently complained that a "hospice mentality" has "hypnotized Catholic leadership in our nation." For years, Dolan grumbled, Church leaders have acted as if "the best thing we can do is prolong [Catholic schools'] death and make them as comfortable as possible."[97] Even the strongest supporters of Catholic schools recognize that, especially in inner cities, additional closures are inevitable. For example, in late 2010, the Archdiocese of New York unveiled an ambitious plan to restructure New York City's Catholic schools — a system in which 40 percent of Catholic school students are non-Catholic, 94 percent are from minority groups, and most live below the federal poverty line. Despite Dolan's calls for "renewed confidence" and demands that Catholics "recover their nerve" to support Catholic schools, this plan will not only remove control of all of the city's schools from parishes and vest it in the Archdiocese but also will result in the closure of more than thirty additional schools.[98]

CHAPTER TWO

Catholic Schools and Charter Schools

This chapter turns to another, equally dramatic, shift in the American educational landscape: the rise of charter schools. Although this book is primarily about what Catholic school closures portend for urban neighborhood health, we include this discussion of charter schools for three reasons: first, charter schools provide us with an opportunity to respond to one obvious objection to our empirical findings. That is, charter schools enable us to test whether Catholic schools' apparently positive neighborhood effects are simply school effects, rather than Catholic school effects—in other words, whether other kinds of schools also benefit urban neighborhoods. A sizable literature, discussed in chapter 7, finds that traditional public schools are associated with neighborhood crime and disorder. But it might be that other kinds of schools, in addition to Catholic schools, generate positive neighborhood externalities. We begin to answer this question in chapter 5, by comparing the effects of Catholic and charter schools on neighborhood crime rates in Chicago. Second, the ascendance of charter schools is closely linked with Catholic school closure trends. Charter schools, which are free, compete with Catholic schools, which are not, and there is little dispute that the declining enrollments in Catholic schools are at least partially attributable to charter schools' success. As Diane Ravitch has observed, "Where charter schools are expanding, Catholic schools are dying."[1] That said, there also is evidence that Catholic schools can compete effectively where expanded school choice exists—that is, where public funds are made available to students attending private schools as well as charter schools.[2] Third, many charter schools operate in closed Catholic schools, either by design (when dioceses opt to "convert" parochial schools to charters) or by default (when charter operators lease closed school buildings from parishes). Additionally, as Catholic schools close, charter schools are stepping in to fill the resulting void by providing educational alternatives to traditional public schools. In contrast to earlier generations, charter schools, rather than Catholic schools, are becoming the dominant schools of choice in many inner-city communities. At the very least, therefore, charter schools are replacing Catholic schools, and the rhetoric accompanying charter conversion decisions suggests that both Catholic and secular leaders hope that at least one kind of charter school—the converted parochial school—also can substitute for Catholic schools.

After a brief introduction to the remarkably diverse and rapidly evolving world of charter schools and to the major questions raised by their exponential rise over the past two decades, we turn to connections between Catholic and charter schools. We first discuss the emergence of quasi-religious charter schools—that is, charter schools that, while technically secular, are operated by religious institutions or leaders or are intentionally designed to incorporate cultural themes that attract and accommodate members of a single religion (for example, Muslims or Orthodox Jews). We then turn to charter conversions—that is, to the intentional conversion of an existing private school to a charter school. Such conversions are permitted in a majority of states with charter laws, and many secular private schools have opted to become charter schools in order to secure access to public funds. More controversial (both inside and outside the Catholic Church) is the decision of some dioceses to convert existing financially struggling parochial schools to charter schools. We discuss the experience of several dioceses undertaking such conversions at the conclusion of the chapter. This conversion trend is also occurring in public education—Congress has appropriated $50 million to fund the conversion of failing public schools into charter schools—although here we leave these efforts to the side.[3]

Charter schools raise many interesting questions that we do not discuss in detail here. For example, we flag, but do not engage, debates about charter schools' academic performance, about charter schools' effects on public schools, about charter school accountability, and about the appropriate institutional design of a charter school law. We eschew these debates for the same reasons that we eschew debates about educational outcomes in Catholic schools: this book is not, primarily, a book about education; it is a book about how educational institutions—especially inner-city Catholic schools—perform as community institutions. There is an extensive and rich literature on charter schools, and we recommend it to readers interested in learning more about these intriguing institutions. Charter schools have revolutionized public education policy in recent years, and we have no doubt that they will continue to do so for the foreseeable future. As Chester Finn, Bruno Manno, and Gregg Vanourek have observed, "[C]harter schools today are more influential than their numbers suggest. They are at the epicenter of America's most powerful education reform earthquake."[4]

CHARTER SCHOOLS IN A NUTSHELL

In contrast to the urban Catholic schools described in chapter 1—some of which have been in operation for over 150 years and most which have been operating for a half of a century—charter schools are educational upstarts. Although charter schools have roots in a number of older reform ideas—including alternative schools, magnet schools, privately operated contract schools, public school choice, and "schools within a school"—charter schools have existed in their current form for just over two decades. Minnesota enacted the nation's first charter school law in 1991, and charter schools have existed in Chicago only since 1997. In 2012, the average number of years a charter school had been open was 7.4, with over 25 percent of all charter schools open less than three years and roughly 33 percent open more than ten.[5] Also in contrast to Catholic schools, the charter schools are opening, not closing. As figure 2.1 depicts, the number of charter schools has increased dramatically in the past two decades, with literally hundreds of new schools opening each year. In 2011, for example, 518 new charter schools opened—over a 9 percent increase over 2010. During the same year, thirty-four new Catholic schools opened and 172 closed—a net decrease of 2.5 percent. Thus while Catholic schools continue to outnumber charter schools, and Catholic school students to outnumber charter school students—in 2012, there were approximately 1,100 more Catholic schools and 90,000 more Catholic school students than charter schools and charter school students—the balance likely will tip in favor of charter schools in the near future.[6]

Charter schools are public-private hybrids—they are publicly funded, but privately operated, schools. Charter schools resemble public schools in that they are tuition-free, secular, and open to all who wish to attend—generally, oversubscribed charter schools must admit applicants by lottery, although some are permitted to test applicants for admission. Charter schools also are more publicly accountable for their results than private schools are

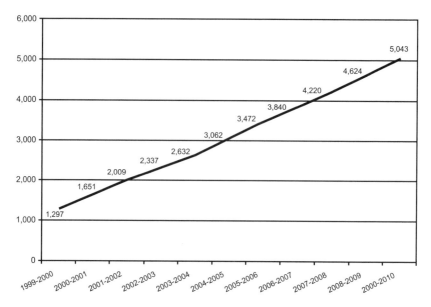

FIGURE 2.1 Charter school growth, 1999–2009

and, arguably, even than traditional public schools are, because underperforming charter schools are more likely to be closed than underperforming public schools are (although charter school accountability is a major point of contention in debates about education reform). Charter schools also have many attributes of private schools. They usually are created as the result of private, entrepreneurial action—that is, the request of a private entity (the charter "operator") for permission to open a school made to a governmental entity (the charter "sponsor"). Like private schools, charter schools also operate more or less independently of local school authorities—that is, they have wide-ranging autonomy over staffing, curriculum, budget, internal organization, and many other matters (although the extent of the autonomy varies by state). And, like private schools, they are schools of choice—that is, parents select them for their children, much as they would a private school.[7] Many of the most successful charter schools—for example, the KIPP schools described below—are operated by regional or national networks (mostly nonprofit, but in some cases for-profit) and follow a uniform instructional model. Others—for example, Detroit's Colin Powell Academy—represent the true grassroots efforts of individual teachers, religious leaders, or parents.[8]

Charter schools enjoy broad, bipartisan political support. During the 2008 presidential election cycle, for example, both John McCain and Barack Obama expressed strong support for charter schools. Soon after his election, President Obama made charter schools a centerpiece of his education policy, pledging $5 billion in federal funds to help create new charter schools and urging states without charter school laws to adopt them and states with caps on the number of charter schools to eliminate them.[9] Within debates about educational finance, many cite charter schools as an alternative to private school-choice programs, such as tax credits or vouchers, that might help stem the tide of Catholic school closures.[10] This procharter/antivoucher position has been echoed in Democratic Party platforms in each of the last three presidential election cycles. As the 2004 Democratic Party platform provided, "Instead of pushing private school vouchers that funnel scarce dollars away from the public schools, we will support public school choice, including charter schools and magnet schools that meet the same high standards as other schools."[11]

Even the teachers' unions have come to grudgingly embrace charter schools, although they routinely represent a stumbling block to charter school expansion in state education reform debates. For example, the American Federation of Teachers—the nation's second largest teachers' union—states that it "strongly supports" charter schools but at the same time condemns school vouchers and tuition tax credits as unwise and dangerous policy. In fact, the term "charter school" is attributed to Al Shanker, who led the American Federation of Teachers for decades. In a 1988 speech, Shanker spoke, hypothetically, about a complete restructuring of the American educational system to "enable any school or any group of teachers . . . within a school to develop a proposal for how they can better educate youngsters and then give them a 'charter' to implement that proposal."[12,13] The National Education Association's (NEA's) position on charter schools is more guarded, urging caution about the risk of diverting public school funds to them, demanding local administrative oversight and teacher unionization, and flatly opposing the conversion of private schools to charter schools. Even this tepid support stands in stark contrast to the NEA's vehement opposition to private school-choice programs. These programs, the NEA warns, undermine accountability and academic standards, threaten civil rights protections, deprive parents of "authentic" choice, "divert essential resources from public schools to private and religious schools," and do not improve student achievement. However, current trends in public education—especially the increasing numbers of public school closures that are fueled in part by the migration of students from public to charter schools and the conversion of failing public schools to charter schools—appear to be undermining support for charter schools among public school advocates.[14]

Despite their widespread political popularity, scholarly opinion about charter schools' performance as educational institutions is mixed. Some studies suggest that traditional public schools outperform charter schools,[15] while others find that charter schools' records surpass those of public schools, at least after accounting for selection bias.[16] Charter school performance varies significantly across states. For example, the available evidence suggests that students attending charter schools in Chicago outperform their public school counterparts on a range of measures, while the students in charter schools in Washington, D.C., do not.[17] There are clearly some very good charter schools, and some charter schools are rightly celebrated for their remarkable success in educating students who fall behind in public schools. Perhaps the most celebrated, and among the most successful, charter schools are a part of the Knowledge Is Power Program (KIPP). KIPP operates 191 schools in twenty states and the District of Columbia, enrolling more than 50,000 students. The KIPP schools were founded in 1994 by two Teach for America alumni with the explicit goal of raising the performance of, and increasing college graduation rates among, low-income urban minority students. KIPP schools, which are primarily middle schools but now also include elementary and high schools, enroll primarily poor minority students—95 percent of KIPP students are African American or Hispanic, and 87 percent are eligible for free or reduced lunches. The KIPP schools' motto, "Work Hard, Be Nice," is reflected in the schools' pervasive focus on discipline, character development, and academic achievement. Students spend eight hours a day in school and attend classes on some Saturdays, even the youngest students have several hours of homework a night, and parents are required to sign commitment forms as a condition of enrolling their children. More than 80 percent of KIPP graduates have enrolled in four-year colleges—a number shy of KIPP's goal of 98.6 percent (body temperature). Most KIPP schools' test scores soar above their local public school counterparts, and, while some skeptics have complained that their success results from intentional "cream skimming" on KIPP's part, a number of academic studies—including those that carefully control for selection bias by comparing KIPP students to those who apply to KIPP schools and are turned away because of overenrollment—suggest that KIPP students do, in fact, perform substantially better than comparable public school students.[18]

In contrast, there also are some clearly bad charter schools, including some that fail miserably as educational institutions, igniting calls for greater accountability and oversight of charter school operations. Charters usually are granted for three to five years to enable periodic review of charter school operations and performance, although some states grant charters for much longer. (In Arizona, for example, charters are granted for fifteen years). Critics argue that, even at the reauthorization stage, oversight is insufficiently rigorous. Still, a number of charter schools have been closed for malfeasance or underperformance. For example, the Marcus Garvey Charter School in Washington, D.C., closed in 1998 after a public scandal that included the conviction of the principal for assaulting a newspaper reporter and two police officers who came to the school to investigate allegations of mismanagement. Dakota Open, a charter school for at-risk Native American students, had its high school program terminated for high absenteeism and failure to produce satisfactory academic results. Some charter schools also have been associated with financial improprieties. For example, the director of the now defunct Citizen 2000 Charter School wrote school checks for her mother's mortgage, her divorce attorney's fees, jewelry, flowers, and swimming pool supplies. Citizen 2000 also exaggerated enrollment figures to get $250,000 more in state funding than it was due.[19] Overall, of the approximately 6,700 charter schools opened between 1992 and 2012, 1,036 were closed. According to the pro–charter-school Center for Education Reform, 42 percent of these closed because of financial deficiencies, 24 percent were closed because of mismanagement, and 19 percent were closed for poor academic performance.[20]

Ultimately, we are ill situated to weigh in on debates about charter school performance and accountability. Although we tend to agree with those who see charter schools as a welcome addition to the educational landscape, we also believe that it is still too soon to tell how charter schools will perform over the long haul as educational institutions (and, of particular relevance here, as community institutions). Given the relative novelty of most of these schools, and the fact that some of them are being operated by individuals who, while well-meaning and enthusiastic, have little experience as teachers and school administrators, it is reasonable to assume that many charter schools are experiencing, and will continue to experience, growing pains. This is one reason why the option of converting Catholic schools to charter schools is attractive to many urban leaders—they introduce established schools with long and successful educational track records into the charter school pool.

INSTITUTIONAL DIVERSITY AMONG CHARTER SCHOOLS

While charter schools are now authorized in forty-one states and the District of Columbia, charter school laws vary dramatically in detail, and the schools created pursuant to these diverse legal regimes vary along with them. Some states tightly control charter schools—for example, by limiting their number and location and subjecting them to substantial governmental regulation. Others have taken a deregulatory "let a thousand flowers bloom" approach. The Center for Education Reform "grades" charter laws according to several criteria—whether the state caps the number of charter schools, the number of charter school authorizers in a state, the extent of charter schools' operational autonomy, and the level of public funding provided. For example, Minnesota, which was the first state to enact a charter school law, earned an "A" for its charter law, which permits a wide range of entities to authorize charter schools (including local school boards, public and private colleges and universities, and nonprofit entities meeting certain criteria), exempts charter schools from the state's educational regulations, allows charter schools to opt out of the teachers' union collective bargaining agreements, and assists schools financially with both operational and capital expenditures.[21] Virginia earned an "F" for a charter law that limits charter authorization to local school boards, requires charter schools to comply with all state and local education regulations and to permit teachers to unionize, and provides only limited operational, and no facilities, funding.[22] These factors predict dramatic institutional variation across states as well as dramatic variations in charter school enrollments, which ranged in 2011 from 354 (in Virginia) to 410,157 (in California). In the same year, Indiana and Arizona—states with roughly equivalent populations, enrolled, respectively, 20,372 students in sixty-three charter schools and 135,930 students in 539 charter schools (respectively, 3.5 percent and 24 percent of total public school enrollment).[23]

The institutional diversity among charter schools is breathtaking. Some focus on a particular curricular theme—for example, Afrocentrism, international studies, fine arts, or classical education. Some charter schools do not exist in the formal, "bricks-and-mortar" sense at all: as of 2012, there also were 228 "virtual" charter schools in twenty-six states. Many charter schools focus on a particular student population, including low-income disadvantaged urban children. The KIPP schools are an example of this model, as are the Catalyst Schools in Chicago, described in detail below.

In fact, 26 percent of charter schools report that "serving a special population," especially poor, urban students, is central to their mission. Perhaps not surprisingly, given widespread dissatisfaction with underperforming urban public schools, the available data suggests that charter schools are particularly attractive to the demographic groups targeted by these schools. In fact, a majority of students enrolled in charter schools are racial minorities. In 2010–2011, 63 percent of students enrolled in charter schools were racial minorities, compared with 47 percent of public school students and 30 percent of Catholic school students.[24] Not surprisingly, charter schools are particularly popular in cities with underperforming public schools. In 2012, 76 percent of public school students in New Orleans and 41 percent of public school students in both Detroit and Washington, D.C., attended charter schools. The proportion topped 30 percent in a number of other cities—Gary, Indiana; Flint, Michigan; and Kansas City and St. Louis, Missouri.[25]

"RELIGIOUS" CHARTER SCHOOLS

There is one universal limit on charter schools' institutional diversity—they must be secular schools. All states prohibit charter schools from teaching religion as religion (that is, from teaching religion as the truth of the matter). State laws express this prohibition in various ways. The majority approach is to simply require that charter schools be nonsectarian. Seven states (and the federal government) additionally prohibit charter schools from being affiliated with religious institutions, and two others (Maine and New Hampshire) prohibit such affiliation to the extent that it is prohibited by the U.S. Constitution. Others (for example, New York) prohibit charter schools from being "under the control" of a religious institution. Still others (for example, Georgia) explicitly permit religious institutions to operate charter schools, so long as the charter schools that they operate are secular schools. Some states' laws are silent on the question, although the universal view—which we evaluate in greater detail in chapter 8—is that the First Amendment's Establishment Clause prohibits religious charter schools.[26]

Although both the Establishment Clause and state laws mandating that charter schools be nonsectarian place an outer limit on curricular content, state laws are generally silent about the extent to which charter schools can incorporate themes with religious connotations, such as cultural or moral education, into their programs. Indeed, character-based or morals-based curricular themes pervade the world of charter schools, although, to be sure, some schools' character education curricula fall closer to the religion line than others. Even those schools that do fall close to that line, however, have survived Establishment Clause scrutiny. For example, in *Daugherty v. Vanguard Charter School Academy*, a federal court rejected an Establishment Clause challenge to a morals-based curriculum that stressed the classical Greek virtues of prudence, temperance, fortitude, and justice and taught students that mercy, compassion, kindness, forgiveness, grace, moral strength, conscience, faith, and self-sacrifice were associated with these virtues. The court reasoned that "the fact that the curriculum employs words and concepts in service of character development that happen to coincide or harmonize with the tenets of some or all religions, does not necessarily betoken endorsement" of religion. The *Daugherty* court also held that the religious use of the school's parent room by a parent prayer group during the school day was constitutional and that a teacher prayer meeting on school grounds before the school day began also did not violate the Establishment Clause.[27] The school at issue in the case, the Vanguard Charter Academy, is one of seventy-five charter schools operated by the National Heritage Academies, each of which employs the curriculum challenged in the case. Collectively, in 2012, the National Heritage Academies educated more than 48,000 children in nine states.[28]

Some charter schools also are structured around cultural themes with strong religious overtones. For example, in litigation in Minnesota, the American Civil Liberties Union (ACLU) claimed that the (now defunct) Tarek Ibn Ziyad Academy (TiZA) in Minnesota was effectively a Muslim school in disguise. Named for the Muslim general who conquered southern Spain in 711, TiZA was founded and was directed by a Muslim imam. Although Islam was not incorporated into the school-day curriculum, the school required a course in Arabic language, which it characterized as the "language of culture that holds together the peoples of the Middle East, South Asia, North Africa and East Africa."[29] The TiZA cafeteria served exclusively halal food, students fasted during Ramadan, and the school vacations were scheduled around Muslim holidays. TiZA's website, which featured young girls wearing the hijab, indicated that the school "provides students with a learning environment that recognizes and appreciates the traditions, histories, civilizations and accomplishments of Africa, Asia and the Middle East" and "aims to help students integrate into American society, while retaining their identity." Moreover, the school avoided teaching subjects contrary to Muslim culture, which appealed to Islamic families. As one commentator has observed, "for many religious appealed to parents, the important part of a religious school is what it does *not* teach."[30,31] TiZA also accommodated parents' religious beliefs by providing for daily opportunities for "voluntary and student-led prayer,"[32] with a large prayer rug in the center of the school set aside for that purpose. On Friday afternoons, students were released for a parent-led prayer service. TiZA staff accompanied students to restrooms for ritual washings before afternoon prayer and the service. In February 2011, the ACLU settled its lawsuit with the state of Minnesota, which promised greater oversight of the school to ensure religion was not a part of the curriculum, and the charter authorizer, a nonprofit organization called Islamic Relief USA, which agreed to withdraw as the school's sponsor. Unable to secure a new sponsor, TiZA was forced to close.[33]

The Ben Gamla Charter School in Hollywood, Florida, also has been the subject of ACLU scrutiny. Ben Gamla, which is named for a historical figure who established Jewish schools throughout ancient Israel, was founded by a Jewish Rabbi and former Jewish day school director. Unlike TiZA, which targeted and attracted primarily religious Muslims, Ben Gamla apparently appeals to a broad spectrum of Hebrew-speaking parents, including both Orthodox Jews who might otherwise attend Jewish day schools and secular Israelis.[34] The school serves only kosher food and requires that one period each day be dedicated to teaching Hebrew and that a second period to be taught in a mix of English and Hebrew.[35] At the school's founding, the local school board rejected the school's first two Hebrew curriculum proposals for "religious references."[36] During the fall of the school's first year, after the ACLU threatened to bring an Establishment Clause challenge, the local school board forced Ben Gamla to freeze Hebrew instruction for three weeks while the curriculum was scrubbed of religious references for a third time.[37] Following this review, and in response to the threatened lawsuit, Ben Gamla replaced the founding principal with an "experienced public school administrator." Since then, the school, which seems to have resolved its differences with the local school board and placated the ACLU, has come to be considered a model for Hebrew charter schools across the United States.[38]

Additionally, especially in inner-city African American neighborhoods, many charter schools have been opened by Protestant clergy members or, where legally permissible, by Protestant churches, almost always as a response to a perceived need for more high-quality educational options. For example, Detroit's Colin Powell Academy was founded by Reverend Ellis Smith, the pastor of Jubilee City Church. Reverend Smith acknowledges that he was responding to a religious calling to open a school for poor urban children and has called upon other African American religious leaders to found charter schools, reasoning that churches are "the most stabilizing institutions" in many urban neighborhoods.[39] As Reverend R.B. Holmes, Jr., a pastor of a Baptist church in Tallahassee, Florida, who formerly chaired the board of a charter school, explained, "[T]here is a role for a community of faith in the public education system. You can't use tax dollars to perpetuate your religious beliefs. But you can use tax dollars to make sure every child gets a good education and parents have some options."[40]

Individual members of Catholic religious orders have responded to a similar call to serve poor children by operating charter schools—including charter schools that closely mimic the Catholic school model. Consider, for example, the San Miguel and Catalyst Schools in inner-city Chicago. In 1995, Brother Edmund Siderewicz, a member of the LaSallian Christian Brothers—a religious order dedicated to operating Catholic schools— founded the San Miguel School in an inner-city Chicago neighborhood. Siderewicz opened a second San Miguel School in a similarly impoverished Chicago neighborhood in 2002. Both schools are explicitly and unapologetically Catholic middle schools (grades 5-8), and both are members of the Nativity Miguel Network, a group of sixty-four Catholic schools that are explicitly "designed to provide families struggling in impoverished neighborhoods with a high quality education."[41] The schools enroll, respectively, eighty-two Latino and 498 African American (out of 507 total) students, virtually all of whom qualify for free or reduced lunches.[42] The San Miguel Schools "specifically target academically underachieving, low income, at risk students and provide them with a model of education that includes extended day schedule and year round calendar, individualized instruction with a 10:1 student teacher ratio, and strong parental involvement." Students are accepted to the San Miguel Schools on the basis of three main criteria: academic underperformance, financial need, and living in proximity to the schools. The schools pair students with academic mentors, guarantee continued academic and financial assistance throughout high school, and provide educational opportunities for adults as well as family counseling services. Each school also has as a goal advancing the development of their surrounding communities through collaboration with local community groups.[43]

In 2002, the Superintendent of Chicago Public Schools, Arne Duncan (who currently serves as President Barack Obama's Secretary of Education) asked Brother Siderewicz to consider opening a public charter school modeled on the San Miguel Schools. Brother Siderewicz agreed and, several years later, opened two Catalyst Schools in inner-city Chicago. (Chicago

Public Schools required Siderewicz to open two schools as a condition of approving his charter application.) The third school was opened in 2010 and currently serves 520 students, 94 percent of whom are African American and 95 percent of whom qualify for free or reduced lunches.[44] The Catalyst Schools' website openly acknowledges that, in founding the Catalyst Schools, Siderewicz attempted "to replicate the San Miguel model as charter schools." And the San Miguel Schools' website lists the two Catalyst Schools as "sister schools." Like the San Miguel Schools, the Catalyst Schools, provide a structured and intensive academic program for low-income students, which features extended school days and a longer school year, low student-teacher ratio, family support and involvement, and graduate support throughout high school. Unlike the San Miguel Schools, the Catalyst Schools are completely secular, although they emphasize character development and acknowledge that "moral values are foundational to the school and to the development of the students' character and life." The Catalyst Schools also, like many charter schools, incorporate many of the structural elements of Catholic schools—uniforms, parental involvement, and a strict disciplinary policy. Currently, Siderewicz is creating a program that would guarantee financial and scholarship support for graduates of both the San Miguel and Catalyst Schools through college.[45]

CHARTER "CONVERSIONS"

Many charter schools operate in closed Catholic schools. This is hardly surprising, given that closed Catholic schools are hardly in short supply in many urban areas and are natural locations for new schools to open. Still, the extent of the practice in some dioceses is remarkable. A spokesman for the Archdiocese of Detroit estimated to one of us that 90 percent of the closed Catholic schools in Detroit are currently occupied by charter schools. Some dioceses, in contrast, have flatly refused to lease their school facilities to charters, citing a concern about the fact that charter schools are attracting students away from Catholic schools. Since canon law entitles parishes to keep the revenue generated by leasing school buildings to charter schools, the incentives for financially strapped pastors to close their schools in order to capture the revenues also are a concern to some Catholic school officials.[46]

The intentional conversions of Catholic schools to charter schools are both different in kind and more controversial—both within Catholic education circles and in the broader education reform world—than any of the phenomena described above (that is, morals-based charter schools, culture-driven charter schools, secular schools operated by religiously motivated individuals, and charter schools operating in closed Catholic school buildings). Some charter school skeptics vehemently object to the conversion of any private school into a charter school. For example, the National Education Association (NEA), the nation's largest teachers union, asserts that "private schools should not be allowed to convert to public charter schools."[47] And, in fact, private school conversions to charter schools are expressly forbidden by law in twelve states, although, in practice, these prohibitions have little bite since school conversions can be structured so as to easily avoid offending them.

In contrast to the NEA's opposition, many urban leaders and charter school proponents welcome the conversion of private and parochial schools to charter schools because such conversions introduce established schools with strong educational track records into a pool of educational upstarts. For example, when the Diocese of Brooklyn sought to convert some of its parochial schools to charters recently, New York City's mayor, Michael Bloomberg, not only welcomed the announcement but actively helped the diocese structure the school closures and reopenings in a way that avoided New York's express prohibition on private school conversions. More recently, when the Archdiocese of Indianapolis announced its decision to close two inner-city Catholic schools in April 2010, the mayor of Indianapolis agreed to serve as the sponsor for the schools' conversion to charter status. "Choices for our students and parents are important especially when it comes to education," the mayor observed. "I am pleased and honored to fully support the transformation of both St. Anthony and St. Andrew & St. Rita into charter schools and look forward to the quality of education the schools will provide."[48]

Charter school conversions are the subject of an intense debate among Catholic leaders and educators. Some Catholics, including some bishops, view the loss of religious identity and autonomy that conversions entail as too high a price to pay for public funding of their struggling schools. Other bishops, facing escalating costs and dwindling enrollments, have reluctantly come to view charter school conversions as preferable to school closures, since they offer the resources to enable the schools to continue serving inner-city children, even if not as Catholic schools. As a senior leader in the Archdiocese of Indianapolis explained, "Many urban Catholic schools are closing across the nation, and we did not want to leave the students or communities we currently serve. Through this transformation, an urgent and unmet need will be filled."[49] Some pastors, weary of the financial and administrative headaches that struggling schools represent, welcome the prospect of a charter school conversion especially because, as mentioned above, under canon law, the school building "belongs" to the parish and therefore parishes generally are entitled to the revenue generated by leasing the school building to a charter operator (although the local bishop has the power to tax these revenues for diocesan purposes). Indeed, as we discuss in subsequent chapters, and as suggested by the Miami experience discussed below, there is reason to be concerned about the financial incentives that school closures in general, and especially charter conversions, create for pastors. To the best of our knowledge, at least four dioceses, Brooklyn, Indianapolis, Miami, and Washington, D.C., have intentionally converted some of their parochial schools to charter schools.

Catholic supporters of charter conversions suggest that there are ways of maintaining continuity with the mission of the former parochial schools. This continuity is generally provided by a morals- or values-based curricular focus. For example, when the Archdiocese of Washington decided to convert seven inner-city parochial schools to charter schools, Archbishop Donald Wuerl assured skeptics that he was determined to "maintain a level of value formation" in the charter schools. Catholic educators also hope that charter schools might incorporate opportunities for voluntary student- or parent-led prayer into the school day and/or enable the Catholic Church to offer religious education classes before or after school. In Catholic education circles, there is significant discussion about the prospect of implementing a "wraparound" model, which would provide before- and/or after-school religious instruction at converted charter schools.[50] In some ways, this model parallels abandoned nineteenth-century experiments, described in chapter 1, with "public" Catholic schools that operated in church-owned buildings with secular subjects taught by teachers jointly selected by pastors and public education officials and Catholic religious instruction provided after school.

The recent experiences of three large dioceses—the Archdiocese of Washington, D.C., the Archdiocese of Miami, and the Archdiocese of Indianapolis—are illustrative of the developing phenomenon of charter conversions. Care should be taken, of course, about drawing conclusions from these vignettes about the long-run implications of converting Catholic schools to charter schools. In particular, early indications suggest that, with the possible exception of the Archdiocese of Indianapolis, church leaders have not achieved their stated goal of maintaining a school character that distinguishes converted parochial schools from other charter schools. We emphasize that we cannot know whether this model might emerge over time. We believe, for reasons we discuss in greater detail in chapter 7, that the emergence of distinctive quasi-Catholic charter schools may well affect their ability to generate positive neighborhood externalities similar to Catholic schools. But, since most of the converted schools in the United States have operated as charter schools for only a few years, it is simply too soon to know what these schools will become. These stories are only the beginning of what likely will be a much broader transformation of the educational landscape.

Dioceses opting to convert some schools to charter status have taken different institutional approaches. The Archdiocese of Washington, D.C., and the Archdiocese of Indianapolis created new charter management organizations to operate converted schools. Technically speaking, these charter operators are independent nonprofit corporations that operate independently of Catholic authorities (as they must by law in most states). But, as a practical matter, diocesan leaders have played a significant role in the formation process and a significant overlap has existed between the early leadership of these newly created charter management organizations and diocesan leadership. The connection between church authorities and charter authorities is particularly close in Indianapolis, where the Archdiocese of Indianapolis is, for all practical purposes, operating charter schools (an option not legally available in many states). Elsewhere, dioceses including the Archdiocese of Miami have enlisted established charter operators to run the schools.

Again with the possible exception of the Archdiocese of Indianapolis, even the active involvement of church leadership in structuring the transition to charter status has not resulted in schools that—at least from the outside—look and feel much different than hundreds of other secular inner-city charter schools. For whatever reason—perhaps some combination of concern about breaching the elusive line between church and state, financial limitations, or pastoral apathy—the charter operators that essentially have been created by the Catholic Church have been less bold than charter operators like TiZA and the National Heritage Academies. That is, the schools' curricula do not depart significantly from the standard "character education" programs that pervade the charter school world, school leaders have not actively sought to imbed opportunities for voluntary religious observance into the school day, and church leaders have not increased religious education courses beyond those offered to members of the parishes that formerly operated the schools.

Washington, D.C.

In September 2007, the Archdiocese of Washington, D.C., announced that it would convert seven inner-city parochial schools into charter schools at the end of the 2007–2008 school year. The seven schools were each a part of the twelve-school Center City Consortium, which had been established in 1997 to enable struggling inner-city schools to take advantage of economies of scale and offload many time-consuming administrative tasks to a central office affiliated with, but independent from, the Archdiocese's schools office. Although the Consortium had made significant progress in improving the academic performance of, and raising money for, its schools, the Consortium had amassed a $1.7 million dollar deficit, which the Archdiocese covered with its operating funds. The relatively new Archbishop of Washington, D.C., Donald Wuerl, found the situation untenable, especially in light of the fact that the vast majority of students enrolled in the Consortium's schools were non-Catholic. Wuerl assembled a forty-member steering committee, made up of parents, principals, and pastors, as well as outside experts, to consider the Consortium's situation. At the end of a prolonged planning process, this steering committee concluded that all of the District of Columbia's Catholic schools could not remain both open and Catholic, and it initiated an investigation of the D.C. charter school law, which specifically authorizes, and provides a process for, converting existing private schools to charter schools.

Acting on the advice of the steering committee, the Archdiocese issued a draft plan that envisioned a smaller Center City Consortium of Catholic schools and the conversion of other schools into a network of charter schools. The Archdiocese also established criteria for determining which of the twelve Consortium schools would remain Catholic and which ones would be converted to charter schools. These criteria included the percentage of Catholic students, enrollment and financial status, number of students supported by the Washington, D.C., voucher program, and the number of available charter school seats in the vicinity of the school. In response, some of the Consortium schools submitted proposals seeking to demonstrate that they could become financially sustainable as Catholic schools. In the end, the Archdiocese opted to maintain a four-school consortium. One other former Consortium school, St. Augustine's, which claims to be "the Mother Church of Black Catholics in the Nation's Capital," decided to become an independent, parish-sponsored school. The remaining seven schools in the Center City Consortium, which collectively enrolled about half of the Consortium students, would be converted to charter schools.

While the D.C. city government welcomed the proposal, citing the advantages of converted parochial schools to charter schools (for example, buildings, strong test scores, and established programs and faculties), the conversions were extremely controversial in Catholic circles. Many teachers and parents vehemently objected to the Archdiocese's decision and expressed dismay and feelings of betrayal. As one parent observed, "If we wanted our kids to go to public school, we would have sent them there." Another expressed her view in more colorful terms, predicting, "When there's not God, the devil gets in it." A new local advocacy group, Black Catholics United to Save Black Catholic Schools, organized to protest the decision, charging the Archdiocese with "backing away from providing Catholic education to African-American children" and "turning its back on the parents who want a Catholic education for their children and the students who are thriving in this environment." Nationally, the president of the National Catholic Education Association expressed concern about the "ripple effect of people thinking that when their Catholic school is in trouble either for enrollment or financial reasons, charter schools are the automatic solution." But the Archdiocese stood firm, justifying its decision as the only way to avoid abandoning the inner city altogether and to maintain "consistency, predictability, and stability" at the schools. Wuerl said at the time, "It's a heartache to know that we wouldn't have these schools anymore. But the sadness is sweetened by the fact that these students would continue to have an education." A pastor at one of the parishes agreed: "It was a little sad to say goodbye to what we knew as Catholic education, but we didn't dwell on it. It was what it was and we were given this wonderful opportunity."

In December 2007, the Archdiocese announced that it had selected Center City Public Charter Schools as the charter management organization for the converted schools. In reality, the Archdiocese directed the formation of the Center City Public Charter Schools, which had been incorporated only one month before the archdiocesan announcement. While the charter management organization was, and remains, completely independent of the Archdiocese, there was significant overlap between the leadership of the Center City Consortium and the Center City Public Charter Schools. The director of the charter management authority, Mary Anne Stanton, was the former director of the Center City Consortium, and the new head of schools, Juana Brown, held the identical position in the Consortium before the conversion. Members of the Consortium board also served on the board of the new charter management organization and dedicated hundreds of hours to ensuring that the transition from parochial to charter status went as smoothly as possible. Once it was up and running, the charter management organization negotiated leases of the parochial school buildings with the Archdiocese, some of which provided for the parishes and schools to share space (for example, some permitted the parishes to use the school space for religious education on Sundays). The Archdiocese also required that some of the leasing revenues, which are substantial—over $1.5 million in the first year—be used to support Catholic schools, although the host parishes also captured a portion of the revenue to use for their own needs as well.

After a whirlwind summer, the seven Center City charter schools opened on schedule for the 2008–2009 school year. At least with respect to staffing, the Archdiocese initially achieved its goal of maintaining continuity between the new and old schools, since 70 percent of the faculty and staff remained in place through the transition. In other respects, however, the charter schools are very different than the parochial schools that they replaced. Despite the high staff retention rate, the public funds made available by assuming charter status enabled the schools to hire additional faculty members and resulted in substantial teacher pay raises, making the Center City schools attractive to teachers and administrators from outside the parochial school system. As a result, 60 percent of the staff in the schools was new when the charter schools opened.

Despite the significant early archdiocesan involvement in the transition and the substantial retention of Consortium staff, the continuity between Consortium schools and Center City Public Charter Schools was short-lived. Both Mary Anne Stanton and Juana Brown left Center City Public Charter Schools within two years, and reports on the ground indicated significant additional staff turnover (including the replacement of many teachers and principals). The Center City Public Charter Schools students also are different in many respects from the Consortium Catholic school students. Perhaps as many as 70 percent of the Catholic school students did not remain in the charter schools. Most transferred to another Catholic school. All but one of the charter schools, which closed after one year because of low enrollment, also experienced a significant influx of new students, who tended to be slightly poorer (75 percent rather than 65 percent qualify for free and reduced lunches) and significantly more likely to have fallen behind academically and/or to have learning difficulties than the Catholic school students they replaced. These realities generated new educational and disciplinary challenges that threatened the parochial schools' relatively strong academic record. In 2009, standardized test scores fell significantly below the levels achieved in the former Catholic schools—students at all of the charter schools tested well below grade level and none of the schools satisfied the "adequate yearly progress" requirement of the federal No Child Left Behind Act.[51]

Finally, despite Wuerl's assurances, the "value formation" in the charter schools required replacing religious instruction with a relatively standard-issue version of character-based instruction. Morning prayer was replaced with a recitation of the school's honor code: "I will arrive at school each day on time and ready to work. I will treat all with respect and dignity. I will solve any conflicts that arise peacefully. I will care for and protect our environment." The Ten Commandments were replaced with ten "core values": collaboration, compassion, curiosity, integrity, justice, knowledge, peace-making, perseverance, respect, and discipline, each of which was to receive a month-long focus during the school year.[52] And, the Archdiocese did not, at least not initially, follow through on its plans for a voluntary before- and after-school program of religious education for charter school students (citing a lack of time to develop and implement the program).[53]

Miami

The recent conversions of seven Catholic schools to charter schools in the Archdiocese of Miami took a very different course. In Miami, the decisions to convert the schools and the postconversion institutional arrangements were driven primarily by the pastors of the parishes where the schools were located, although the financial impetus for these pastors' decisions to close their parish schools was a change in archdiocesan fiscal policy. In November 2008, the Archdiocese of Miami announced that it would be suspending all parish subsidies—including $3 million per year specifically earmarked for Catholic schools in the poorest parishes. The Archdiocese also required repayment of any money it had lent to parishes since they had opened, sometimes decades earlier. Unlike the procedures followed in many dioceses, the Archdiocese of Miami allowed pastors to decide whether to keep their schools open in the wake of the subsidy suspension, and seven pastors concluded that they could not continue to operate their schools without the subsidies, especially facing the pressure to repay their archdiocesan debt. Other pastors determined that they could continue operating their schools by raising tuition, redoubling fundraising efforts, and aggressively recruiting new students. The pastors who desired to close their schools complained that the schools sapped resources needed for myriad expenses, from upkeep on the physical plant of their church, to community outreach, to religious education courses for public school children.

Even before the Archdiocese announced that it was suspending parish subsidies, one of the pastors, Father Jose Luis Menendez, approached the Archbishop about the possibility of closing his school and leasing the building to a charter operator. He presented the charter option as a money-making opportunity for both his parish and the Archdiocese. Menendez also identified a potential charter operator, Academica, which operates a number of charter schools throughout Florida. Initially, the Archdiocese rejected Menendez's proposal, but, following the 2008 decision, the Archbishop agreed to permit one parish, Menendez's Corpus Christi, to allow a charter school to operate on its grounds on a one-year trial basis. By February 2009, however, the Archdiocese was working with the pastors of all seven parishes where schools would be closed to identify charter operators. Because of the short time frame, the Archdiocese determined that it could not organize its own charter management organization and apply for new charters, but rather allowed parishes to reach agreements with existing operators that already held charters. The pastors toured several schools operated by different charter management organizations, and many were attracted to the structured environment offered by Academica (the charter operator preferred by Menendez), which featured uniforms, a strict disciplinary code, and high academic standards.

After the pastors selected charter operators for their closing schools— six opted for Academica and two for independent operators—the Archdiocese worked with the parishes to structure facilities license agreements that enabled parishes to share the school space for religious education classes and other services after school and on weekends. Unlike the leases used in Washington, D.C., the license provided that the charter schools had access to the school buildings only during school hours; after school and on the weekends, authority of the school buildings reverted to the parish. Also in contrast to the situation in Washington, D.C., the Archdiocese allowed the parishes to keep all the licensing revenue, rather than claiming a portion of it for the support of open Catholic schools—although, as a practical matter, the Archdiocese will receive the lion's share of the revenue until the parishes repay their archdiocesan debts.

Both archdiocesan leaders and pastors in parishes with the charter schools trumpeted the conversions as a way to bring new educational options for families and new financial resources for the parishes and the Archdiocese. In contrast to the experiences in other dioceses, however, the primary focus in Miami was on the benefits of the latter. As Brother Richard DeMaria, the head of schools for the Archdiocese stated, "I worked very hard to find a solution to keep the inner-city Catholic schools open, but when I finally came to the conclusion that I couldn't save them, I chose to help save the inner-city parishes through the charter school process." Father James McCreanor, the pastor at one of the parishes, concurred. "We were spending $300,000 a year on top of tuition on a school with only 185 students. In a parish of nearly 3,000 families, it became more difficult to justify that. Over time, a myth had developed that the Archdiocese would never close Sacred Heart's school. It took the financial crisis and the Archdiocese's decision to end the subsidy to really force everyone to face the reality that our parish could no longer afford to operate a school." Menendez put it more succinctly, "*I am free.*" As elsewhere, the decision to convert the schools received a hostile reception in some Catholic circles, including among the parents of the children enrolled in the schools and, initially, the archdiocesan leadership itself, which objected to the loss of Catholic identity and feared competition for its remaining schools. The director of Academica, Victor Barroso, reported that one priest called him "the Devil;" he also complained that some parents and teachers at the closing schools did not understand the "win-win" nature of the conversion—"with the parish gaining much-needed rent for an empty building and our schools accessing good facilities."

In contrast to Washington, D.C., where the vast majority of Consortium students chose to enroll in another Catholic school rather than remain through the transition to charter status, the converted charter schools in Miami retained about 75 percent of the former Catholic school students and attracted many new students. Overall, enrollment increased at least twofold over Catholic school enrollment in all of the schools and tripled in one school. Also in contrast to the Washington, D.C., experience, a majority of the teachers in the closed Catholic schools did not remain through the transition (and the handful that did remain either left or were terminated during the charter schools' first year of operation).

The Miami experience, however, does parallel the Washington experience in one important respect: as in D.C., charter schools created as a result of the Miami Catholic school closures do not appear, at least from the outside, distinctive from hundreds of other charter schools emphasizing character education and academic rigor. This is, in a sense, hardly surprising, since, in contrast to Washington, the Archdiocese enlisted an established, secular charter operator to run most of the converted schools. Nor was the Archdiocese of Miami any more proactive in attempting to implement the wraparound model of religious education. Father Menendez in particular marketed his charter conversion plan as enabling "more effective religious education programs that could reach many more young people." Still, neither the Archdiocese nor the parishes where the schools are located have implemented religious education programs that specifically target the charter school students. The pastors where the charter schools operate report that enrollment in existing religious education programs has increased, which it logically should since Catholic parents of public school children are obligated to enroll their children in religious education classes. In 2009, Menendez reported that he would like to offer after-school religious education classes but cannot yet afford it because he is still paying off the debt to the Archdiocese. He also stated that his director of religious education "has plans to increase CCD [Confraternity of Christian Doctrine] enrollment" by advertising "our after school religious program in a different way." Another pastor expressed more pessimism, worrying that once the charter school students who "grew up steeped in the Sacred Heart culture" graduate, "I don't know what the impact will be."[54]

Indianapolis

Most recently, the Archdiocese of Indianapolis decided in 2010 to close two inner-city Catholic schools, Saint Anthony Academy and Saint Andrew/ Saint Rita Academy, and reopen them as charter schools, Padua and Andrew Academies.[55] As in Washington, D.C., and Miami, the Archdiocese justified the decision to convert the schools to charter schools as a means of "saving" the schools, explaining in a press release, "Many urban Catholic schools are closing across the nation, and we did not want to leave the students or communities we currently serve. Through this transformation, an urgent and unmet need within urban Indianapolis will be filled."[56] And, as in Washington, D.C., the local government welcomed the conversions, with the mayor of Indianapolis agreeing to serve as the sponsor of the converted charter schools.

Padua and Andrew Academies are the closest thing to true wraparound charter schools that exist in the United States. Before the fall of 2010, the schools were a part of a consortium of schools, the Mother Theodore Catholic Academies, which the Archdiocese created in an effort to strengthen schools serving inner-city communities. Technically, Padua and Andrew Academies are no longer part of this network. The charter operator is an independent corporation called ADI Charter Schools (for "Archdiocese of Indianapolis"). However, ADI Charter Schools, by contract, delegates responsibility for day-to-day operations to the Mother Theodore Academies, and, as a result, schools continue to be directly managed by the Archdiocese.[57]

Students continue to wear uniforms, and the schools' curricula continue to mimic in many respect the traditional Catholic school formula—high expectations for both student academic performance and parental involvement, a disciplined and orderly school environment, and an emphasis on character education. Moreover, the Archdiocese offers religious education classes after school for charter school students. While attendance at these classes is not mandatory (and cannot be, by law), an archdiocesan official reported to us that participation rates exceed 50 percent at the predominantly Latino Padua Academy and falls just shy of that level at Andrew Academy, where the student body is predominantly African American and non-Catholic.[58]

Padua and Andrew Academies are, in some respects, sui generis: the Archdiocese of Indianapolis appears to be the only diocese in the United States directly operating charter schools, and it also appears to be the only diocese that provides after-school religious education targeted specifically for charter school students. But, of course, the facts underlying the Archdiocese's decision to close Saint Anthony and Saint Andrew/Saint Rita are anything but sui generis. Given the financial pressures on many dioceses to close their schools, the experience in Indianapolis points the way toward more charter conversions, of a more aggressive "religious" nature than previously, in the future.

CHAPTER THREE

Catholic School Closures and Neighborhood Social Capital

Obviously, the changes discussed in the preceding chapters—namely, the closure of Catholic schools and the opening of charter schools—have effects not only on the students attending the schools but also on the neighborhoods surrounding them. These latter effects are not well understood. In the chapters that follow, we report the findings of novel research seeking to measure them.

This chapter contains our empirical analysis of the effects of school closures on social cohesion and disorder in Chicago neighborhoods. After a brief description of the Archdiocese of Chicago's school system, we analyze, first, what factors influenced school closure decisions and, second, how school closures between 1984 and 1994 affected subsequent levels of neighborhood disorder and social cohesion. To test these latter effects, we rely on data compiled by the Project on Human Development in Chicago Neighborhoods (PHDCN), which has amassed enormous amounts of information about Chicago neighborhood life. Importantly, for our purposes, in 1994 and 1995, as part of the PHDCN project and in an effort to test the "broken windows hypothesis," which is described in detail in chapter 4, sociologists Robert Sampson and Stephen Raudenbush collected survey information about both observed and perceived disorder and about perceived levels of social cohesion in nearly two hundred Chicago neighborhoods. By matching this data to information about Catholic school closures in Chicago between 1984 and 1994, we are able to measure the effects of school closures on perceived levels of disorder and social cohesion in the PHDCN neighborhoods. We find evidence that a school closure is strongly predictive of increased levels of disorder and suppressed levels of social cohesion in the neighborhood where the school closes. For reasons elaborated in detail at the conclusion of this chapter, these findings are serious and disturbing. They suggest that residents' quality of life diminishes after a school closes in a neighborhood, that residents will be more fearful of victimization (in many cases not unreasonably so), and that they will find it harder to organize and address neighborhood problems.

CATHOLIC SCHOOLS IN CHICAGO

The Archdiocese of Chicago, which encompasses Illinois's Cook and Lake Counties, operates the largest private school system in the United States. During the 2012-2013 school year, the Archdiocese's Catholic school system included 256 schools—216 elementary schools (which are our exclusive focus here) and forty high schools. Over 87,000 students were enrolled in these schools—more students than all but approximately thirty U.S. public school systems (although far fewer than the 300,000 students who attended the Archdiocese's schools in 1965). Of the students recently enrolled in archdiocesan schools at that time, 22 percent were non-Catholic and nearly 30 percent were racial minorities.[1] The Archdiocese reported that the average per-pupil cost of education in its schools was $4,514 for elementary students and $12,858 for high school students. Tuition and fees covered over 60 percent of these costs, with the remainder funded by various sources, including school fundraising efforts, subsidies by parishes and the Archdiocese, and debt.[2] Additionally, a private philanthropic organization known as the Big Shoulders Fund provides substantial support for ninety schools serving poor children, and a number of high schools depend partially on income from endowments and other investments.[3] Tellingly, but not surprisingly, in sharp contrast to the parish school model described in chapter 1, during the 2008-2009 school year, parish financial support made up less than 8 percent of elementary school operating funds.[4]

Between 1984 and 2004, 130 Catholic elementary schools in the Archdiocese of Chicago closed completely or merged with other schools; 110 of these schools were located within the Chicago city limits.[5] The schools that remain open in the Archdiocese heavily blanket downtown Chicago and are scattered through the suburbs to the north and southwest of the city. The schools that have closed were concentrated in central-city neighborhoods,[6] many of which experienced the significant demographic shifts during the second half of the twentieth century described previously. In some cases, the Archdiocese closed several schools in the same neighborhood, which is not surprising given the density of parishes in some neighborhoods. We focus here exclusively on the 225 elementary schools that were open in the City of Chicago proper in 1984, sixty-three of which closed by 1994.

EXPLAINING SCHOOL CLOSURES:
BEYOND DEMOGRAPHICS

A key component of our study was an effort to identify instrumental variables, that is, factors influencing school closure decisions that were exogenous (or unrelated) to demographic variables that might predict neighborhood decline. We recognized that we needed to do this in order to establish a causal link between school closures and subsequent neighborhood changes. The fact that a neighborhood declined after a school closed is suggestive of a connection between urban Catholic schools and social capital. Without disaggregating the school closure decisions from demographic variables that would also predict neighborhood decline, however, we would be unable to demonstrate a cause-and-effect relationship. It might be simply that the Archdiocese closed schools in struggling neighborhoods (which may be the case for many of our observations) and that these neighborhoods continued to decline afterward for reasons unrelated to the closures. If so, the fact that neighborhoods with viable schools were healthier than those where schools had closed might simply reflect the fact that the schools remaining open tended to be located in healthier neighborhoods (again, likely true in many cases). On the other hand, since many Catholic schools in poor Chicago neighborhoods remain open (at least thus far), we also knew that factors other than demographics influenced school closure decisions. Moreover, even a cursory review of financial records of open schools reveals that nearly all of the Archdiocese's elementary schools are struggling financially. Thus, we needed to understand why some poor, financially struggling schools closed and others remained open.[7]

We therefore began by seeking to understand what factors influence archdiocesan school closure decisions. Sister Mary Paul McCaughey, the superintendent of Catholic schools in the Archdiocese, generously offered to meet with us and introduce us to other key members of her staff. These conversations with archdiocesan school officials confirmed our initial assumption that school finances play a huge role: schools that are self-supporting or attached to parishes that provide substantial financial support are unlikely to be targeted for closure. Other financial factors—including the level of debt, dependence on archdiocesan support, and the ability to harness private philanthropy—also influence closure decisions. The Archdiocese's *Catholic Schools Viability Assessment* lists, among the signs of a healthy school, "diverse sources of revenue," "viable development program," and "Endowment Fund with local plan to grow the endowment." We also learned that elementary school enrollments below two hundred are considered unstable—although many archdiocesan schools' enrollments hover just above or below that number—and that schools with consistently low scores on standardized tests raise concerns as well.[8]

Our conversations with archdiocesan officials, however, also confirmed our suspicion that school closure decisions are far from scientific and that the factors discussed above are influential but not determinative. Although archdiocesan practices varied over the time of our study, generally, before a school is closed, it is placed on a "threatened" list by the archdiocesan schools office. At this point, a school's fate is largely determined by intangible factors. In particular, we learned that a school's chances of remaining open increase exponentially if its parish rallies to its support. With a handful of exceptions, the elementary schools operating in the Archdiocese are traditional parochial schools—that is, the schools are operated by a Catholic parish. Except in extraordinary circumstances, this means that the pastor of the parish, who must be a Catholic priest, is the chief administrative officer of both the church and school, although each school also has a principal, who is usually a layperson, charged with day-to-day school operations. Within individual school closure debates, archdiocesan school officials repeatedly emphasized the critical importance of the support and leadership provided by the priest who is the pastor of the parish operating the threatened school. In fact, Sister McCaughey suggested that the pastor-school relationship is the single most important factor driving a school closure decision. Although the final decision to close a school is made by the Archbishop, harried, financially strapped priests who wish to "unload" a school often get their way.

Parish-school relationships are complex, especially because a school represents a significant financial investment, especially for financially strapped inner-city parishes. Some parishioners may resist the suggestion that their parish should financially support the education of non-Catholic children, and parishioners with children in public schools may want their parish to focus instead on religious educational programs (traditionally referred to as CCD for Confraternity of Christian Doctrine). Pastors may see the school as an unnecessary drain on scarce resources, which must also go toward paying salaries for the parish staff as well as, among other things, utilities and upkeep on aging church buildings, which may hold architectural and historic value but frequently have experienced decades of delayed maintenance.[9] Sister McCaughey offered several recent anecdotal accounts of extern priests (that is, priests serving Chicago parishes who are from other dioceses or foreign countries) who lacked a strong commitment to Catholic education generally and their associated schools in particular. In several of these cases, the students in the school were not, by and large, members of the parish, and the parish members did not, by and large, live in the neighborhood. These priests tended to see the schools as unnecessary burdens and the school buildings as a potential source of revenue. If the school is closed, the pastor has the option of leasing the building—often for use as a charter school.[10] Sister McCaughey explained that the financial incentives created by school closures were a source of concern because the parish (rather than the Archdiocese) keeps any revenue from the lease or sale of the school building.

As an aside, we suspect that these intraparish political and financial factors partially explain what initially appeared to be a curiosity: our analysis of data from the last three censuses revealed that schools in neighborhoods with higher Latino (and presumably Catholic) populations were slightly more likely to close than those in white or African American neighborhoods. Although Latinos will soon make up a majority of Catholics in the United States, only 3 percent of Latino children in the United States attend Catholic schools.[11] Moreover, while less than 5 percent of U.S. Catholics are African American, African Americans account for approximately 12 percent of urban Catholic school students. The Latino share of Catholic school students has steadily increased over the past two decades and now exceeds the African American share by approximately 5 percent.[12] In many cases, however, African American families have a longer history of turning to inner-city Catholic schools to educate their children. From a public choice perspective, therefore, black families may be better positioned to mount more successful "save our school" campaigns. Thus, while we do not suggest that these demographic factors are causal, we do believe that current demographic trends suggest that efforts to attract Latino families to Catholic schools are critical to the future of many urban schools.

Our conversation with Sister McCaughey led us to hypothesize that parish leadership characteristics might predict, perhaps to a greater extent than demographics, which schools close. In particular, we hypothesized that characteristics of the pastors in parishes affiliated with a school might independently explain some of the variance in school closure patterns, that is, that pastor characteristics might be the instrumental variables we sought. We suspected, for example, that if something was "broken" in the parish leadership structure—a pastor was removed suddenly and unexpectedly or was accused of abuse—the school operated by his parish would be more likely to close. We also thought that a pastor's age might predict school closures. Since schools are administratively and financially burdensome, we hypothesized that older pastors might lose the energy needed to run a school, especially as the parish membership aged and the student population became increasingly non-Catholic. Alternatively, we thought it equally plausible that younger priests, who are more likely to have attended public schools, might not value Catholic schools as much as older priests who experienced Catholic schools as students. We also, taking hints from Sister McCaughey, hypothesized that priests from outside the diocese might feel less committed to local Catholic schools.

In order to test these hypotheses, we examined information about the leadership of the parishes with schools in the Archdiocese. We learned who led the parishes associated with closed schools at the time of their closing. If, as was usually the case, the parish was led by a priest, we recorded his age, how long he had been in the parish, whether he was ordained in the Archdiocese, or, alternatively, whether he belonged to a religious order such as the Jesuits or Franciscans. We also checked whether any priest assigned to the parishes with schools had been accused of sex abuse. Much of the publicly available data on pastors came from a publication called *The Official Catholic Directory*, which is published annually and lists each parish and school in each diocese and archdiocese, along with the name of the pastor and other priests assigned to a parish—or, in relatively rare cases, information on parishes led by administrators who might not even be priests. *The Official Catholic Directory* also provides the year of ordination for every priest in the United States, as well as the names of the members of religious orders working in every diocese. By tracking pastoral assignments, *The Official Catholic Directory* enabled us to know when each pastor arrived at, and left, a parish. In a few cases, when we could not identify parish leadership, we called the parish or relied on Internet searches and/or the encyclopedic memory of Sister Margaret Farley, who has worked in the archdiocesan schools office for decades. We gathered information on clergy abuse both from an official archdiocesan report on substantiated accounts and from a website that tracks accusations, including many unsubstantiated accounts.[13] Finally, we grouped all of this information into a number of "pastor variables," which we describe in greater detail below.

Using this data as well as demographic variables from the 1980 and 1990 censuses, we then performed a binomial regression to determine how strongly each of our variables affected the likelihood that a school would close. As we anticipated, increasing poverty in a neighborhood was positively related to school closings. As the percentage of African Americans and Hispanics increased in a PHDCN neighborhood, again as we expected, the likelihood of a school closing also increased. Interestingly, the probability that a school would close also increased when a neighborhood began to improve economically (as indicated by rising incomes and, in Sampson and Raudenbush's observations, by the presence of "upscale restaurants and lounges"). We surmise that this is because gentrifying neighborhoods experience "yuppification" as families are replaced with residents who have no, or few, children and who might be less interested in Catholic schools than their working-class predecessors.[14]

But, importantly, factors other than these demographic variables also predicted school closures. Our analysis confirmed our suspicion that there are several pastor variables (instrumental variables) that predict school closures as much or more than neighborhood demographics. While we did not find the number of externs that Sister McCaughey led us to expect,[15] we did find patterns of pastor-school relationships that differentiate schools that closed from those that did not: First, we found a slight, but not statistically significant, distinction between the two kinds of priests in the Roman Catholic Church—"diocesan" (or "secular") and "religious." Diocesan priests commit themselves to working in the geographic diocese where they are ordained; they take a vow of obedience to the local bishop, who assigns the priests to a ministry, almost always within the diocese. Religious priests belong to religious orders—such as the Jesuits or Franciscans—that are not tied to any specific geographic location. Religious priests take a vow of obedience to the superior of their order. The superior, rather than the bishop, determines a religious priest's ministerial assignment, which may be anywhere in the world. We suspected that diocesan priests might be more vested in the work of the Archdiocese, including its parish schools. And indeed we found that schools led by a religious priest closed slightly more frequently than those led by a priest ordained in the Archdiocese of Chicago (26 percent for the closed schools compared with 23 percent for the open schools). Second, again confirming Sister McCaughey's emphasis on the importance of a priest's commitment to a school, many schools closed when a long-standing pastor reached retirement age and a new priest, who did not share his predecessor's long history with the school, became pastor at the parish and school. Indeed, about 22 percent of the closed schools had pastors in their first year of service to the parish when the school closed.[16] Third, the age of the pastor was also strongly predictive of school closures. In fact the likelihood that a school would close increased by 1 percent per year elapsing since a pastor's ordination (the only date for which we could obtain reliable information). We assume that the date of ordination is a rough proxy for age since most (but not all) priests are ordained as young men.[17]

Finally, the factor that most predicted that a school would close—more so than income or race—was whether there was something "irregular" about the parish leadership. Some of the schools tragically were part of parishes where a priest was alleged to have abused children. Several of the parishes were being run by interim "administrators" on temporary assignment from the Archdiocese—usually priests, but also some laymen and -women or re-ligious sisters. According to Sister McCaughey, a priest in the Archdiocese of Chicago is usually appointed as pastor in a parish for a six-year term. Pastors are frequently renewed for another six years, although after two terms, renewal occurs only if a priest would otherwise retire during his next term. If a pastor is unable to complete his term, the Archdiocese typi-cally appoints an "administrator" to complete the term. This might occur if a priest dies, becomes seriously ill, or develops substance abuse or mental health problems. In some cases, a pastor may leave the priesthood to marry or assume life as a layperson for other reasons. In any of these cases, the parish and its parishioners likely would be severely distressed and therefore less likely to rally to the cause of saving a school. The outsider appointed to administer the parish for a short time also likely would be less committed to keeping the school open in cases of doubt. Schools affiliated with these troubled parishes, captured in the "Irregularity" variable in table 3.1, were ten times more likely to close as healthy parishes led by pastors in regular rotation.[18]

BEGINNING TO UNDERSTAND THE NEIGHBORHOOD EFFECTS OF CATHOLIC SCHOOL CLOSURES

Having identified factors that were both more predictive of whether a school closed and unrelated to the demographic predictors of neighborhood de-cline, that is, instrumental variables, we were satisfied that school closures could be disaggregated from factors influencing neighborhood health. We therefore were able to turn to the question at the heart of this book: What does a Catholic school mean to an urban neighborhood? We review our

TABLE 3.1. Variables predicting school closures

Variable	B	Exp(B)
Irregularity in the parish	−2.304	10.010
	(.160)	
Years priest has been ordained	−0.012	1.012
	(.004)	
Share black in census tract 1990	−2.189	8.923
	(.149)	
Share Hispanic in census tract 1990	−2.266	9.645
	(.182)	
Poverty rate in census tract 1990	−1.629	5.099
	(.342)	
Constant	−2.758	.063
	(.163)	

Note: Table 3.1 summarizes our binary logistic regression analyzing factors influencing school closures. The first column shows the coefficient for each characteristic that will form the best predicting ability from the data in the sample, as well as the standard deviation (in parentheses). The statistical significance in each case was at less than .01 probability of error. The whole equation predicted 21.2 percent of the variance from the mean. In this equation, guesses made based upon the equation would be right 72.8 percent of the time. The final column explains the economic significance of each coefficient.

findings here, all of which strongly suggest that a Catholic school means a great deal and that closures have significant negative neighborhood impacts. We found that school closures were associated with increased levels of disorder and decreased levels of social cohesion in a neighborhood, factors which, for reasons we explain in the concluding pages of this chapter, are all signs of serious neighborhood distress.

Our analysis of school closure effects involves three primary sources of data. The first source is data obtained from the Archdiocese of Chicago's Office of Catholic Schools on school closings (and the small number of openings), including the addresses of the schools and occasionally information about the reassignment of students (in case of a merger) or the school buildings (in case of rental to a charter school or demolition).[19] The second is demographic data by census tract from the decennial censuses of 1980 and 1990.[20] The third comes from the PHDCN, which we briefly described above and which is now housed at the University of Michigan's Interuniversity Consortium for Political and Social Research (ICPSR). Three types of PHDCN data were made available to us. The first type consists of systemic and very detailed observations made of observable disorder in eighty of the 323 PHDCN "neighborhood clusters." In 1994, Robert Sampson and

Stephen Raudenbush enlisted trained observers, driving sport utility ve-
hicles, to videotape and catalog visible disorder along nearly 25,000 face
blocks in selected Chicago "neighborhood clusters." They then observed
the videotapes and coded the presence of nine manifestations of physical
disorder and seven manifestations of social disorder. The second type of
data was a survey, conducted in 1994 and 1995, of 4,000 Chicago residents
from all of the 343 neighborhoods, which was designed to elicit information about perceptions of neighborhood crime, social cohesion, and physical and social disorder. Additionally, we were provided with data from a
longitudinal survey of 8,782 Chicago residents measuring all kinds of demographic, educational, psychological, labor, and other variables. We were
disappointed that the latter survey response rates were spotty, rendering the
data extremely unreliable and, as we discuss in the Introduction, preventing
us from using it to analyze how school closures affected disorder and social
cohesion over time.[21]

To measure school closure effects on these variables, we plotted the geographic location of the closed schools using a mapping program (ArcGIS),
which enabled us to associate each closing in its particular year to the
census tract data preceding and following it. Personnel at the ICPSR then
matched the school closing and neighborhood tract data so that we knew
whether, and in what year, a Catholic elementary school (or more than one)
had closed in any of the PHDCN neighborhoods. ICPSR personnel also told
us whether or not a Catholic elementary school had been open between
1984 and 2004 in each of the 343 PHDCN neighborhood clusters. Only
four neighborhoods within the PHDCN survey data set did not contain at
least one Catholic elementary school in 1984. These were excluded from the
sample analyzed. We also excluded information on Catholic high schools,
although preliminary estimates suggested that they exhibit similar results.
We excluded this data for two reasons. First, because high schools draw
students from a larger geographic area than most elementary schools, we
thought that they were less likely to be neighborhood institutions. Second,
because very few Catholic high schools are associated with parishes, we
were unable to employ the pastor variables that enabled us to disentangle school closure decisions from the demographic variables predictive of
neighborhood decline.

In an ideal world, we would have used Sampson and Raudenbush's systematic (that is, videotaped) observations to measure the connections between school closures and disorder. Unfortunately, we could not use this
data because not enough neighborhoods that included closed schools were

selected for systematic observation. In other words, many of our closed schools were in neighborhood clusters that were not selected, as were many of our open schools. Instead we relied on the PHDCN's "community survey" of 4,000 residents who answered questions about their neighborhood, including the levels of perceived physical and social disorder as well as social cohesion in their communities. We recognize that this survey data is not a precise measure of actual disorder and social cohesion in Chicago neighborhoods since resident perceptions may be skewed by a number of factors, including, as Sampson and Raudenbush have themselves demonstrated, neighborhood demographics. These surveys, however, were the best measures of disorder and social cohesion available for our project, and we have high confidence in the survey design and results given the quality of researchers designing it.[22]

Using this survey data, we sought to measure whether Catholic school closures were associated with positive or negative neighborhood effects. The available empirical evidence, discussed previously, suggests that public schools are associated with increased disorder and crime. Given what we knew about Catholic schools' success vis-à-vis public schools as educational institutions, we wondered whether they might work very differently as community institutions as well. That is, we wondered whether they might create and maintain social capital, especially in poor neighborhoods where there are frequently few other viable community institutions. We therefore set about modeling causation directly using both the variables predicting school closure described above and, with several demographic variables, a school closure's effect on a neighborhood.

To do so, we estimated the effect of a Catholic school closure on perceived disorder and social cohesion efficacy using a two-step regression analysis.[23] This method is appropriate for our study because there are possible feedback loops in the variables that we are seeking to measure. That is, the school closure may cause neighborhood change, but closure may also be caused by neighborhood change. The model allows us to simultaneously predict both whether or not a school will close (the endogenous variable, which might both be affected by neighborhood changes and/or generate them) and the effects of the closure on the PHDCN neighborhood where the closed school was located. In other words, the model first estimates the likelihood that a school will close, as in table 3.1. The predicted values for each neighborhood are then fed into an equation predicting, for example, perceived neighborhood social disorder. The basic idea is that by including not only the socioeconomic factors that might explain both neighborhood decline and school closings, but also variables that should not directly affect neighborhood health (in our case, the pastor variables described above), we can show the effect of a school closing, independent of the demographic variables. In other words, the two-step model enabled us to move from correlation toward causation. While ideally we would have preferred a dynamic model of the kind utilized in the next chapter, our one-time PHDCN survey data precluded this more sophisticated approach, which is available where there is longitudinal data.

School Closures and Perceived Social Disorder

Using the two-step regression model and the variables described above, we first sought to measure how a school closure affected perceived social disorder in a neighborhood. The PHDCN community survey asked residents "how much of a problem" they considered three manifestations of social disorder—drinking in public, selling or using drugs, and teenagers causing disturbances.[24] Respondents were offered three possible responses—"big problem, "somewhat of a problem," "not a problem"—which were scored from 3 to 1, totaled, and averaged to obtain the scaled result. As table 3.2 reflects, taking into account whether or not a school closed, the estimated equation predicted more than 55 percent of the variation in perceived social disorder in a neighborhood [R^2(adj.) = 0.556]. In fact, a Catholic school closure was nearly as predictive as the demographic variables in the census tract. The median family income in the census tract had the opposite sign (in other words, as income increased, social disorder decreased), was also

TABLE 3.2. Variables predicting perceived neighborhood social disorder

Variable	Unstandardized coefficient	Standardized coefficient
(Constant)	1.876 (.113)***	
Predicted value of whether Catholic school in neighborhood closed before 1995	.338 (.171)*	.196
Share black in census tract, 1990	.245 (.108)*	.249
Share Hispanic in census tract, 1990	.544 (.144)***	.362
Median family income in census tract, 1990	−7.703E−6 (.000)***	−.306

*$P < .05$.
**$P < .01$.
***$P < .001$.

statistically significant, and the effect was larger than the effect of the increased Latino population or whether the Catholic school closed.

School Closures and Perceived Physical Disorder

As with social disorder, we relied on the PHDCN community survey to measure the effects of Catholic school closures on perceived physical disorder. The survey instrument asked three questions pertaining to physical disorder: "How much of a problem is litter, broken glass or trash on sidewalks and streets" in your neighborhood?; "How much of a problem is graffiti on buildings and walls?"; and "How much of a problem are vacant or deserted houses or storefronts?" Possible responses ranged from "not a problem" to "a very big problem"; the responses, scored from 1 to 3, were totaled and averaged over the survey respondents to obtain the scaled result. As above, we conducted a two-step regression using the same demographic variables and pastor-related variables to predict whether a school closed in the relevant time period and the predicted value plus demographic variables to measure the effects of a Catholic school closure on perceived physical disorder. School closures, taken with other variables, predicted nearly 53 percent of the variation in perceived physical disorder between neighborhoods [R^2(adj.) = 0.528]. Table 3.3 indicates that an increase in perceived physical disorder predicted by a Catholic school closing in a neighborhood was larger than the increase predicted by an increase in the percentage of black residents in the census tract and about two-thirds the size of a the effect of a decrease in median family income. Once income was taken into account,

TABLE 3.3. Variables predicting perceived neighborhood physical disorder

Variable	Unstandardized coefficient	Standardized coefficient
(Constant)	1.599 (0.095)***	
Predicted value of whether Catholic school closed in neighborhood before 1995	0.322 (0.142)*	0.204
Share black in census tract, 1990	0.106 (0.090)	0.239
Share Hispanic in census tract, 1990	0.423 (0.120)**	0.001
Median family income in census tract, 1990	−6.429E−6*** (−.000)**	.000

*$P < .05$.
**$P < .01$.
***$P < .001$.

the share of African Americans in the census tract did not have a statistically significant effect on perceived levels of physical disorder.

School Closures and Social Cohesion

For our measure of social cohesion, we again relied on the PHDCN community survey, which asked residents to indicate their level of agreement and disagreement with the following statements: (a) "People around here are willing to help their neighbors"; (b) "This is a close-knit neighborhood"; (c) "People in this neighborhood can be trusted"; (d) "People in this neighborhood do not generally get along with each other"; and (e) "People in this neighborhood do not share the same values."[25] Taking into account school closures and census variables explained nearly 45 percent of the variance in social cohesion between neighborhoods [R^2(adj.) = 0.449]. The predicted value for whether or not the Catholic school closed and the share Hispanic in the census tract were both statistically significant, with the Catholic school impact larger than any of the census variables (table 3.4). As was the case with social and physical disorder, median family income in the census tract had the opposite sign (in other words, as income increased, social cohesion increased). Income had a statistically significant effect on social cohesion. As with perceived physical disorder, once income was taken into account, the share of African Americans in the census tract on the perceived level of social cohesion was again not statistically significant.

TABLE 3.4. Variables predicting neighborhood social cohesion

Variable	Unstandardized coefficient	Standardized coefficient
(Constant)	3.506 (.089)***	
Predicted value of whether Catholic school closed in neighborhood before 1995	−.377 (.135)**	−.308
Share black in census tract, 1990	.085 (.085)	−.122
Share Hispanic in census tract, 1990	−.311 (.114)**	−.293
Median family income in census tract, 1990	3.973E−6 (.000)*	.223

*$P < .05$.
**$P < .01$.
***$P < .001$.

DISORDER, SOCIAL CAPITAL, AND
URBAN NEIGHBORHOOD LIFE

All of these results suggest that Catholic schools are important, stabilizing
forces in urban neighborhoods and that school closures lead to less socially
cohesive, more disorderly, neighborhoods. The remainder of this chapter
explores the important, and previously unexplored, implications of our findings for urban neighborhoods that lose their Catholic schools. In contrast
to previous studies focusing on what urban Catholic schools mean for their
students, we seek to understand what they mean for their neighborhoods.
In order to do so, we situate our findings within broader debates about the
costs of disorder and the benefits of social capital on urban neighborhood
life. For the present time, we leave to one side the debate about the "broken
windows hypothesis," which posits a causal link between disorder and serious crime. The question is a hotly contested one, which we save for the following chapter in order to focus here on the uncontested effects of disorder
on neighborhood life. We have just demonstrated, as best we can using the
one-time survey data, that Catholic school closures lead to elevated levels of
disorder and suppressed levels of social cohesion in a community. Based on
these findings, we can conclude—without taking sides in the broken windows debate—that Catholic school closures do not portend good things for
urban neighborhoods. We base this conclusion on two simple and uncontested facts: first, disorder suppresses the social capital that a community
needs to organize informally to address neighborhood problems, including
serious crime, and second, disorder increases the fear of crime, which in
turn also tends to suppress social capital. In other words, disorder, social
capital, and fear have feedback effects upon one another, which likely, over
time, will increase crime and, even in the interim, are certain to decrease
the quality of life in a neighborhood.

Disorder and Social Capital

To begin, it is important to note that—even leaving to one side questions
about the effect of disorder on urban neighborhoods—our findings suggest that Catholic school closures are associated with lower levels of social
cohesion in a neighborhood. This finding, standing alone, is sobering. We
believe that it is safe to assume that levels of social cohesion and levels of
social capital are correlated. Social capital is the subject of a large and somewhat contentious literature that we discuss in greater detail in chapter 7.[26]

For present purposes, Robert Putnam's "lean and mean" definition—that is, "social networks and the norms of reciprocity and trustworthiness that arise from them"—suffices.[27] There is little question that social capital is critically important to urban neighborhood health. The best evidence for this proposition comes from numerous empirical studies of collective efficacy, the term that sociologists and social psychologists use to describe the "ability of neighborhoods to realize the common values of residents and maintain effective social controls."[28] These studies universally find that neighborhoods with low levels of collective efficacy are more dangerous, more disorderly, and have lower levels of residential stability—a factor that in turn mediates the demographic variables associated with low levels of collective efficacy—than neighborhoods with higher collective efficacy levels.[29] Not surprisingly, a resident who counts on her neighbors to address community problems has less cause to seek to move to a new community; a resident who does not know her neighbors, or—worse—does not trust them, tends not to enlist their assistance in efforts to address neighborhood problems.[30]

While collective efficacy and social capital are not synonymous, we assume that high levels of collective efficacy correlate with high levels of social capital. We also assume that neighborhood social cohesion is an important input into both social capital and collective efficacy. In fact, Sampson and Raudenbush's own formula for measuring collective efficacy incorporated their measure of social cohesion, although we do not attempt to replicate that analysis here. Collective efficacy is one way that members of a community can successfully harness social capital. Since social networks and trust between neighbors are almost certainly needed to catalyze effective informal collective action, it is entirely reasonable to assume that social capital is a foundation of collective efficacy—and also that social cohesion is needed to form social networks and trust between neighbors.[31]

Thus, even if our findings had only linked Catholic school closures with low levels of social cohesion, we could expect that, over time, the neighborhoods where schools closed would decline. Our finding that school closures are also linked to increased levels of physical and social disorder strengthens this prediction because disorder in itself tends to suppress collective efficacy in a neighborhood. In their important study, which generated the data upon which we rely here, Sampson and Raudenbush compared levels of observable disorder to levels of serious crime in a neighborhood as part of an effort to test the broken windows hypothesis by determining whether more disorderly neighborhoods were, in fact, more dangerous. When they compared neighborhood disorder levels to crime levels, Sampson and Raudenbush initially found a strong correlation between disorder and both crime and collective efficacy—that is, higher levels of disorder correlated strongly with higher crime rates and lower levels of collective efficacy in a neighborhood. The direct correlation between disorder and crime largely disappeared, however, when they controlled for neighborhood structural factors such as race, income, and residential stability.[32]

Sampson and Raudenbush also found, however, that, even after controlling for these neighborhood structural factors, disorder was strongly linked to reduced levels of collective efficacy. Moreover, they found that collective efficacy was strongly predictive of higher crime rates. Thus, they were able to link disorder indirectly with increased crime in a multistage causal chain. Disorder triggered decreases in collective efficacy, which in turn predicts higher crime rates. Thus, disorder, they predicted, may have a "cascade effect," that indirectly affects crime rates by undermining collective efficacy. They hypothesized that perceptions of disorder may color residents' judgments about the level of cohesion and control in their community—a hypothesis that is consistent with previous research suggesting that perceptions of disorder strongly influence individual perceptions of collective efficacy. Disorder, they suggested, might therefore "turn out to be important for understanding migration patterns, investment by businesses, and overall neighborhood viability." In other words, even if disorder is not directly linked to serious crime, disorder may, by suppressing social capital in a neighborhood, set off a chain of events that eventually leads to more crime.[33] We return to this possibility in the next chapter.

Disorder, Fear, and Social Capital

Disorder, including the disorder apparently triggered by Catholic school closures, and social capital are linked in another way: disorder causes people to be afraid, and fear tends to suppress social capital. While the causal connection between disorder and crime is hotly contested, the connection between disorder and the fear of crime is not. Nearly all efforts to measure the connection between disorder and fear find a strong positive correlation between them. People intuitively associate disorder and crime. Apparently, the average observer agrees with the broken windows hypothesis; when she sees physical disorder or experiences social incivilities in a neighborhood, she assumes that serious crime is prevalent there as well. Indeed, disorder may prove more fear inducing than actual personal experience with crime itself because residents who live in disorder-plagued neighbor-hoods encounter disorder on a daily basis, even if they are rarely, if ever, victimized.

Disorder generates fear at both the neighborhood and individual levels. At the neighborhood level, disorder is not only positively correlated with fear of crime, but higher levels of disorder correspond to higher levels of fear. At the individual level, residents within the same neighborhoods ex-perience different levels of fear depending upon their individual percep-tions of the amount of disorder in their communities. That is, the more disorder a person sees, the more fearful she is. For example, Jeanette Cov-ington and Ralph Taylor interviewed over 1,500 residents about the levels of disorder in sixty-six Baltimore neighborhoods and then compared these responses with physical assessments of neighborhood conditions conducted by trained observers. They found that fear was most strongly influenced by the disorder levels within a respondent's neighborhood. Residents of neigh-borhoods with higher levels of observed physical and social disorder had higher fear levels. They also found that individual perceptions of disorder were strongly linked to individualized, within-neighborhood, differences in fear. Residents who saw more disorder than their neighbors, or expressed greater concern about disorder, were more fearful.[34] Moreover, there is evi-dence that police efforts to reduce disorder cause people to be less fearful of crime, even when crime itself does not decrease.[35]

The relationship between disorder and fear of crime is important for the present purposes because fear, like disorder, is negatively correlated with collective efficacy and therefore—in our view—neighborhood-level social capital. It is easy to hypothesize why: when individuals are fearful, they tend to take steps to minimize the risk of victimization. For this reason, the level of precaution-taking in a community is a common measure of fearfulness.[36] These precautions are costly, in both economic and social terms. Economi-cally, Americans spend more on these private precautions—estimates range from $160 billion to $300 billion—than on the total U.S. law enforcement budget.[37] In other words, private individuals spend more to avoid being vic-timized than U.S. governments at all levels (federal, state, and local) spend on police, prosecutors, judges, and prisons. And these figures do not reflect the total cost of crime avoidance, such as the opportunity costs of remaining inside behind locked doors to avoid victimization.[38]

Many economists condemn private precautionary measures as socially wasteful, reasoning that they do not reduce the total amount of crime but rather simply displace it. That is, precautions only deter criminals from victimizing protected individuals, not from committing crimes. Instead, criminals will choose to victimize those who have not taken steps to protect themselves. And precaution taking may prove counterproductive for another reason. Social influence theory predicts that people will be law-abiding when they perceive that their neighbors are obeying the law. As Dan Kahan has observed, "Individuals don't decide to commit crimes in isolation; rather . . . individuals are much more likely to commit crimes when they perceive that criminal activity is widespread."[39] But private actions taken to avoid victimization cannot, by definition, support such a perception. Not only should residents take fewer steps to protect themselves from victimization if their neighbors are law-abiding, but the private deterrence measures that fearful individuals are most likely to take—including neighborhood watch groups, alarm systems, extra locks, bars on windows, and so on—tend to signal that crime is prevalent in a community. In other words, when a resident takes steps to prevent victimization, especially visible steps such as installing bars on her windows, she may signal to her neighbors that she does not trust them. Even if neighbors do not interpret precautionary measures as evincing a lack of trust—perhaps because the community is plagued by criminals from other neighborhoods—precautionary measures likely still undermine collective efficacy and suppress social capital. Consider, for example, the likely effects of one of the simplest and most common crime-avoidance strategies—remaining indoors. Not only does this "prisoner in my own home" phenomenon likely turn the public spaces in a community over to social deviants, but it also reduces opportunities for the informal, interneighbor socialization needed to build social capital.[40]

In light of all of this evidence, we can begin to answer this book's central question: What does a Catholic school mean to an urban neighborhood? Based upon our findings, we can predict with some confidence that neighborhoods where Catholic school closures occur will be less socially cohesive and more disorderly than neighborhoods with viable schools. At a minimum, we know that residents in neighborhoods where schools close experience higher levels of disorder—which, regardless of any secondary effects, tends to make life unpleasant. Moreover, since we know that social cohesion promotes—and disorder suppresses—social capital and that, over time, suppressed levels of social capital are correlated with increased crime, we can predict that the initial effects of school closures may trigger a course of events that leads to serious crime. We now turn to that hypothesis.

CHAPTER FOUR

Catholic School Closures and Neighborhood Crime

Our findings in the previous chapter—that Catholic school closures reduce neighborhood social cohesion and increase neighborhood disorder—naturally led us to wonder whether Catholic school closures also might affect rates of serious crime. Given the well-established connections between collective efficacy and crime, the social capital generated by Catholic schools should enable neighbors to organize and address the kinds of social problems that lead to serious crime. Or, to flip the hypothesis, if Catholic schools generate social capital, and their disappearance from a neighborhood erodes it, then we can surmise that neighbors in places losing Catholic schools will find it more difficult to organize and address those problems—a reality that should, in the short or long term, lead to more crime. Our curiosity about the extent and nature of the connection, if any, between urban Catholic school closures and rates of serious crime was also fed by the ongoing debate over the "broken-windows hypothesis," which posits a causal connection between disorder and serious crime.

We turn to these questions here. Using crime data provided at the police beat level by the Chicago Police Department, we test whether and how Catholic school closures between 1990 and 1996 affected the rates of six major crimes reported between 1999 and 2005. We find, as we suspected we would, that Catholic school closures do affect crime rates. During the period for which we have crime data, crime declined dramatically across the city of Chicago, in keeping with national trends. We therefore expected that crime rates would decline in a beat, regardless of whether a school previously closed in it. What we wanted to understand, however, was whether a Catholic school closure might cause a police beat to have more crime than it would have had if the school had not closed. And this is exactly what our analysis suggests.

Specifically, we find that previous Catholic school closures affected the slope of the decline in serious crime in a police beat. That is, even after controlling for numerous other factors that might affect crime rates and for variables other than these factors that predicted school closures (specifically, the instrumental variables relating to parish leadership discussed in the previous chapter), crime decreased more slowly between 1999 and 2005 in police beats where Catholic schools closed between 1990 and 1996 than in beats where schools remained open. This chapter reviews these findings and, as previously, situates them within broader debates about the connections between crime, disorder, and social capital.

CATHOLIC SCHOOL CLOSURES AND CRIME

To recap, the hypotheses we seek to test here are as follows: first, given the apparent connections between Catholic school closures and suppressed levels of social cohesion, we hypothesized that Catholic school closures might trigger increases in serious crime—an important and sobering finding in its own right, but one only indirectly relevant to the debate about the putative link between disorder and crime. Second, we also hypothesized that school-closure–related disorder might also be linked to serious crime, a finding that would tend to support the broken-windows hypothesis, which links disorder and serious crime. Our empirical analysis clearly confirms the first hypothesis. That is, we link Catholic school closures to the trajectory of crime in a police beat in the years following a closure. The investigation of the second hypothesis generated new evidence for the broken-windows debate in a way that was, we admit, somewhat unexpected to us. We were not able, because of data limitations, to definitively link the disorder triggered by earlier school closures to later crime, although our findings are strongly suggestive of such a link. What we did find, however, was a link between levels of perceived disorder in 1995 (as captured by the Project on Human Development in Chicago Neighborhoods [PHDCN] survey) and the intercept, or starting level, of serious crime in 1999. This finding lends support to the broken-windows hypothesis. We discuss the import of these findings below.

Again we rely on multiple sources of data, including data on Catholic schools provided by the Archdiocese of Chicago, data on parish leadership from *The Official Catholic Directory*, data on clergy abuse allegations, the PHDCN data on social cohesion and disorder, and demographic data from the 1990 census and the 2000 census. Additionally, we obtained police beat-level data from the Chicago Police Department on the incidence of six major crimes (aggravated assault, aggravated battery, murder, burglary, robbery, and aggravated sexual assault) from 1999–2005. The total number of incidents during this period was as follows: 53,882 aggravated assaults; 101,828 aggravated batteries; 4,105 murders; 185,074 burglaries; 125,628 robberies; and 14,082 sexual assaults. As with the survey data, we recognize that this data does not perfectly track actual crime levels in Chicago. This is because it reflects both the crimes that citizens choose to report and law enforcement activities and priorities. In particular, we are aware that crime-incidence data might be affected by the policing strategies employed in Chicago. In 1994, the Chicago Police Department instituted a comprehensive community policing effort, known as the Chicago Alternative Policing Strategy (CAPS). CAPS represents a devolutionary approach to policing policy, which—like all community policing efforts—seeks to increase the frequency and quality of police-citizen interactions, in part by enlisting community members to help shape policing priorities. Nine or ten officers are assigned to each beat and supervised by a sergeant. In order to maximize their "turf orientation," these officers are given long-term assignments and primary responsibility for responding to calls in their beat. CAPS officers also hold monthly community meetings in their beats, and district advisory committees, made up of residents, community leaders, business owners, and other stakeholders, meet regularly with police leaders to discuss community priorities. During the 1990s, approximately 250 beat meetings were held each month. During the period of our study, the policing strategies that resulted from the CAPS program necessarily varied across neighborhoods. For example, a community prioritizing the elimination of drug-related violence might have opted to hold a "smoke-out"—bar-b-que picnic—on corners or in parks where dealers congregate; a neighborhood most concerned about a prostitution problem might have engaged in "positive loitering" to deter solicitations.[1] The upshot is that the police priorities varied by beat, and these variations may have affected the data we draw upon in this study. For example, if residents came to have more confidence that police would respond to their concerns, then presumably they would be more likely to report crimes to the police. Since resident confidence and involvement may have varied across beats, we assume that the accuracy of beat crime statistics does as well. And, of course, we cannot rule out the possibility that officers' accuracy in recording criminal incidents also varied across beats. Still, we believe that the crime data is arguably more reliable than the survey data since it was compiled for important direct purposes other than academic consumption.

Using this data, we sought to test the connection, if any, between 1990–96 school closures and 1999–2005 crime. We also sought to test whether Catholic school-closure-related effects on disorder trigger subsequent increases in crime. In order to do so, we used a latent growth curve model and boosted logistic regression to predict crime from 1999 to 2005 in the police beats surrounding the 159 Catholic schools that were open in 1989. Because we describe the full statistical model employed in this analysis in detail elsewhere,[2] we summarily describe the process and the results here.

Overall, crime declined nationally and in Chicago during the period of our data. Figure 4.1 shows a very slight decrease between 1999 and 2000, a rapid decrease until 2004, and a leveling between 2004 and 2005. We therefore expected crime to decline in most police beats in Chicago, regardless of whether a Catholic school closed during the relevant time period. If Catholic school closures made no difference to crime rates, the line (curve) for beats containing closed Catholic schools would be superimposed upon the line shown in figure 4.1. The latent growth model allows us to generate and contrast the lines for beats in which schools remained open and for which

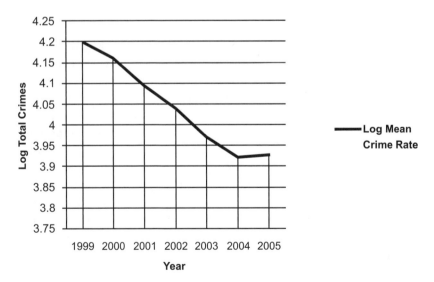

FIGURE 4.1 Basic mean of the log crime rate per year (1999–2006)

TABLE 4.1. Summary of effects of closing and disorder from boosted logistic regression

	Effects on intercept factor (standard error)	Effects on slope factor (standard error)	Effects on disorder (standard error)
Disorder	0.237* (0.106)	−0.017 (0.129)	
Closing	−0.082 (0.154)	0.541** (0.183)	0.184 (0.127)
1990PCA1			0.719*** (0.034)
1990PCA2			0.223*** (0.049)
1990PCA3			−0.004 (0.059)
2000PCA1	0.237* (0.106)	−0.462*** (0.133)	
2000PCA1	−0.328** (0.055)	−0.388*** (0.115)	
2000PCA3	0.208** (0.071)	−0.312*** (0.075)	
R^2	0.342	0.461	0.601

Note: Dependent variable is crime rate/1,000 by police beat (logged) for 1999–2005. It was created using a boosted logistic regression (Trevor Hastie, *The Elements of Statistical Learning* [New York: Springer-Verlag, 2009]) using the Twang Package in R. PCA are the coefficients derived using principal component analysis, as defined in the text.
*$P < .10$.
**$P < .05$.
***$P < .01$.

they closed by examining two characteristics of these curves for all police beats—the starting level of serious crime in a police beat in 1999 (which we refer to as the "intercept") and direction and rate of change in the crime rate between 1999 and 2005 (which we refer to as the "slope").

In order to overcome possible objections that any differences are caused by other characteristics of the neighborhoods represented by these beats, we statistically equalize them across a number of variables. These variables include the parish-/pastor-based instrumental variables that we previously described and that continued to strongly predict school closures during this later time period, as well as a number of socioeconomic factors (drawn from the 1990 and 2000 decennial censuses) that are associated with crime[3] and with school closing disorder (also gathered as a composite variable by the PHDCN). We use data from the 1990 census to predict school closures between 1990 and 1996 and perceived disorder in 1995 and 2000 census data to predict serious crime between 1999 and 2005. In table 4.1, collections of these demographic variables, which reflect relative social deprivation, immigration, and residential stability, are grouped into PCAs (or principal components). As we model each year's crime rate for each beat we observe, we also consider the effect of the location of the beat, since crime in one neighborhood might affect crime in adjacent neighborhoods (as crime spreads or is deflected elsewhere) or more distant ones (as law-abiding citizens move).

We find that crime rates in police beats with open Catholic schools throughout the period of our study differ in two ways from those in which the schools closed. First, the starting points, or intercepts (the level of crime in 1999), were lower in the 118 police beats with open schools than in the forty-one police beats with schools that had closed. The model (in the first row of numbers, first column of table 4.1) indicates that this difference in intercepts was likely caused by the difference in perceived disorder in the two types of police beats. This finding will be discussed below since it tends to confirm the broken-windows hypothesis. The second significant finding (in the second line, third column of table 4.1) is that the rates of decline in serious crime, or slopes, in beats that contain open Catholic schools were steeper than those where the Catholic schools closed. The latter finding is the most critical for this book.

Both effects can also be seen pictorially in figures 4.2 and 4.3. Figure 4.2 depicts the actual intercepts (related to disorder) and slopes (related to school closing) of the crime rates for a random selection of twenty of the 159

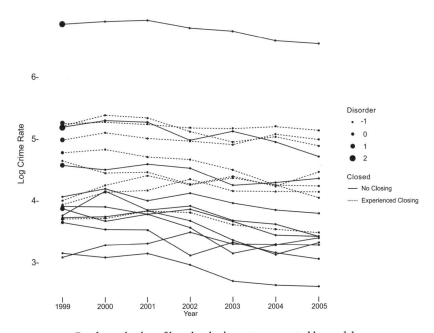

FIGURE 4.2 Random selection of beat-level crime rates generated by model

beats that contained Catholic schools in 1993, some of which later closed and others of which remained open. These slopes illustrate that the crime rates across the time period varied across police beats, as we would expect that they would, but that the rates generally declined. Figure 4.2 also pictorially represents the level of perceived disorder recorded by Sampson and Raudenbush in 1995 with the varying sized dots at the beginning of each crime slope—larger dots indicating more disorder in a police beat in 1995.

A complete picture of the effects of Catholic school closures across all police beats in Chicago is provided by figure 4.3, which represents the effect of school closings in a scatterplot of the average of slopes (or rates of decline). The larger markers, representing the average slopes for beats with open and closed schools, indicate that the slope of the decline in serious crime

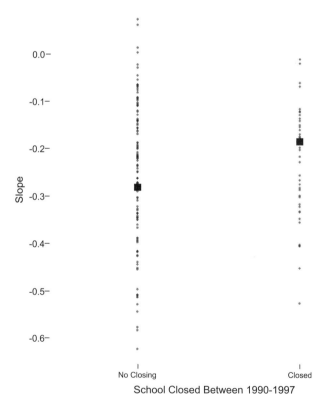

FIGURE 4.3 Slope/closing relationship

in police beats with open Catholic schools was, during the relevant time period, significantly steeper than that of beats in which schools closed. In other words, crime declined faster in beats with open Catholic schools than in beats where schools had closed. The average rate of crime's decline from 1999–2005 was nearly 25 percent, while for those beats where the schools closed it also declined, but only by roughly 17 percent.[4] Whatever caused crime rates to decline over this time period was more potent in the beats that contained Catholic schools than in those where the schools had closed.

CATHOLIC SCHOOLS AND BROKEN WINDOWS

Our findings suggesting that Catholic school closures are linked to higher crime rates are, standing alone, significant and novel. But we remained curious what these findings might suggest (if anything) about the highly contested broken-windows hypothesis, which posits a causal link between disorder and crime. At least since the publication of James Q. Wilson and George Kelling's enormously influential 1982 essay, "Broken Windows: The Police and Neighborhood Safety," urban policy—especially urban policing policy—has become intensely focused on curbing disorder and reinvigorating neighborhood social networks and the healthy informal norms of conduct that flow from them. In "Broken Windows," Wilson and Kelling first articulated the broken-windows hypothesis, which posits a causal link between disorder and crime. "Disorder and crime," they argued, "are usually inextricably linked, in a kind of developmental sequence." Communities that fail to curb physical and social disorder, they reasoned, become vulnerable to serious crime for at least two related reasons. First, unchecked disorder frightens law-abiding citizens, causing them to avoid public places, and eventually leads those with financial means to move away from the disorderly community. The law-abiders' departure, first from parks and sidewalks and eventually from struggling communities to more stable ones, in turn further weakens social controls. Second, disorder sends signals to would-be offenders that communities plagued by disorder are "safe" places to commit crimes: the community's failure to check disorder suggests that residents cannot—or choose not to—control socially detrimental behaviors and conditions. "If the neighborhood cannot keep a bothersome panhandler from annoying passersby," Wilson and Kelling predicted, "the thief may reason, it is even less likely to call the police to identify a potential mugger or to interfere if the mugging actually takes place."[5]

"Broken Windows" challenged nearly a century of thinking about the role of police in urban communities.[6] Wilson and Kelling argued, contrary to the decades of reformers' assumptions, that police should integrate themselves into the social fabric of the communities that they protect and that they should prioritize efforts to control physical and social disorder and to address low-level, "victimless" crimes. They reasoned that, by intervening to check disorder, officers could help communities send the right signals—namely, that, in this neighborhood, residents do not tolerate social deviancy. The disorder-control efforts of the police officers, Wilson and Kelling hypothesized, would also kick-start the informal social norms needed to check deviancy—norms that had been crippled by the disorder plaguing all too many urban neighborhoods. Thus, police intervention to enforce the kinds of antidisorder norms that operate naturally in healthy communities would both check the spiral of urban decay and reduce more serious crime.

Policing policies flowing from the broken-windows hypothesis are numerous and diverse.[7] Some, such as former New York City Mayor Rudolph Giuliani's famous quality-of-life campaign and the antigang ordinance at issue in the *Chicago v. Morales* decision (527 U.S. 41 [1999]), directly target perceived "disorders"—gang members, squeegeemen, turnstile jumpers, and so on. Others, such as ubiquitous community policing efforts, including the CAPS program in place in Chicago at the time of our study, build upon Wilson and Kelling's arguments about the importance of police-citizen interaction. Community policing efforts seek to build stronger relationships between police officers and the citizens whom they protect, both through policing techniques—for example, foot and bike patrols—that ensure more frequent informal interactions and by soliciting citizen input about policing priorities. While community policing practices influence all aspects of police operations, they are closely intertwined with order-maintenance efforts for at least two reasons. First, removing officers from patrol cars and replacing them with foot and bike patrols encourages police-citizen interaction, but it also maximizes officers' ability to monitor and control disorder and enables them to intervene early and prevent serious crime before it occurs. Second, and perhaps most tellingly, when citizens are asked to help shape policing priorities, they frequently prioritize the elimination of "prevalent and low-key troubles"—loitering, vandalism, prostitution, gangs—which are the very disorders at the heart of the order-maintenance agenda.[8]

The broken-windows hypothesis and its order-maintenance progeny have generated an intense academic debate and a sizable empirical literature, most of which seeks to test, in various ways, whether disorder and serious crime are in fact causally linked.[9] Social-norms champions of order-maintenance policies extrapolate the following causal chain from the commonsense observation that our behavior is shaped by, and frequently conforms to, our perceptions of others' behavior: first, it is reasonable to assume that people tend to be law-abiding when they perceive that their neighbors are obeying the law; second, relatively minor disorders like vandalism and public drunkenness signal that their neighbors are not obeying the law; third, these signals create an environment that fosters more serious crime. Disorder, according to social-norms scholars like Dan Kahan, "erode[s] deterrence by emboldening law-breakers and demoralizing law-abiders."[10] Put differently, the social-norms scholars argue that by failing to curb disorder, a community signals to wrongdoers that the informal social controls that tend to keep disorder and crime in check in healthy communities are broken. A would-be wrongdoer may therefore infer from the presence of disorder that the community plagued by it also does not, or cannot, control more serious crime. If so, he is likely to perceive that the disorder-plagued community is a "safe" place to commit crime, that is, that the risks of criminal behavior are low and the rewards high. Disorderly neighborhoods are also dangerous ones, social-norms scholars argue, and the danger is a direct result of the presence of disorder. Moreover, social-norms scholars assert, echoing Wilson and Kelling, that order-maintenance strategies can act as a circuit breaker that disrupts the causal relationship between disorder and serious crime, both by directly curbing disorder and by helping to reinvigorate the important informal social controls that keep disorder in check. If disorder emboldens law breakers, social-norms scholars reason, then governmental (usually police) efforts to curb disorder should embolden law-abiders. As law-abiding citizens begin to assert control over their communities, the need for governmental intervention will wane.[11]

The empirical support for these social-norms arguments is quite mixed. Some scholars have purported to demonstrate a connection between neighborhood-level variations in disorder and serious crime. For example, in his influential book, *Disorder and Decline*, Wesley Skogan collected and analyzed data from forty urban neighborhoods with dramatically different crime rates. Skogan found a strong positive correlation between disorder and robbery rates, even after controlling for race, poverty, and other demographic variables commonly associated with crime.[12] Other scholars have purported to prove the broken-windows hypothesis by demonstrating the effectiveness of order-maintenance policies, reasoning that if disorder causes crime, then real-world efforts to curb disorder should reduce real-world serious crime.[13] Other scholars, including most notably Bernard

Harcourt, have replicated and challenged many of these studies' findings,[14] and still others—including, notably, Jeffrey Fagan—have argued that order-maintenance tactics "succeed" by disproportionately targeting racial minorities and other disfavored groups for enforcement.[15]

Robert Sampson and Stephen Raudenbush's exhaustive study of the effects of disorder in Chicago, which we discuss in the previous chapter and which generated the data for our study of Catholic school closure effects on disorder and social cohesion, is of particular relevance to us here. To recap, Sampson and Raudenbush found that the correlation between disorder and crime that they initially observed largely disappeared when they controlled for neighborhood structural factors such as race, income, and residential stability. The direct nexus between disorder and crime held true only for robbery rates—a finding consistent with Skogan's earlier work. As discussed previously, Sampson and Raudenbush also found, importantly, that disorder reduced collective efficacy—a factor that continued to strongly predict higher crime rates, even after they controlled for neighborhood structural factors. Sampson and Raudenbush's findings led them to reject the strong version of the broken-windows hypothesis, which posits a direct causal link between disorder and serious crime. But they took care not to dismiss disorder as irrelevant. Instead they concluded that even if disorder and crime are not directly causally linked, disorder may have a "cascade effect" that indirectly affects crime rates by undermining neighborhood collective efficacy.[16]

CATHOLIC SCHOOLS AND DISORDER CASCADES

We did not undertake this project to prove or disprove the broken-windows hypothesis. Moreover, this question is somewhat beyond the scope of our current investigation, which seeks to explore school closure effects rather than disorder effects on their own. Thus, we emphasize that our bottom-line finding—that Catholic school closures slowed the rate of decline in serious crime in Chicago police beats between 1999 and 2005—is, standing alone, an important one. In light of our previous findings about the effects of school closures on social cohesion, we believe that a large part of the explanation of why Catholic schools suppress crime is that they generate neighborhood social capital. The fact that neighborhoods with strong social institutions and healthy informal social networks are safer and more stable than those with fewer strong institutions and weak networks has been repeatedly demonstrated in the studies, discussed above, linking collective efficacy with low levels of crime and high levels of residential stability. Catholic schools appear to be one of the informal social institutions capable of generating the social capital that fosters collective efficacy in a neighborhood.

Our study, however, is at least consistent with, and arguably provides evidence supporting, Sampson and Raudenbush's predictions about the effects of disorder over time. In the previous chapter, we discussed our findings that school closures triggered elevated levels of perceived disorder, and here we link school closures to serious crime in a police beat. It is reasonable, therefore, to assume that the disorder triggered by Catholic school closures may be linked to the later crime we observe here. We do not, however, attempt to demonstrate a causal link. In chapter 3, we linked Catholic school closures between 1984 and 1994 with the level of perceived disorder in Chicago neighborhoods in 1995. Given the long time period between these earlier closures, however, and our crime data, which begins in 1999, causation would be too difficult to demonstrate definitively. Too many intervening causes of crime might have occurred in a neighborhood between 1984 and 1999, which we could not adequately control for using even the most sophisticated statistical analysis.

That said, our findings here are consistent with, if not strongly suggestive of, Sampson and Raudenbush's predicted "disorder cascade." During our initial statistical analysis of this crime data, which compared, in a less sophisticated way than we do in this chapter, the connections between school closures in a beat and more temporally proximate rates of specific crimes, we observed a lag of several years between a school closure and a spike in serious crime. That is, a school would close, and several years later, crime would increase in the beat. These findings, combined with our more sophisticated analysis described above, lead us to surmise that Catholic school closures may be a trigger that sets off the cascade predicted by Sampson and Raudenbush by increasing disorder and decreasing social cohesion and collective efficacy (as suggested by our prior study).

Additional evidence supporting the disorder cascade is suggested by our finding linking the level of perceived disorder in a police beat in 1995-96 to the intercept (the starting level) of serious crime in 1999. This finding was initially somewhat surprising to us because Sampson and Raudenbush, who collected the disorder data upon which we rely, rejected a direct causal link between contemporaneous levels of disorder and serious crime. Yet we find that disorder (at least as it is perceived by residents) is linked, in a statistically significant way, to subsequent levels of serious crime—even after we control for the same structural predictors they used. The most plausible explanation for why this is so, in our view, is that the cascade that Sampson and Raudenbush predicted began to occur during the years between their measurement of disorder (1995) and the first year of our crime data (1999).[17]

Unfortunately, the one-shot nature of the observations upon which we relied to measure the connection among school closures, social cohesion, and disorder in the previous chapter creates something of a chicken-and-egg problem. We cannot know the order of the causal chain linking school closures, disorder, social cohesion, and crime. It might be that a school closure causes first an erosion of social capital that in time triggers disorder and later crime. Or, since disorder signals to residents that social control is eroding, school closures may trigger increased disorder, which in turn erodes social capital, which leads to more crime. Alternatively, the disorder and social capital effects of school closures may occur simultaneously. Whatever the precise sequence of the causal chain, however, our findings tend to support the conclusion that disorder is linked to an erosion of social control that eventually leads to increased crime.

Our findings here also do not speak directly to the core policy question in the broken-windows literature — namely, whether order-maintenance efforts are efficacious. Arguably, our findings lend support for urban policies, including community policing practices, which seek to strengthen informal neighborhood networks — for example, Chicago's CAPS program, described above; police work with local community leaders (including pastors) to organize marches in high-crime areas; prayer vigils at the site of gang- or drug-related shootings; smoke-outs in drug market areas; and positive loitering campaigns to harass prostitutes and their customers. At least to the extent that our findings suggest a connection between religious institutions and neighborhood social capital (in other words, to the extent that Catholic schools' crime-suppressive effects are linked to the schools' religiosity), our study lends particular support for efforts to enlist religious institutions and leaders in crime prevention efforts (for example, police-organized anticrime prayer vigils). As Tracey Meares has argued, collaboration between the police and religious leaders holds particular promise because these efforts provide a public platform for religious leaders who enjoy significant moral authority in many inner-city communities.[18] We cannot know, based upon our data, however, whether these publicly sponsored efforts will generate the same robust levels of social capital as the informal networks generated by private institutions (including the Catholic schools we study). And we admit skepticism that they will. Endeavors like Chicago's positive loitering campaigns, smoke-outs, and prayer vigils are far from perfect substitutes for the organically generated collective efficacy present in healthier neighborhoods. Somewhat ironically, James Q. Wilson—who is now seen as the godfather of such efforts—questioned their promise over four decades ago. In his 1968 essay, "The Urban Unease," Wilson laid blame for the burgeoning urban crisis on the failure of informal community controls in urban neighborhoods. And he fatalistically argued that "there is relatively little government can do directly to maintain a neighborhood community. It can, of course, assign more police officers to it, but there are real limits to the value of this response."[19]

The irony of Wilson's past skepticism aside, the intuitive appeal of his argument is strong. Governmental efforts like community policing seek to help residents generate the social capital that exists organically in healthy neighborhoods, where the need for governmental intervention to address social problems, including serious crime, is dramatically reduced. Our findings suggest that urban Catholic elementary schools are one kind of neighborhood institution (and, as we discuss in chapter 7, there undoubtedly are others) that acts organically to generate neighborhood social capital. The findings also suggest that these schools' disappearance triggers a chain of events that eventually necessitates police intervention. As we discuss in chapter 7, scholars have begun to explore whether strong local social institutions can mitigate the effects of neighborhood structural disadvantage. Our findings here suggest that Catholic schools are one such social institution. Therefore, it may be the case that maintaining Catholic schools in a community represents a more effective (and perhaps also more cost-effective) method of curbing crime than the intensive police interventions that populate the community policing tool kit. We return to the policy implications of this possibility in the concluding chapter of the book.

CHAPTER FIVE

Charter Schools, Catholic Schools, and Crime

In this chapter, we turn to questions raised, but unanswered, by the findings reported in previous ones. That is, we seek to understand—to the extent that our data allows—whether the negative effects of Catholic school closures reflect Catholic school effects on neighborhood life, rather than school effects or community institution effects. We tackle this question in two ways. First, we seek to learn whether the negative effects of Catholic school closings reflect the fact that, as we strongly suspect, open Catholic schools suppress neighborhood crime or, alternatively, whether these effects are the result of a loss of a community institution. We believe that this distinction is an important one. A finding that open Catholic schools are associated with lower crime rates in a police beat would tend to confirm our suspicion that Catholic schools generate social capital. It would also provide concrete evidence that Catholic schools behave differently, in terms of neighborhood citizenship, than public schools do, since other scholars have documented a link between open public schools and increased crime. Alternatively, if our findings are instead loss effects—that is, reflective of the fact that Catholic school closures trigger an increase in crime, rather than Catholic schools themselves suppressing it—we would be left wondering whether the loss of other kinds of community institutions might also erode neighborhood social controls. (And, indeed, our analysis does not rule out this possibility.) In order to test the effects of open Catholic schools on crime rates, we use regression analysis to compare the rates of serious crime in police beats with Catholic schools with those without them.

Second, in order to separate school effects from Catholic school effects, we add charter schools to our analysis. We do so for a number of reasons. Charter schools are, in our view, imperfect proxies for public schools, especially in Chicago, where many charter schools function as neighborhood schools. In contrast to traditional public schools, moreover, charter schools are not present in many police beats, making a comparison between beats with and without charter schools possible. Charter schools also are a relatively recent phenomenon, enabling us to test the effects of school openings, and they are schools of choice, enabling us to partially address the selection bias difficulty present in any effort to compare Catholic and public schools. Additionally, charter schools likely drive some Catholic school closures, both because they compete with Catholic schools for students and because, as archdiocesan officials emphasized in our discussions, the revenue available from leasing Catholic school buildings to charter operators incentivizes some pastors to urge the Archdiocese to close their schools. (Again, this is because while the decision to close a school ultimately rests with the Archdiocese, the school building "belongs" to the parish under canon law, and therefore the default rule under canon law is that a parish is entitled to keep any revenue generated by leasing it.) Charter schools are frequently offered as an alternative to broader school-choice programs that include private and religious schools that might stem the tide of Catholic school closures. And, finally and importantly, charter schools fill—and likely will continue to fill—the educational void left when Catholic schools close. They almost certainly will increasingly come to fill the physical space once occupied by closed Catholic schools, as they have already begun to do in many cities.

During the 2012–2013 school year, there were 110 charter schools (or, technically, thirty-seven charter schools operating on 110 campuses) in Chicago.[1] (Illinois law caps the number of charter schools permitted in Chicago at seventy-five,[2] but the Chicago Public Schools—which serves as the sole authorizer in the city—interprets this requirement as permitting multiple campuses of the same school.) Thirty-five of these schools opened during the period of our study. Chicago's charter schools are institutionally diverse. They include elementary schools, junior high schools, and secondary schools as well as nontraditional age groupings (for example, grades 6–12). A least two are single-sex schools, and several have themed curricula. Charter schools enroll a higher proportion of African American students (60 percent) than does the district as a whole (41.6 percent) and a smaller proportion of Hispanic, white, and Asian students. Chicago's charter schools also enroll a slightly higher proportion of low-income students (91 percent) than does the Chicago Public Schools as a whole (87 percent). The Chicago Public Schools reported that 63 percent of charter school students are "from the neighborhood."[3] Fourteen of the twenty-eight charter schools in the study reported here were operating in closed Catholic schools.

Our analysis tends to confirm our suspicion that we are, in fact, finding a Catholic school effect on neighborhood health. First, we find that police beats with Catholic schools have consistently lower rates of serious crime than those without Catholic schools—even, as before, after we control for numerous demographic factors that would correlate with neighborhood distress. Second, in contrast to Catholic schools, we find that the presence of a charter school appears to have no statistically significant effect on crime rates in a police beat. These results hold true even when a charter school is operating in a closed Catholic school. Indeed, in these circumstances, although the results do not reach statistical significance, the direction of the results is not promising. That is, in beats with charter schools operating in closed Catholic schools, crime rates appear to increase.

DATA

As previously, we rely on multiple sources of data. The Archdiocese of Chicago's Office of Catholic Schools provided us information on closed and open Catholic schools in the City of Chicago, including their location, name, and parish affiliation. Data on charter schools came from the Chicago Public Schools, Office of New Schools, which provides detailed annual reports of all of the charter and contract schools operating in the city, and from the Illinois Network of Charter Schools.[4] To parallel our information on Catholic schools, we restricted our analysis to charter elementary schools located in the City of Chicago proper. That is, we excluded all charter schools enrolling only grades 6 and above, including high schools and free-standing middle schools. Since many of the Catholic schools in the city enroll students through the eighth grade, we included K–8 charter schools in our data set. Our decision to exclude free-standing middle schools was influenced by the literature suggesting that adolescents tend to perform and behave worse in such schools than in K–8 schools. We therefore suspected that charter middle schools' neighborhood effects are more likely to parallel those of high schools than those of elementary schools. Demographic information by census tract comes from the 2000 decennial census.[5] The crime data is the same as that used in the last chapter—data on the incidence of six major crimes (aggravated assault, aggravated battery, murder, burglary, robbery, and aggravated sexual assault) at the police beat level from 1999 to 2005.

EXPLAINING SCHOOL CLOSURES/OPENINGS

As we describe in earlier chapters, we recognize the obvious endogeneity problem presented by such a research effort. That is, we recognize that the same factors that cause charter schools to open, and Catholic schools to remain open, in a neighborhood might also cause or suppress crime. It might be the case that the Archdiocese of Chicago is less likely to close schools in safe neighborhoods, and it might be the case that charter operators are more likely to open schools in dangerous ones. In previous chapters, in order to separate the two possible effects (that is, demographics and school closures), we employed closure-predicting variables unrelated to neighborhood demographics (or other things closely associated with crime)—specifically, the parish leadership characteristics described previously. We began our comparative analysis of Catholic versus charter schools similarly, by seeking to identify variables that would predict why Catholic schools remained open for the relevant time period (1999-2004). Again we found that certain characteristics of the parish leadership structure were strongly connected with school closings or viability—over and above neighborhood demographics. Specifically, schools operated by parishes with "irregular" leadership—that is, parishes operated by an administrator (rather than a pastor) or associated with a clerical abuse allegation—were far more likely to close than schools operated by parishes without such irregularities. Or, put differently, a school located in a parish that had not been associated with any abuse allegations and that was operated by a pastor, rather than a parish administrator, was far more likely to remain open. Since neither parish irregularity nor the length of time since ordination would seemingly have anything to do with demographics or neighborhood crime, we were comfortable concluding that the parish leadership variables are an appropriate way to address the endogeneity problem.

Although these findings left us satisfied that we could address the endogeneity problem when comparing police beats with and without a Catholic school, we chose not to employ these predictive variables in our analysis here. This is because we are unable to identify similar variables that would enable us to disentangle the locations of charter schools from neighborhood demographics. We assume that the location of charter schools is the result of a complex mix of factors, including the entrepreneurial energy

and educational mission of charter school operators, the quality of and parental satisfaction with local public schools, and the availability of space
suitable for a new school. We recognize that some charter school operators
intentionally choose to locate in poor urban neighborhoods where crime
is likely to be more prevalent. Indeed, some charter schools in Chicago articulate an explicit mission of educating poor children living in difficult
neighborhoods.[6] We therefore cannot deal with the endogeneity problems
surrounding charter school openings as we did to explain Catholic school
closures. It is simply impossible to identify variables predicting where
charter schools will open that are like the parish leadership characteristics
that predict where Catholic schools will remain open. To avoid comparing "apples to oranges," therefore, we do not employ the nondemographic
variables predicting which Catholic schools remain open. While our analysis takes account of neighborhood demographics by controlling for various
demographic variables throughout, we cannot completely disaggregate the
locations of the schools that we study from the neighborhood factors that
may affect crime rates. Thus, in contrast to the evidence presented in chapters 3 and 4, we do not claim to demonstrate causation here—although our
previous analysis of school closure effects and of the continued predictive
effects of parish leadership variables leads us strongly to suspect that the
link between open Catholic schools and reduced crime is a causal one.

CATHOLIC AND CHARTER SCHOOL EFFECTS ON CRIME

In 2004, there were Catholic schools in eighty-four (out of 279) police beats
in Chicago and charter schools in twenty-eight police beats. In fourteen
police beats, a charter school was operating in a closed Catholic school. All
of the Catholic elementary schools open in the city of Chicago in 2004 had
been open since the 1930s, although some of them had received children
originally attending other schools closed since 1984. (In 2004, the Archdiocese opened a new school in Chicago, but that school only enrolled pre-
schoolers; it has since grown to include grades pre-K through 8.) In contrast
to the Catholic schools, none of the charter schools in the city opened before
1997. We therefore cannot rule out the possibility that the Catholic school
effects we observe are a product of longevity in a community, nor can we
know whether, over time, as charter schools take root in a community, they
will come to have similar positive neighborhood effects.

Whether or not Catholic elementary schools generate or maintain social
capital in a neighborhood poses an interesting empirical question, as does

whether charter schools, and perhaps especially charter schools operating in closed Catholic school buildings, do the same work. Neighborhood social capital is of course influenced by social and demographic factors, which in turn affect the rates of crime that we investigate here. In fact, neighborhoods with Catholic and charter schools are quite different, both from each other and from the average Chicago census tract, so it becomes important to control for these dissimilarities. Thus, we began by matching Catholic and charter schools, census tracts, and police beats using the mapping program ArcGIS, as previously.[7]

Prior work indicates that the relationship between crime rates and other neighborhood characteristics is best represented by taking the natural logarithm of the crime rates — that is, total crimes divided by the census track populations.[8] Our analysis here includes the same characteristics found to explain crime in Chicago by a host of other researchers.[9] As in chapter 4, we employ a technique called principal component analysis (PCA), which uses regression results to group many factors into a smaller number of variables; thus, for some equations, the demographic variables were reduced to three factors.[10] Because there are fewer variables, the coefficients for the different types of schools are larger, although statistical significance and direction do not change. To produce figure 5.1, we first separated the data into two groups: the police beats with and without an open Catholic school. Then, for each of the seven years, we used regression analysis to predict the average crime rate in that year. In effect, we held constant the presence or not of a charter school (located or not in a closed Catholic school), plus the computed composite socioeconomic factors.

While crime was declining in Chicago between 1999 and 2005, the crime rate, controlling for demographic factors, was lower in each year in those beats with Catholic schools than in those that did not include them. The adjusted mean predicted value of the logged crime rates, controlling for the demographics of principal component analysis for each year, make up the points in figure 5.1. In other words, figure 5.1 was created by using the predicted values of closing using the variables from Model 1 from table 5.2 for each of the seven years of crime rate data, comparing results for cases in which there was and was not an open Catholic elementary school.

We also analyzed each of the demographic factors separately. The regression result was similar in all the cases, as reported in table 5.2. The regression coefficients employing principal component analysis are displayed as Model 1. The other two models are very similar, and graphing them would produce nearly identical results. Model 2 displays regression coefficients,

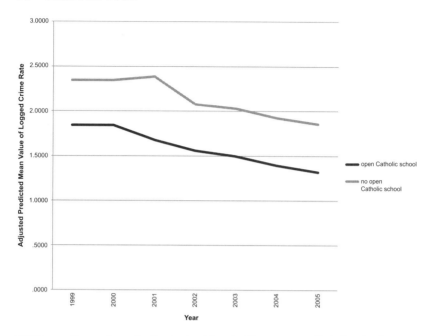

FIGURE 5.1 Comparison of police beats with and without an open Catholic school

standard errors, and statistical significance for an equation where, instead of grouping the demographic characteristics, these are broken out into original census data for each police beat and tract combination.[11] The difference between Model 2 and Model 3 is that Model 2 uses individual race characteristics, while Model 3 groups them together.[12] The various columns of table 5.2 show that regardless of how we account for the sociodemographic variables that generally predict serious crime, an open Catholic elementary school in a beat is associated consistently with a statistically significant decrease in the rate of serious crime.[13] Although the percentage difference varied by year, the crime rate in police beats with Catholic schools was, on average, at least 33 percent lower than in police beats without them.

Table 5.2 also reflects regression analysis of the effects of having a charter school located in the police beat (which, as with the inverse for Catholic schools, essentially holds constant the presence of a Catholic school). Charter schools appear to have no statistically significant effect on crime in either direction, although in a few years, regressions for individual crimes suggest a statistically significant link between charter schools and elevated rates of aggravated assault and aggravated battery. To the extent we can note anything about the charter schools that were operating in closed Catholic school buildings, the direction of the coefficients is not encouraging. That is, in these cases, the crime rate seems to increase.

We emphasize that the findings presented here lend themselves to less firm conclusions than those presented in the previous two chapters. This is primarily because we do not, and for the reasons we articulate above cannot, fully disentangle the locations of charter schools from neighborhood demographic factors that would tend to predict crime—although we do control for these factors using regression analysis. We therefore do not

TABLE 5.2. Regression results: Crime rates and Catholic/charter schools

	Model 1	Model 2	Model 3
	B (standard error)	B (standard error)	B (standard error)
(constant)	4.035 (.018)***	5.871 (.164)***	5.751 (.167)***
Open Catholic school	−.276 (.109)*	−.125 (.068)*	−.164 (.069)*
Charter school	−.071 (.214)	−.023 (.133)	.065 (.136)
Charter in Catholic	.045 (.282)	.117 (.176)	.157 (.179)
PCA1, deprivation	.470 (.018)***		
PCA2, immigration	−.162 (.018)***		
PCA3, stability	−.219 (.018)***		
Total population, 2000		.000 (.000)***	.000 (.000)***
Share nonwhite, 2000			.926 (.060)***
Share foreign born, 2000		−.396 (.161)*	−.395 (.147)**
Same household, 2000		−.399 (.108)***	−.198 (.109)
Percent in labor force		−.711 (.157)***	−.626 (.161)***
Percent below poverty line		−1.165 (.144)***	−1.065 (.147)***
Percent youth ages 15–25		.079 (.188)	.227 (.190)
Percent renter		.202 (.087)**	.183 (.088)*
Percent female head, 2000		−1.186 (.119)***	−1.143 (.119)***
Percent linguistically isolated, 2000		−.301 (.218)	.217 (.214)
Median income, 2000		−5.233E−6 (.000)***	−5.847E−6 (.000)***
Percent households with public assistance, 2000		1.874 (.176)***	1.685 (.180)***
Percent black, 2000		.987 (.064)***	
Percent Hispanic, 2000		.978 (.067)***	
R^2, adjusted	.259	.714	.702
F	160.459	428.335	432.535

Note: PCA are the coefficients derived using principal component analysis, as defined in the text.

***$P < .001$.

**$P < .01$.

*$P < .05$.

claim to show causation here. However, when viewed in light of our previous findings about the effects of Catholic school closures in Chicago—and of the continued predictive value of nondemographic factors associated with Catholic schools remaining open—we strongly suspect that the link between open Catholic schools and reduced crime is a causal one. We have no similar hunches about charter schools.

Even if we could prove causation, we would be left with many questions. We could not know whether opening a new Catholic school (or reopening a closed one) would lead to decreased crime in a neighborhood. We also could not know whether charter schools will ever have a statistically significant effect on neighborhood crime (in either a positive or negative direction). Indeed, given their tremendous institutional diversity, we suspect that it may always be impossible to make broad generalizations about charter schools' neighborhood effects—other than, perhaps, that they are not the same as Catholic schools' effects (perhaps in part because Catholic schools are less institutionally diverse). We certainly hope that, over time, some charter schools will develop into good neighborhood citizens. We might expect this, in particular, of charter schools that mimic the aspects of the Catholic schools' educational formula emphasized in chapter 7—intentional community building; discipline and character building; and an emphasis on trust among school personnel, students, and teachers. Our research here does not give insight into the question of whether converting Catholic schools to charter schools, rather than closing them altogether, could maintain the Catholic schools' positive effects. Although our findings suggest that operating a nonsectarian charter in a closed Catholic school does not do so, none of the schools in our study opened as a result of a conversion decision by the Archdiocese of Chicago. Moreover, some of the charter schools moved into a closed Catholic school several years after it was shuttered. The lack of continuity alone likely dramatically reduces the ability of the new school to establish itself as the natural successor to the Catholic school.

CHAPTER SIX

A Replicable Story?

One obvious question raised by the findings just presented is whether Catholic schools generate the same level of social capital—and thus, whether Catholic school closures generate the same negative effects—in cities other than Chicago. Our findings regarding the implications of Catholic school closures in Chicago—the third largest city in the United States—are, standing alone, important ones. But clearly we would be ill advised to extrapolate universally applicable conclusions from findings from one city, no matter how robust the result or careful the study.[1]

Thus, we explore, in more summary fashion than we did for our work in Chicago, similar studies that we conducted in two other large American cities, Los Angeles and Philadelphia. We chose these cities for a variety of reasons. To begin, they are, respectively, the second and fifth largest American cities, and each had, at the beginning of our period of study, a large number of open Catholic schools. They also add geographic diversity (as, say, Milwaukee and Detroit would not). We selected Los Angeles because its Catholic history and land use patterns are quite different from Chicago's, and Philadelphia because both its Catholic history and land use patterns are similar to those in Chicago. Like Chicago, the archdioceses incorporating these two coastal cities are among the largest in the United States in terms of number of Catholics— first (Los Angeles) and sixth (Philadelphia). Their importance to the Catholic Church is also reflected in the fact that each has traditionally been governed by an archbishop who is also a cardinal—a prelate called to assist in the governance of the Church in important ways, including the election of the pope. Both cities were attractive to study since, like Chicago, we gained access to survey data measuring social capital variables.

PHILADELPHIA

As we discussed previously, Philadelphia's parochial school history is similar to that of Chicago, although it begins far earlier, with one church, St. Mary's, even boasting a visit by George Washington. As in Chicago, while the original growth in the number of Catholic parishes was attributable to Irish immigration, many parishes also were established to serve non-English-speaking immigrant ethnic groups. (These are called "personal" or "national" as opposed to "territorial" parishes, and several still exist in Philadelphia.) Of the 159 parishes in the City of Philadelphia listed in *The Official Catholic Directory* in 2004, all but three originally operated schools. Many of these schools had closed or consolidated with other parish schools by our period of interest (1998–2005), and some of the parishes themselves closed prior to 1990 as well. By 2010, only sixty-eight schools remained open in Philadelphia proper; sixty-five of the original 156 closed after 1980. While some of these schools, such as St. Mary Magdalen de Pazzi (Italian) and Sacred Heart (Hungarian), belonged to personal parishes, most others, like Blessed Sacrament (which, according to its website, was once the largest parochial school in the United States), belonged to territorial parishes.

Our study of the effects of school closures on levels of social capital and crime in Philadelphia yields results consistent with those found in Chicago. As in Chicago, we sought to measure the effects of school closings (here, between 1998 and 2004) on later crime (here, between 2005 and 2009). There are a few differences in the data collected for Philadelphia. From *The Official Catholic Directory*, in addition to the information on pastors used for instrumental variables in the Chicago studies, we added the number of additional clergy residing in the rectory, reasoning that additional hands available to handle time-consuming school issues might make it easier to keep the schools open. We also separately considered the effects of clerical abuse allegations on school closures since, tragically, priests assigned to parishes with schools in Philadelphia were accused of abusing children significantly more often than had been the case in Chicago. In fact, 32 percent of parishes with schools that remained open after 1990 had priests living in the rectory who were eventually accused of abuse, according to official archdiocesan records. Some of those accused, including a number subject to church discipline, civil liability, and even criminal punishment, were the

TABLE 6.1. Parish leadership variables, Philadelphia

Variable	Description	Mean
Order	Pastor was member of religious order	0.14
Other clergy in rectory	Count of other clergy in rectory 2004 or when school closed	1.72
Length of time since ordination of pastor	Length of time since pastor ordained (from 2004 or date school closed)	27.50
Abuse by clergy while school open	Priest in rectory accused of abuse during time school was open	0.34

pastors of parishes with schools. Table 6.1 contains descriptive information on Philadelphia parishes with schools open in 1994.

In contrast to the Project on Human Development in Chicago Neighborhoods data described in chapter 3, the social capital data we employed for Philadelphia, which was collected by the Public Health Management Corporation, did not include perceptions of disorder. Instead, survey data was collected on what might be called social cohesion variables, with relevant questions including how likely a subject was to feel a part of the neighborhood ("Please tell me if you strongly agree, agree, disagree, or strongly disagree with the following statement: I feel that I belong and am a part of my neighborhood"); how likely people in the neighborhood were to help others in the neighborhood ("Using the following scale, please rate how likely people in your neighborhood are willing to help their neighbors with routine activities such as picking up their trash cans, or helping to shovel snow. Would you say that most people in your neighborhood are always, often, sometimes, rarely, or never willing to help their neighbors?"); to work on a project to improve the neighborhood ("Have people in your neighborhood ever worked together to improve the neighborhood? For example, through a neighborhood watch, creating a community garden, building a community playground, or participating in a block party?"); or to trust others in the neighborhood ("Please tell me if you strongly agree, disagree or strongly disagree with the following statement: Most people in my neighborhood can be trusted").[2] These, like census-based social indicators related to poverty, were reduced to a single variable through principal component analysis (PCA) as described in chapter 4. Descriptive statistics for the individual questions are reported in table 6.2.

The Philadelphia Police Department sent us a comprehensive list of all crime reports, by geographic coordinate, for each crime reported during 2005–2009. For example, during the period January to June 2005, there

TABLE 6.2. Social capital variables, Philadelphia

Variable	Mean	Standard deviation	Median	Min	Max
Participation	0.743	0.366	0.685	0	1.73
Helping neighbors	3.473	0.537	3.445	1.5	5
Improving the neighborhood	4.636	0.206	4.60	4	5
Belonging	4.135	0.285	4.11	3.33	5
Trusting	3.768	0.423	3.75	2.89	5

were 37,298 such reports. Each was identified by a three-digit number keyed to the department's specification of Uniform Crimes. For example, crimes in the range 100–200 were homicides. Because we had physical locations (geographic coordinates) for each crime as well as for each Philadelphia neighborhood, we were able to intersect the crimes with each census tract as well as each police beat. Finally, as in Chicago, we used a variety of demographic census variables at the census tract level, as reported in table 6.3.

Since we employed nearly the same empirical methodology here as we had for Chicago in chapter 4, we will not rehearse the rationale for each step here. The results can generally be described as follows: Catholic schools in Philadelphia were significantly more likely to close when, in addition to poverty and changes in the demography in the neighborhood, the parish included a priest accused of abuse. In fact, they were nearly seven times more likely to close. They were significantly less likely to close (closing only half as often) for each additional priest living in the parish rectory. Together with sociodemographic variables, these two clergy variables explained nearly 30 percent of the variance in whether or not a school closed between 1998 and 2004. In fact, without any sociodemographic controls, these two instrumental variables predicted 20 percent of the variance in closings. These findings support our hypothesis suggesting that attitudes and conduct on the part of individual pastors significantly affect whether schools close in the first place.

As they had in Chicago, Catholic school closings negatively and significantly affected the amount of social capital in a neighborhood, however social capital was calculated. In fact, the effect was larger than various demographic factors, including, say, percent Hispanic or percent graduating from high school. The effect of school closures on social capital, however, became insignificant once the PCA capturing poverty was considered—although the direction remained consistent with our findings in Chicago.[3]

As in Chicago, crime generally was lower in the last year of our data than in the first. Unlike in Chicago, however, the overall pattern was not an even decline, and the differences between starting and ending levels of crime was not as pronounced. Figure 6.1 depicts the average crime rates for five serious crimes during our period of interest, and figure 6.2 depicts actual predicted overall crime rates for ten census tracts in Philadelphia.

The variations in crime rates complicated the use of a latent growth model such as the one employed in chapter 4. The results reported are for a mixed-effects maximum-likelihood regression model only. As in Chicago, we found that Catholic school closures explained a large amount of the variance in crime rates (with our equations having an R^2 (adjusted) of .621).[4] In addition to the crime rate's profile not showing a steady decline, the smaller population tracts in Philadelphia (i.e., population of less than five hundred)

TABLE 6.3. Descriptive statistics (2000 census), Philadelphia

Variable	Mean	Min	Max
Tract population	5,144.98 (2,064.352)	185	10,479
Median family income, $	32,062.27 (14,239.44)	7,500	119,036
Unemployment, rate	0.1133 (.0065)	0.028	0.399
Youth 15–25, rate	0.2811 (6.067)	0.094	0.487
Single mothers, rate	0.1921 (.9932)	0.0029	.531
Public assistance, rate	0.0096 (.00966)	0	0.629
Poverty, rate	0.1796 (.1333)	0.00	0.75
High school graduation, rate	0.6833 (.1100)	0.367	0.969
Foreign-born, rate	0.080 (.0660)	.004	0.286
Linguistic isolation, rate	0.1049 (.1106)	.006	0.472
Rental housing, rate	0.3522 (.1454)	0.074	0.941
Lived in same house 5 years ago, rate	0.6479 (.0811)	0.465	0.818
Nonwhite, rate	0.4809 (.3798)	0.015	1.00

Note: Standard errors are in parentheses.

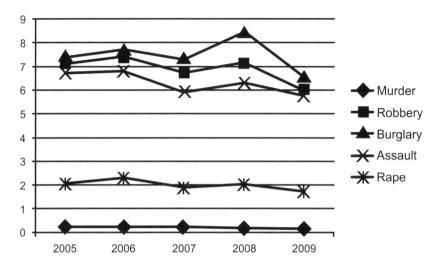

FIGURE 6.1 Average crime rates, Philadelphia

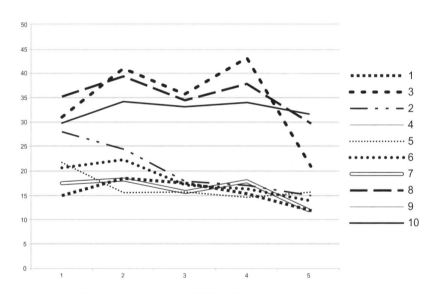

FIGURE 6.2 Crime rates for ten tracts, Philadelphia

TABLE 6.4. Variables predicting crime, Philadelphia

Variable	Coefficient (standard error)
School closed 1998–2004	.2593754
	(.1017428)**
PC1, poverty	.1686999
	(.0212451)***
PC2, youthful, mobile foreign	−.0282923
	(.0379547)
PC3, older foreign	−.0282923
	(.0379547)
PC4, general population	.0324132
	(.1072853)
Social capital component	−4.012481
	(1.206842)***
Weights, from propensity scores	−.8507271
	(.3126932)**
Local Moran's, geographic	−.9056816
	(.3225967)**
Log of population	−.1185392
	(.2042917)
Constant	4.815475
	(1.750148)**

***$P < .001$.
**$P < .01$.
*$P < .05$.

did not demonstrate regular effects (see fig. 6.2, showing tracts at the top and bottom with huge variations among years). When socioeconomic variables (poverty in various attributes, explaining about 42 percent),[5] geographic proximity, weights derived from the propensity of a Catholic school to close, population, and the (positive) social capital indicators were considered, the Catholic school closings again substantially and significantly affected the overall rate over our period of study (with an estimated coefficient of .2594, $p < .001$).

The standardized coefficient for the school's closing (.2593754) was greater than that of the poverty factor (.1686999, $p < .01$). Likewise, higher social capital in a beat was significantly related to a lower initial rate of crime as well as to a lower overall rate (with an estimated coefficient of −4.012481, $p < .001$). The coefficient here was nearly ten times as large as that for the closed schools.[6] Thus, we can conclude that the Philadelphia results corroborate those from Chicago, suggesting the deleterious effect of school closings on neighborhood crime.

Our findings in Los Angeles, however, diverge from the pattern of the other two cities that we studied. We obtained restricted (not available to the public) crime data from the Los Angeles Police Department (with addresses, as in Philadelphia), the Los Angeles Sheriff's Department, and various independent municipalities in Los Angeles County.[7] In this way, our study of Los Angeles departs from our studies of Chicago and Philadelphia. In these locales, we limited our inquiries to Catholic schools located in Chicago and Philadelphia proper. Our data in Los Angeles allowed us to expand our analysis to incorporate suburban schools. We also obtained social capital data from the Los Angeles Family and Neighborhood Study (LA FANS), which collected survey data in 2000 and 2001 similar to those collected by the Public Health Management Corporation in Philadelphia and employed above, but they also included questions about perceived levels of disorder.[8] Further, we collected demographic data at the census tract level.

As previously, we employed PCA to calculate regression results. Describing the variants in crime rates is itself problematic. While for Chicago and Philadelphia, the principal component variables predicted upwards of 60 percent of the variance in crime, for Los Angeles, the R^2s are less than half as large, taking roughly the same factors into account.[9] While PCA on racial demographic variables is roughly as predictive as elsewhere, the poverty component is insignificant as a determinant of the crime rate ($p < .872$).[10] Nor do any of the social capital variables appear to have a statistically significant effect on crime. Most important for our analysis here is that, in contrast to our findings in Chicago and Philadelphia, open Catholic schools had no statistically significant effect at all on overall crime rates, although the signs are consistent with what we found in the other cities.[11]

These divergent findings clearly prevent us from predicting that Catholic schools always benefit neighborhoods as they do in Chicago and, apparently, Philadelphia. However, we think that there are several plausible explanations for why our findings in Los Angeles diverge from those in Chicago and Philadelphia, each of which is at least consistent with the main thesis of this book. These include the following.

We Were Unable to Test School Closure Effects

To begin, we were unable to test the effects of closed Catholic schools in Los Angeles on social capital and crime because the Archdiocese has closed very few of its schools. As a result, we limited our analysis to comparing police beats with and without Catholic schools. We found that the presence of an open Catholic school does not appear to affect either social capital or crime. As we discuss in detail in chapter 7, it is possible that the closure of a Catholic school has a stronger, negative effect on social capital and crime than the presence of an open Catholic school. If so, if the Archdiocese of Los Angeles begins to close schools, we would expect to see neighborhood social capital decline and crime increase. We cannot, of course, know if this is the case at this time. We do note, however, that in chapter 5 we did find that open Catholic schools in Chicago appeared to suppress crime, suggesting that we are not just finding school-closure effects. In this way, our findings for Los Angeles do diverge from those in Chicago.

Los Angeles Simply Has Less Social Capital Than Chicago and Philadelphia

The available evidence strongly suggests that levels of social capital in Los Angeles are much lower than in other major American cities. For example, in Putnam's massive Social Capital Benchmark survey,[12] respondents' reported level of trust varied widely from the U.S. sample, as reported in table 6.5.

The wider survey, including rural as well as urban areas, shows that on the variable *social capital equality* (measuring the equality of civic engagement across the community), for example, Los Angeles scored 64 as its community quotient (where less than 100 is lower than demographics would predict; less than 70 is one standard deviation less). Chicago scored 94. (Philadelphia was not measured.)

There are a number of reasons why social capital may be low in Los Angeles. To begin, Los Angeles residents are more transient than the national norm. According to the Social Capital Community Survey, 40 percent of the

TABLE 6.5. Level of (dis)trust, Los Angeles

Trust only a little or not at all:	Los Angeles	United States
People in your neighborhood	32	17
People you work with	23	13
People at your place of worship	14	6
People who work where you shop	35	23
Local news media	43	Not statistically different from Los Angeles
Local police	21	17

Note: All data are percentages.

Los Angeles survey sample had moved to their community within the past five years, compared with 29 percent of the national sample. As economists Edward L. Glaeser, David Laibson, and Bruce Sacerdote have documented, social capital increases with residential tenure (and homeownership, itself a predictor of residential stability) and declines with mobility and expected mobility.[13] As the Community Benchmark Survey noted, "While it is clear that Los Angeles scores relatively low on measures of trust, it is equally clear that the low scores are due in part to the relatively high incidence of newcomers in Los Angeles, who are less trusting than persons who have been here five years or longer. In other words, Los Angeles is a relatively new home to many of its residents, and when people are new in town, they are more cautious than long-term residents. . . ."[14]

In keeping with Robert Putnam's work suggesting that ethnic diversity suppresses social capital, the Community Benchmark Survey also hypothesized that the low levels of social capital in Los Angeles are linked to the level of ethnic diversity in the metro area.[15] The Community Survey originators also conclude that what drove down Los Angeles's rating in Putnam's 130-question national social capital survey was the high levels of distrust displayed by Hispanics. (This is an important qualifier, since both Chicago and Philadelphia are also very diverse.) While no more than 12 percent of Los Angeles whites said they trusted other races "only a little or not at all," 37 percent of Los Angeles Latinos doubted Asians, 43 percent distrusted other Hispanics, and 54 percent were anxious about blacks.[16] Table 6.6 provides information about the percentage of respondents indicating that they trusted members of racial groups only a little or not at all.[17]

The Los Angeles Community Foundation researchers collecting the survey data we employed here drew similar conclusions, observing that "ethnically diverse communities tend to show far greater socioeconomic differences in levels of social capital than in the nationwide sample." It is also possible that Los Angeles residents may not join community building

TABLE 6.6. Level of distrust by racial group, Los Angeles

	White	African American	Asian American	Hispanic
Whites?	11	22	5	37
African Americans?	12	23	12	54
Asian Americans?	11	27	4	40
Latino/Hispanics?	11	18	5	43

Note: All data are percentages.

institutions. For example, the California Community Foundation project showed that while respondents in Los Angeles are as religious as people elsewhere in the United States, they are significantly less likely to have joined a church or other religious institution than the national norm.[18] Finally, there is some evidence that social ties in Los Angeles are more likely to cross neighborhood boundaries than in other cities.[19]

All this said, it is not immediately apparent to us why suppressed levels of overall social capital would alter how a Catholic school affects neighborhood crime. We would assume, in fact, the opposite—that the relative effects of Catholic schools would be unaffected by overall levels of social capital in a broader community. We leave open the possibility that the positive effects of community institutions, including Catholic schools, are suppressed where levels of social capital are suppressed.

Catholic School Effects Are More Pronounced in Dense, Urban Neighborhoods

One of the reasons that we selected Los Angeles for additional study is that the city has very different land use patterns than either Philadelphia or Chicago. To begin, Los Angeles is far less dense than the other cities we study. In the 2010 census, Los Angeles averaged 8,092.3 people/square mile, compared with Chicago's 11,841.8 and Philadelphia's 11,379.5. The neighborhoods where most school closures occurred in Philadelphia and Chicago are traditional mixed-use, dense, urban neighborhoods, most of which developed before the enactment of zoning laws that mandate low-density, single land use development patterns. Los Angeles also developed far later than Chicago or Philadelphia, experiencing major growth, attributable in significant part to immigration, far more recently. In contrast to our studies of Philadelphia and Chicago, our analysis included all Catholic schools in the Archdiocese of Los Angeles, including those located in suburban locales. As a result, most of the development in the neighborhoods we studied proceeded according to a plan established by public zoning laws. There is some evidence that social connections fall sharply with physical distance, so the relative low density of the Los Angeles area may not be conducive to building social ties.[20]

As we discuss in detail in chapter 7, in her classic book, *The Death and Life of Great American Cities*, Jane Jacobs influentially challenged the prevailing wisdom that mixing residential and nonresidential land uses suppresses social capital and increases disorder. Jacobs reasoned that while busy city neighborhoods may appear disorderly and uncoordinated, the vitality generated by mixing land uses is critical to urban health. A diversity of land uses, she argued, gives people a diversity of reasons to be present in a community throughout the day and night. Therefore, mixing residential and commercial uses helps guarantee private "eyes upon the street" to monitor and suppress disorder and crime. Moreover, she predicted that nonresidential land uses—parks, corner shops, neighborhood taverns—provide opportunities for informal social interaction among relative strangers in a neighborhood.[21] These kinds of establishments can help build social capital by, to borrow from Putnam again, "bridging" diverse groups of people who would not otherwise encounter one another.[22]

A sizable empirical literature suggests that, by and large, Jacobs's hypothesis that nonresidential land uses foster social capital and suppress disorder and crime is simply wrong. Most of the researchers conducting these studies reject Jacobs's hypothesis as intuitively appealing but empirically unsustainable. They find instead that exclusively residential neighborhoods have lower crime rates, less disorder, and higher levels of collective efficacy than mixed residential and commercial neighborhoods.[23] We discuss this literature and the reasons why Catholic schools may behave differently, as neighborhood citizens, than other nonresidential land users in chapter 7. In short, we suspect that Catholic schools perform the functions that Jacobs predicted other kinds of nonresidential land uses would—that is, they generate social capital by drawing together members of a community who might not otherwise meet and generate the eyes upon the street that suppress disorder and crime. But it may be that Catholic schools cannot effectively perform these functions in less dense, single land use neighborhoods like those that dominate Los Angeles's built environment.[24]

Los Angeles's Parish Schools Resulted from Planned, Rather than Organic, Growth

Our results might also be influenced by the fact that most of Los Angeles's parochial schools were built as a part of a master plan—fitted neatly on the single land use zoned landscape rather than allowed to develop organically as part of an unplanned urban environment. The city's oldest (and for a long time, only) church is the Nuestra Señora Reina de los Angeles (known as the Plaza Church), founded in 1814, dedicated in 1822 for the first settlers in the city, and rebuilt in 1869 as Our Lady Queen of Angels. Most churches in Los Angeles, however, were located as a result of centralized planning, rather than arising organically with immigration as they did in

Chicago and Philadelphia. The most significant expansion of the Catholic schools' footprint in Los Angeles occurred under the direction of Cardinal James Francis McIntyre, who led the Archdiocese from 1948 to 1970. Soon after his installation as archbishop, McIntyre, dismayed by the fact that limited capacity forced Catholic schools to turn away tens of thousands of applicants each year, announced an ambitious capital campaign (the Youth Education Fund) and a plan to build dozens of additional schools. (In the first six years of the campaign, McIntyre oversaw the construction of sixty-two elementary and eleven high schools.) McIntyre's plan called for dividing his four-county Archdiocese into twenty-four districts and constructing schools along a plat system. Also as a result of the timing of the development of Catholic schools, a lower percentage of parishes in Los Angeles originally included a school than in Philadelphia and Chicago.[25] For all these reasons, Catholic schools may never have been established as neighborhood institutions in the same way that they were in the two older cities that we study.

The studies we conducted on Philadelphia and Los Angeles leave us unable to definitively say that Catholic schools are always good for urban neighborhoods. Indeed, we would need a much broader geographic sample than three cities to make such a claim. Our ability to replicate our results in Philadelphia leads us to suspect that Catholic schools likely benefit neighborhoods in cities like Philadelphia and Chicago—that is, older, denser cities with more organic "urban" land use patterns. We cannot say, without additional research, whether Los Angeles is aberrational or whether Catholic schools might be less beneficial in other, less dense, newer cities (for example, Las Vegas). Regardless of whether they would be, it is important to note that the bulk of Catholic schools are located in dense, older, urban centers—and that, therefore, this is where the majority of Catholic school closures are occurring as well. In these places, our research sounds a strong word of caution about the shrinking universe of Catholic schools.

CHAPTER SEVEN

Explaining Catholic Schools'
Positive Externalities

As we suggest in the introduction, we believe that our findings are best explained by the fact that urban Catholic schools generate social capital—and that, therefore, Catholic school closures lead to the dissipation of social capital—in a community. Our hypothesis builds upon, but is distinct from, previous research linking Catholic schools' success as educational institutions to their ability to generate social capital among members of a school community. It also flows naturally from the extensive literature connecting serious crime with low levels of "collective efficacy," the term used by sociologists and social psychologists to describe the ability of a community to organize and address problems.

We begin here by explaining our conception of social capital, before turning to several possible explanations for why Catholic schools generate it.

THE CONCEPT OF SOCIAL CAPITAL

Capital, as economists see it, is one of the necessary elements of producing any goods. It can take several forms. The original formulation (as seen in Adam Smith's *Wealth of Nations*) saw capital combined with land and labor in firms' production functions. In the twentieth century, Theodore Shultz[1] and his students, among them Gary Becker,[2] saw that tools like education and job training made labor much more productive and so gave birth to the field of "human capital," familiar to policymakers and educators as well as economists. The conception of social capital—that is the capital produced by social relationships—followed naturally on this work. As James Coleman explained, "Like other forms of capital, social capital is productive, making possible the achievement of certain ends that would not be attainable in its absence."[3]

The term "social capital" was apparently independently invented at least six times over the course of the twentieth century. Of particular relevance to our current work is the fact that the first person to use the term was apparently a Progressive-era education reformer, L.J. Hanifan, who stressed the importance of community involvement as an input for successful schools, and the third person was "urbanist" Jane Jacobs, who used the term in the 1960s to describe the informal social relationships needed to ensure healthy city neighborhoods.[4] The concept became part of the standard social science discourse thanks to the work of sociologists Mark Granovetter—who recognized that the market system proposed by Adam Smith did not completely depend upon individual pursuit of self-interest but rather was "embedded" in social relationships, which generate trust, establish expectations, and create and enforce norms—and James Coleman—who in the late 1980s once again connected social capital and human capital formation in the education context, especially in the Catholic school context.[5]

Because the social capital literature has developed in a variety of fields, its terminology and means of measurement also vary. As Robert Putnam put it, "By analogy with notions of physical capital and human capital—tools and training that enhance individual productivity—'social capital' refers to features of social organization such as networks, norms, and social trust that facilitate coordination and cooperation for mutual benefit."[6] Putnam's *Bowling Alone* popularized the concept, and it has since become the focus not only of a good deal of sociology and political science scholarship[7] but also of writings in economics. In his "Economics of Social Capital," Cambridge economist Partha Dasgupta describes social capital as a means to create trust. He maintains that social capital (which he also sometimes calls interpersonal networks) can stem from a number of sources but never requires resort to an external enforcer of agreements (that is, as in government enforcement of contracts or, in our case, police enforcement of criminal laws).[8]

Our conception of social capital is a fairly simple, bare bones one that does not draw the distinction, emphasized by both Granovetter and Putnam, between deep and casual social bonds (or, in Putnam's formulation, between "bonding" and "bridging" social capital). By social capital, we mean social networks that make urban neighborhoods function smoothly— the connections that draw residents together and enable them to suppress evils like crime and disorder. As Coleman observes, social capital "not only facilitates certain actions; it constrains" others.[9] For us, social capital need not produce more voting or other participation in the political process, as suggested by Putnam and his recent coauthor David Campbell, although it probably is correlated with good citizenship.[10] It need not be based, as some literature claims, upon "who you know" as in James Buchanan's "Theory of Clubs."[11] As we see it, social capital may be reflected in the act of collecting a vacationing neighbor's mail, or calling the authorities to report suspicious activity, or picking up a discarded fast food container from the street. Social capital will be highly correlated with trust and will facilitate the extension of trust beyond the family and into the neighborhood.

Interpersonal networks cost something to establish. In many cases, they may involve transactions costs — the costs of negotiating agreements, making written ones where required, and enforcing them by formal or informal means. In the neighborhood context, they are likely to involve opportunity costs, meaning that the participants could be spending their time and money doing something other than getting to know their neighbors.[12] Once established, however, social capital should not only minimize transaction cost in dealings among network members but also should have (typically positive, but not always) external effects. Social networks help us to produce human capital and sometimes are better than impersonal markets in promoting exchange.[13] Briefly, they will be more effective when they function in a complementary, as opposed to a substitutionary, way. That is, some kinds of networks can prevent markets from functioning well because they dilute personal incentives to invest for prosperity.[14] In the neighborhood context, social networks will also be ineffective when they and the market are substitutes (cooperative trash pickup and disposal on a neighborhood level may be less efficient than trash services provided by for-profit firms, but cooperative litter pick up is more so). On the downside, since they are exclusive by their very nature, social capital networks can act to reinforce inequalities and prejudice,[15] and since they generate trust (and therefore vulnerability), they may be subject to opportunism.[16]

SOCIAL CAPITAL, SCHOOLS, AND EDUCATIONAL OUTCOMES

Of particular relevance to our study is the literature exploring the connection between social capital and educational outcomes. We emphasize that our research builds upon, but goes beyond, this previous scholarship

to explore the impact of Catholic schools on neighborhoods. This literature generally falls into two categories. The first discusses the role of social capital within schools as an important input for student achievement.
This literature suggests that successful schools, including Catholic schools
in particular, are characterized by high levels of within-school social capital. The second focuses on the intersection between levels of social capital
in a community and the performance of students and schools situated in
those communities. This is the context within which the concept of social
capital was first articulated by Hanifan, and the literature exploring this
connection suggests, as Hanifan originally predicted, that the level of social
capital in the community where students live is an important predictor of
school performance. The godfather of both categories of both social capital
literatures is the godfather of the conception of social capital itself, sociologist James Coleman. According to Coleman's formulation, social capital
"inheres in the structure of relations between actors and among actors,"
and institutions that foster these relationships are incubators of social capital.[17] Coleman used schools to illustrate this conception of social capital,
arguing that successful schools tended to be distinguished by parents' connections to their children's school and to the parents of their children's
peers.[18] These connections, he reasoned, "closed the loop" among school,
teachers, and parents, thus guaranteeing the enforcement of appropriate
norms.[19] Coleman further argued that these kinds of connections—and the
norm-enforcement authority that they enable—helped to explain Catholic
high schools' high graduation rates.[20]

Coleman's hypothesis was further explicated and tested in the influential book *Catholic Schools and the Common Good*. In the book, sociologists
Anthony Bryk, Valerie Lee, and Peter Holland linked Catholic high schools'
educational successes to the fact that they are intentional communities, fea-
turing high levels of trust among students, parents, teachers, and administrators. Bryk and his colleagues observed that Catholic school teachers and
administrators saw their role as not just educational but formative. These
communitarian features, according to Bryk and his colleagues, are one of
two important reasons why Catholic schools succeed as academic institutions. In their words:

> Schools organized as communities have direct consequences for both teachers
> and students. For teachers, working in communally organized schools should
> enhance the likelihood of attaining the intrinsic rewards so essential to the
> profession. In such contexts, teachers should express greater satisfaction with

their work, and their morale should generally be higher. Further, the presence of highly committed teachers is likely to be infectious. Drawing faculty
together results in a social solidarity that also draws students into the mainstream of school life. . . . The personal interest of individual teachers in individual students fosters a social bonding of these students to the school and to
the core activities that manifest the school's goals. When this social activity is
widespread, a normative environment is created in which caring and a sense of
hope and purpose come to characterize the personal experience of both adults
and students.[21]

Bryk and his colleagues further suggested that the communitarian organization of schools, and the high level of trust it enabled, was an important
input into the other factor explaining Catholic schools' success at educating
low-income minority students—namely, the high academic expectations of
Catholic schools for all students regardless of race or class background.[22]
Bryk's conclusions are in keeping with an earlier test of Coleman's hypothesis by Stephen Morgan and Aage B. Sorensen. Morgan and Sorensen concluded that while some of the so-called Catholic school effect on minority
student outcomes can be explained by the fact that Catholic schools expect
all students to take a rigorous academic curriculum, the performance gap
between public and Catholic schools is best explained by the social capital
formed between members of a Catholic school community, that is, the connections formed among faculty members, students, and parents.[23]

In more recent work, Bryk has, along with other colleagues, applied
these lessons to the public school context, arguing that social capital/trust
within a school community is an important predictor of public school performance and improvement, especially in disadvantaged urban communities. In a recent study of Chicago, for example, Bryk, Penny Sebring, Elaine
Allensworth, Stuart Luppescu, and John Easton argued that the level of
relational trust can enable a school to overcome structural impediments to
improvement. Bryk and his colleagues studied a radical experiment by the
Chicago Public Schools, which in 1988 devolved significant resources and
authority to local school councils and mandated that the councils reform
their schools. In the years that followed, some schools experienced a dramatic improvement, against the odds suggested by community and student
demographics, while others stagnated or declined. Bryk and his colleagues
found that the level of relational trust within a school—particularly the trust
among teachers, parents, and administrators—was one of the most important factors predicting improvement among the schools that faced similar
levels of structural impediments to student improvement.[24]

Bryk and others also have demonstrated that the level of social capital in the community surrounding a school is a critical input into a school's success (or failure), especially in the urban context. For example, in their 2010 study of the Chicago decentralization experiment, Bryk et al. found that decentralization was less likely to catalyze improvements in student performance in schools located in disadvantaged neighborhoods. This was hardly a surprising finding given what we know about the connection between student demographics and student performance. When they delved deeper into the picture, seeking to understand what explained variations in improvement between schools located in similar neighborhoods, however, they also found that schools located in neighborhoods with higher levels of social capital (as measured by the same Project on Human Development in Chicago Neighborhoods data that we employ here) and lower levels of crime were more likely to improve. For example, over a third of schools in neighborhoods characterized by high levels of collective efficacy improved, compared with only 22 percent of those located in low collective efficacy neighborhoods. The results were more pronounced for crime: again, one-third or more of schools in low-crime neighborhoods improved, compared with only 15 percent of those in high-crime neighborhoods. Neighborhood religiosity—for which Bryk and his colleagues employed a separate measure of social capital—also strongly predicted improvements; schools located in neighborhoods with high levels of religious participation were more than twice as likely to improve than those in communities with weaker participation. All of these factors (except perhaps religiosity), admittedly, are correlated with a neighborhood's socioeconomic status, but Bryk et al. suggest that variations in social capital and crime go a long way to explaining the relative success of schools in more stable, integrated settings (as well as the ability of some schools to overcome their structural odds and succeed).[25]

These findings about the role of social capital both within a school and in the school's surrounding neighborhood take center stage in Charles Payne's recent reflection on reform efforts in urban public schools, *So Much Reform, So Little Change*. Drawing upon both the academic literature on school improvement and his own extensive experience with reform efforts, especially in the Chicago Public Schools, Payne attributes the persistent failure of reform efforts to the dual realities that most urban public schools are characterized by a lack of trust and support among the various school constituencies and by the fact that the schools draw students from communities with very low levels of social capital.[26] Levels of social capital (both inside a school and in the surrounding communities) also have effects beyond academic performance, as suggested by a recent study of teacher and student safety in Chicago Public Schools. The researchers found that, while factors beyond the control of schools (neighborhood crime, poverty, the academic achievement of incoming students) affected the level of safety in a school (and students' perception of safety), students and teachers consistently reported feeling more secure—regardless of the level of crime in the surrounding neighborhood—in schools characterized by high levels of trust and collaboration among members of a school community.[27] In other words, there are feedback effects between the level of social capital in a school and levels of social capital in the community surrounding a school. This research suggests that social capital in the community affects educational outcomes, and also that social capital inside a school can overcome structural impediments to learning coming from the community (including low levels of social capital).

More recently, scholars have begun to explore whether, and how, school-choice programs affect levels of social capital within school communities. As we explore in greater detail below and in chapter 8, scholars have generally found a positive school-choice effect on social capital, evidenced by increased levels of civic knowledge and tolerance of diversity among students transferring from public to private schools as part of a school-choice program.[28] While some have questioned whether higher levels of social capital in choice schools results from the fact that parents opting to participate in the programs themselves exhibit higher levels of social capital, many of these studies are able to control for selection effects because scholarships are allocated through randomized lottery systems.[29]

CATHOLIC SCHOOLS AS GENERATORS OF NEIGHBORHOOD SOCIAL CAPITAL

While all of this research demonstrating that social capital within a school (and especially within Catholic schools) produces positive educational benefits and that neighborhood social capital can make schools better is relevant to our research, we make a distinct claim here. We believe that Catholic schools do not simply generate social capital within classroom walls but also beyond them. But our bottom-line conclusion is that they generate social capital. For reasons that we articulate at the conclusion of this chapter, we believe that the social capital inside the Catholic schools we study does more than simply make these schools effective educational institutions—it also makes them effective community institutions.

Before we turn to this bottom line, however, we first explore several alternative explanations for our findings.

The Jane Jacobs Explanation

One possible explanation for Catholic schools' success as neighborhood institutions is offered by Jane Jacobs's classic defense of urban life. Since the early twentieth century, single-use, suburban land use patterns have dominated in the United States, in large part because our dominant form of land use regulation—zoning—rests upon a long-standing assumption that nonresidential land uses inhibit social capital. As Richard Chused has persuasively argued, the Progressive-era proponents of zoning were "positive environmentalists" who firmly believed that "changing surroundings would change behavior." They believed that single land use patterns were not only superior to the mixed land use patterns characterizing urban communities, but that they would foster a physically and morally healthier citizenry.[30]

This long-standing view received its sharpest, and most influential, challenge in Jane Jacobs's classic work, *Death and Life of Great American Cities*. Jacobs vehemently disputed the prevailing wisdom that mixing residential and nonresidential land uses suppresses social capital and increases disorder. American land use practices, she countered, have it exactly backwards: Jacobs reasoned that while busy city neighborhoods may appear disorderly and uncoordinated, the vitality generated by mixing land uses is critical to urban health. A diversity of land uses, she argued, gives people a diversity of reasons to be present in a community throughout the day and night. Therefore, mixing residential and commercial uses helps guarantee private "eyes upon the street" to monitor and suppress disorder and crime. Moreover, she predicted that nonresidential land uses—and especially small-scale commercial enterprises like corner stores and neighborhood taverns—provide opportunities for informal social interaction among relative strangers in a neighborhood.[31] According to Jacobs, these kinds of establishments can help build social capital by, to borrow from Putnam, bridging diverse groups of people who would not otherwise encounter one another.[32] It may be the case, in other words, that Catholic schools are engines of social capital for the reasons that Jane Jacobs championed mixed landuse urban environments—they, like other nonresidential land uses, draw together and build connections between community members who might otherwise not interact.

Today, nearly a half-century after the publication of her important book,

Jacobs's ideas may be at the peak of their influence. In particular, her views about the value of nonresidential land uses in urban communities, now popularized by the self-styled "new urbanists," are shaping both suburban design and the design of urban "infill" and redevelopment projects. Furthermore, and importantly, Jacobs's influence—or at least the version of it promoted by the new urbanists—is beginning to be reflected in incremental changes to long-standing land-use regulations, including a gradual trend toward the adoption of mixed-use zoning. All of these efforts implicitly endorse Jacobs's argument that mixed land use environments are, at least under some circumstances, socially beneficial.[33]

The popular and academic commentary on Jacobs's arguments, however, frequently overlooks the empirical literature testing her hypothesis that nonresidential land uses foster social capital and suppress disorder and crime. In a number of studies, criminologists, sociologists, and environmental psychologists have sought to examine the connection between different land use patterns (that is, exclusively residential versus mixed use) with disorder and crime. The relative neglect of this work in the literature on land use policy is unfortunate. Most of the researchers conducting these studies reject Jacobs's hypothesis as intuitively appealing but empirically unsustainable. They find instead that nonresidential land uses suppress social capital and increase crime and disorder.[34] Researchers comparing the crime rates (and in some studies, the presence of observable physical disorder) in two neighborhoods with similar demographic profiles but different land use patterns generally find that exclusively residential neighborhoods have lower crime rates, less disorder, and higher levels of collective efficacy than mixed residential and commercial neighborhoods.[35]

The researchers conducting these studies link their findings to the "routine-activities" theory of crime. Routine-activities theory builds on the insight that most predatory crime is opportunistic. That is, as Robert Sampson and Stephen Raudenbush summarize, crime "involves the intersection in time and space of motivated offenders, suitable targets, and the absence of capable guardians."[36] Land use patterns are relevant to this thesis for two reasons: first, nonresidential land uses (such as schools, stores, parks, etc.) may serve to invite strangers—including would-be offenders—into a neighborhood. By providing places for neighbors to congregate, these land uses may also generate a larger pool of potential victims than residential ones. Thus, while Jacobs was right that nonresidential land uses increase the number of individuals present in an urban neighborhood, the routine-activities theory suggests that higher numbers of "eyes upon the street" actually may increase the number of potential offenders rather than the opportunities for informal surveillance.[37]

Second, contrary to Jacobs's intuition, commercial uses may decrease private surveillance efforts. This argument flows from Oscar Newman's important work on "defensible space." Newman argued that architectural and urban design can decrease crime by increasing opportunities for residents to exercise "ownership" over public spaces.[38] Proponents of routine-activities theory suggest that the desire to exercise control over our environment is strongest closest to our homes. Events occurring in one's yard are more important than those occurring on the sidewalk, sidewalk events are more important than neighborhood events, and so on. According to this theory, by introducing strangers into a community, nonresidential land uses create "holes in the resident-based territorial fabric" or "valleys in the topography of territorial control."[39] Resident surveys conducted for these studies suggest that nonresidential land uses reduce informal monitoring by residents. In one study, for example, residents on blocks with nonresidential land uses reported that they recognized other block residents less well, felt that they had less control over events in the neighborhood, and were less likely to count on a neighbor to monitor suspicious activity than residents of exclusively residential blocks.[40] The researchers conducting these studies hypothesize that the increased traffic generated by nonresidential uses makes it more difficult to discern who belongs in a community. It is also possible that residents place a higher value on residences than businesses and thus are more vigilant about monitoring them.

Our evidence suggests, however, that urban Catholic elementary schools apparently work as Jacobs predicted nonresidential land uses should work: they increase social capital and suppress disorder and crime in the neighborhoods where they are located. We do not believe therefore that parochial schools foster community because they are nonresidential land uses but rather despite the fact that they are.

The Night Watchman Explanation

One reason why Catholic schools may behave differently as neighborhood citizens than other kinds of nonresidential land uses simply may be that Catholic parishes are more secure. In most parishes, for example, the pastor lives on site and may serve as a night watchman. A partial explanation may also be that Catholic school facilities that might otherwise serve as recreational hangouts for teenagers or staging areas for illicit activities—such as playgrounds and parking lots—are fenced and inaccessible. Conversely, it is also possible that increased crime rates in a police beat following a school closure stem from the fact that vacant buildings are, as a sizable literature attests, themselves magnets for crime.

We are skeptical, however, that these factors alone are sufficient to explain our findings. To begin, we do not understand why the presence of a night watchman would necessarily foster neighborhood social interactions. Moreover, even if it did, a school closure rarely removes the night watchman from the neighborhood since most parishes in our study remained open, and the pastor remained in residence, after the school closed. And, although vacant buildings certainly are detrimental to a community, we suspect that most closed school buildings do not remain vacant but rather are used for other parish functions or (increasingly) leased to charter schools.

The School Effects Explanation

Another possibility is that we are observing simply (or perhaps more accurately, simple) school effects on community life. In other words, it is possible that Catholic schools are effective community institutions not because they are *Catholic* schools but rather because they are *schools*. For any number of reasons, schools generally, rather than Catholic schools specifically, may generate social capital. In our view, it is entirely logical to assume that institutions dedicated to the formation of human capital also generate social capital. This was James Coleman's hypothesis—that the social-capital and human-capital formation functions of schools intersect. This hypothesis is strongly supported by the literature, discussed above, which suggests that social capital within a school is a critical input into educational performance.

Public schools, in particular, have long been associated with community building. (Consider, for example, the movie *Hoosiers*.) Historically, this may have been particularly true in rural communities, where, as the common school movement gained ground, local communities were responsible for raising the funds to support a school for local children—a communal enterprise that undoubtedly both generated and reflected high levels of social capital. More recently, skeptics of school choice also have defended public schools on communitarian grounds. As discussed in greater detail in chapter 8, for example, economist William Fischel has justified neighborhood public schools on the grounds that they generate what he calls "community specific social capital." As Fischel observes, "[M]y approach to social capital formation simply requires that parents get to know other parents. Investment in community-specific social capital is simply adding local names to your address book, and sending your child to a local school does that more effectively than any other means." Fischel cites, as evidence for this proposition, data suggesting that states with smaller (and therefore presumably more community-friendly) school districts have higher levels of social capital. If the location of social capital matters—and the sizable literature connecting collective efficacy with neighborhood stability tends to suggest that it does—then Fischel is correct to emphasize the opportunities for community building generated by neighborhood schools.

Fischel's observation that many adult social relationships are formed through parent interactions in their children's schools likely resonates with most parents of school-aged children. Further, Fischel is correct that, to the extent that the "names in the address book" generated by neighborhood public schools are more likely to be neighborhood names, the social capital that the names represent is more likely to be community specific in nature.[41] Still, although local public schools undoubtedly are important community institutions, the available empirical evidence casts doubt upon whether urban public schools in fact are effective at generating neighborhood social capital. Consider, for example, the empirical literature examining the effect of land use "hot spots"—that is, land uses associated with high levels of crime and disorder and low levels of collective efficacy. These studies have linked a variety of nonresidential land uses, including, importantly for our purposes, public schools, with increased crime in a community. For example, a number of studies document that residential blocks containing public high schools and immediately adjacent blocks experience a statistically significant higher incidence of crime. At least one study found that public elementary schools also appeared to generate crime as well—perhaps more crime than public high schools.[42] In contrast, there is little indication in these studies that private schools generate crime and disorder. Although one study of Cleveland found a slight, but not statistically significant, increase in crime in neighborhoods with private high schools, other studies have generally found no effect.[43] These studies cast doubt upon the possibility that the beneficial effects of Catholic schools that we find would also be generated by urban public schools. These findings are entirely in keeping with those of Fischel, who predicts that urban public schools are likely to be, for a variety of reasons discussed below, less effective social capital producers than suburban ones.

These studies, to be sure, were not conducted at the same time and place, using the same data, as the results that we report here. Therefore, we cannot definitively say that their results are generalizable to the conditions on the ground described in this book. We cannot know for certain whether public schools might have been generating social capital and suppressing crime in Chicago during the time that we study. Moreover, the studies described above measure the effects of open schools, and we are primarily measuring results of school closures. Ideally, we would have measured the effects of both closed and open public schools in our study. We considered doing so, but, for a number of reasons rejected the possibility as unwieldy: far fewer public than Catholic schools closed during our period of interest. Moreover, there were far more public schools than Catholic schools, making comparisons between police beats with and without schools over time much more difficult.

Current trends in public education suggest that the study of public school closures is, or is becoming, a fruitful area for future research. As briefly discussed in the introduction, many districts are closing or consolidating schools. For example, in March 2013 alone, Philadelphia and Chicago announced plans to close, respectively, 23 and 53 schools, prompting massive protests by teachers, students, and parents[44]—decisions driven both by enrollment trends and financial woes.[45] A number of urban districts also have converted public schools to charter schools. After Hurricane Katrina, for example, over half of the public schools in New Orleans reopened as charter schools,[46] and significant numbers of public schools have become charter schools in other cities, including Philadelphia and Washington, D.C. In addition, many state and federal policies, including the controversial No Child Left Behind Act, require that persistently failing schools be closed or restructured. All of this suggests that more closures may be on the horizon—especially in light of the budgetary and enrollment realities facing many urban districts, and the fact that, under current standards, as many as three-quarters of all U.S. public schools could be labeled "failing."[47] Studies of these phenomena will shed light on whether our results in fact reflect a Catholic school effect on community life as well as on the intersection between school structure and community social capital.

All that said, we do include a proxy for public schools—that is, charter schools in the city of Chicago—in our study. And our results suggest that open Catholic and open charter schools do not generate comparable levels of social capital—at least insofar as social capital is reflected in crime rates. As discussed in chapter 5, we find that open Catholic schools were consistently associated with lower crime rates in a police beat and open charter schools were not. These results held true even for charter schools operating in closed Catholic schools. These results are necessarily more tentative than our results for Catholic schools—for reasons we explained in greater detail previously. Combined with previous studies of the effects of public schools, the divergence between our results for Catholic and charter schools in Chicago leads us to strongly suspect that we are not simply finding school effects.

The Student Body Explanation

Our results also might be explained by the fact that Catholic schools enroll different types of students than do public and charter schools. For example, most (but not all) of the Catholic schools in our study enrolled grades kindergarten (or prekindergarten) through 8, and most (but not all) of the charter schools we include did not. The educational psychology literature on school transitions suggests that students perform better—in terms of behavior, academic achievement, and self-esteem—in K–8 schools.[48] If older students are more likely to generate disorder—and researchers have linked the greater incidence of crime near public middle and high schools with the presence of large numbers of adolescents—then Catholic schools' practice of combining elementary and middle school students may generate positive neighborhood externalities by encouraging good behavior among an age cohort that is, generally speaking, more likely to get into trouble. Our comparative study of Catholic and charter schools in Chicago, however, leads us to discount the grade structure explanation. Unlike Catholic schools, very few of the charter schools in our study extended into the middle school years. Moreover, we intentionally excluded stand-alone charter middle schools as well as high schools, making it unlikely that the divergent effects that we find of open charter and Catholic schools are middle school effects.

Another possibility is that our findings result from selection effects. Catholic schools' control over student body composition is frequently cited as contributing to their relative educational success, as is the fact that better educated, highly motivated, parents are more likely to choose Catholic schools for their children.[49] Both factors may help explain Catholic and public/charter schools' divergent neighborhood effects. Public schools usually exercise far less enrollment discretion than do Catholic schools. Traditional public schools generally must accept all comers, and even charter schools must conduct a lottery for admission if demand exceeds capacity (although in Chicago, public schools and charter schools may give priority to students residing within their neighborhood attendance boundary—if one is designated).[50] Public and charter schools may also find it more difficult to expel disruptive students who may act out both inside and outside the class-room setting. Moreover, although Catholic school tuition is relatively low relative to tuition at secular private schools,[51] a decision to send a child to a Catholic school signals a threshold level of parental motivation—and moti-vated parents may be better able to control their children's behavior before and after school. Finally, Catholic schools frequently place demands on par-ents that public schools do not or even cannot: Many require parents to vol-unteer in the school and/or provide parents with the option of volunteering in order to reduce tuition burdens.[52] These requirements may help gener-ate parental networks as well as building, as Bryk et al. have suggested, a school-parent community that encourages parents to endorse Catholic schools' more rigorous and structured academic program. These require-ments also may have the side effect of guaranteeing a stable flow of respon-sible adults into a neighborhood who help keep disorder and crime in check.

That said, it is important not to overstate the explanatory value of stu-dent body factors. To begin, a substantial body of empirical evidence tends to refute the claim that Catholic schools' educational success is attributable to selection bias.[53] Indeed, the available evidence suggests that the educa-tional benefits of Catholic schools are greatest for the poorest, most disad-vantaged, students. As Darlene York summarizes in describing the evidence as it applies to African American students, "family background variables such as income, parental education levels, and parental educational aspira-tions seem less important in the achievement gains" of minority students in Catholic schools.[54] Moreover, there also are selection effects in charter schools, which our study suggests do not have the same positive neighbor-hood effects as those of Catholic schools. Since a parent selecting a char-ter school must opt out of the traditional public school system and choose among a range of alternatives, it is reasonable to expect that charter schools, like Catholic schools, attract the students of more motivated parents.[55] Fur-thermore, while charter schools are free (and Catholic schools are not), most Catholic schools deeply discount tuition and also provide significant financial assistance, practices that blur the charter-Catholic distinction for low-income students and enable Catholic schools to enroll students from disadvantaged backgrounds.

The Neighborhood Networks Explanation

Another possible explanation for our findings is that urban Catholic schools generate neighborhood networks, and especially (as Fischel predicts) neigh-

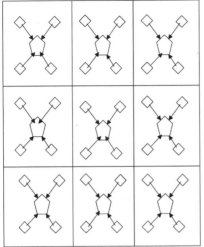 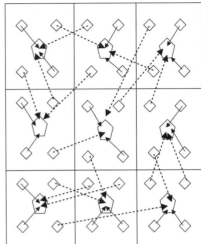

FIGURE 7.1 Parental networks
at neighborhood public schools

FIGURE 7.2 Parental networks
at private schools

borhood parental networks, because they are neighborhood institutions. Recall that Fischel argues that local public schools generate community-specific social capital in large part because they are geographically bound community institutions that provide a meeting place for neighbors. Figure 7.1 reproduces Fischel's depiction of the parental networks generated by neighborhood public schools. Fischel expresses skepticism about school choice because he worries that the parental networks at private schools selected by participating parents would be more geographically diffuse, as depicted in figure 7.2. Thus, while the sum total of social capital generated by parental networks at choice schools would not necessarily be lower than that generated by local public schools—as Fischel acknowledges, parental networks at private schools are no less extensive than those in public schools—the social capital would not be concentrated in a single neighborhood or community.

We certainly are open to the argument that schools are particularly efficacious community institutions. We believe that Fischel may well be correct about the unique function of neighborhood schools in generating community-specific social capital, but the important qualifying criteria may also be the "neighborhood-ness" of a school rather than its "public-ness." That is, we believe it is plausible that the schools we study generate neighborhood social capital because many of them are neighborhood institutions. This was certainly true historically, as discussed previously, for the Catholic schools that are the focus of our study. And, while factors other than proximity undoubtedly influence parents' decisions about where to send their children to school, it is reasonable to assume that many Catholic school students continue to attend the Catholic school closest to their home.[56] Moreover, as Fischel acknowledges, not all public schools are neighborhood schools. For example, while Fischel's hypothesis about the social capital production function of local public schools leads him to expresses skepticism about statewide voucher programs, he also suggests that school choice makes the most sense—and may actually increase social capital—in large urban districts, where various factors, including public school choice, make it more difficult for parents to get to know one another.[57]

In fact, given the prevalence of public school choice in large urban districts like the Chicago Public Schools, students attending a Catholic school may be more likely to live in the surrounding neighborhood than public school students. In 1980, in a response to a federal desegregation decree, the Chicago Public Schools implemented an open enrollment program. Each resident is guaranteed admission into a geographically assigned public school but is also entitled to apply for admission to more than two hundred magnet programs throughout the city. Selection of students to attend non-neighborhood schools is generally determined by randomized lotteries, although entrance into some competitive schools is determined by entrance exams. In 2000–2001, more than one-third of all elementary school students in the Chicago Public Schools enrolled in a school other than their assigned neighborhood school.[58]

If we are correct that many Catholic schools are neighborhood institutions, then Fischel's depiction of the parental networks in local public schools also yields insight into why Catholic school closures reduce neighborhood-level social capital. Without question, a school closure disrupts the school's parental networks and community-specific social capital that these networks generate. If many parents live proximately to the closed school, then the closure disrupts neighborhood networks as well. Building upon Fischel's illustrations, we can depict the hypothetical effects of such a disruption for actual school closures in Chicago. In 1984, the Archdiocese of Chicago "merged" three schools on the far south side of the city—Saints Peter and Paul School, Immaculate Conception School, and Saint Mary Magdalene School. The result of the merger was that Saints Peter and Paul and Immaculate Conception were closed and the students in these schools

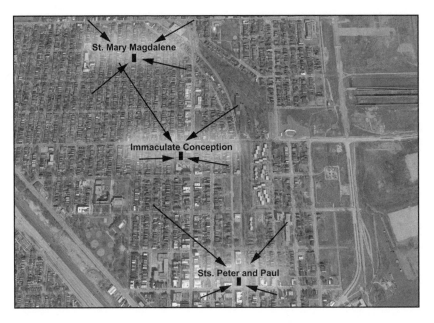

FIGURE 7.3 Parental networks in three Chicago Catholic schools

were transferred to Saint Mary Magdalene, which was renamed Jesus Our Brother. Figure 7.3 depicts, following Fischel's lead, the location of the parental networks prior to the merger. We assume that most parents would prefer to send their children to a proximate school, although we account for those who live farther away with the longer lines on the map.

Obviously, the merger disrupted the preexisting networks when the children transferred to Jesus Our Brother. The merger also likely disrupted existing parental networks at Jesus Our Brother (formerly Saint Mary Magdalene), as the school absorbed new students and parents. After a period of transition, we can assume that the parental networks at Jesus Our Brother were as strong as the preexisting networks, although, as depicted in figure 7.4, these networks are now less localized than premerger. Moreover, some Saints Peter and Paul and Saint Mary Magdalene parents probably chose not to send their children to Jesus Our Brother—perhaps transportation was unavailable to the merged school or the parents were upset with the Archdiocese's decision to close their children's school. These parents may have opted for another Catholic school or a public school instead. If so, some of the parents, as depicted in figure 7.4 did not join the reconstituted parent network at Jesus Our Brother at all.

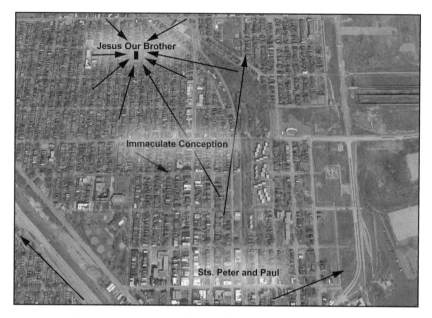

FIGURE 7.4 Parental networks following school merger

In 1994, the Archdiocese closed Jesus Our Brother School, again disrupt-
ing parental networks. We do not have information about where children
displaced by the closure were assigned by the Archdiocese. If these stylized
images are, in fact, reflective of the reality on the ground in Chicago during
the years that we study, we believe they go a long way toward explaining
our findings. Put simply, Catholic school closures do not remove just any
schools from neighborhoods; they remove neighborhood schools, and the
effects of their removal are therefore completely consistent with Fischel's
hypothesis about the social-capital-generation function of neighborhood
schools.

We still suspect that the neighborhood schools explanation is incomplete. To begin, we do not know with any degree of certainty how many of
the Catholic schools that we study are, in fact, neighborhood schools. Since
we do not know how many students enrolled in a school at the time that it
closed lived in the neighborhood, our neighborhood networks explanation
is purely conjectural. (Indeed, we doubt that the data that would enable
us to determine where students lived who enrolled in a closed school at
the time of the closure exists today.) Moreover, as we discussed in greater
detail in chapter 5, we find that charter schools in Chicago do not, thus

far, appear to be as efficacious in generating neighborhood social capital as Catholic schools. Yet, according to the Chicago Public Schools, a majority of the city's charter schools are, in fact, neighborhood schools. Illinois law authorizes the designation of an attendance boundary for charter schools and permits charter schools to give priority to students residing within their boundaries. During the 2008–2009 school year, Chicago charter schools, on average, drew approximately 63 percent of their students from the surrounding neighborhood, although the percentage of neighborhood students ranged from a low of 6.7 percent to a high of 100 percent.[59] Taken together, the fact that we know that many charter schools are neighborhood schools, and that we do not know for certain how many Catholic schools are not, leads us to conclude that the neighborhood school explanation is incomplete.

It is possible, therefore, that Catholic schools generate social capital not (or perhaps not only) because they are educational institutions that connect parents but also because they are community institutions that connect neighbors. That is, they may generate community-specific social capital not because they are schools but because they are neighborhood institutions. This possibility is supported by a fairly extensive literature discussing the role of various community institutions—for example, community centers, community gardens, and, as discussed below, churches—in building social capital.[60] As one of us has written about extensively, this hunch about the importance of neighborhood networks is also reflected in popular community policing policies designed to draw neighbors together to build the social capital needed to address neighborhood problems.[61] And there is evidence that residents of poorer communities are less likely to interact for a variety of reasons, a reality that, not surprisingly, suppresses the level of social capital in a community. Community institutions (and perhaps also community policing) provide a forum for interneighbor interaction that helps residents overcome this social isolation.

While plausible, both the narrow (neighborhood school focused) and broad (community institution focused) version of the neighborhood networks explanation seem incomplete to us. Without knowing more, for example, we cannot say why Catholic schools would perform more effectively as community institutions than public schools or charter schools (especially neighborhood public schools or neighborhood charter schools, which we also would expect to have neighborhood network effects). We also do not know whether Catholic schools would perform effectively as community institutions if they were not neighborhood schools, and we cannot say definitively how many of the schools that we study were neighborhood schools. We turn therefore to two factors that may make Catholic schools distinctive.

The Religious Institution Explanation

Catholic schools also may succeed as community institutions because they are religious institutions. There are extensive literatures linking both religion and religious institutions with social capital. (Indeed, religious participation is itself a common measure of social capital.) As Putnam has argued, "Faith communities in which people worship together are arguably the single most important repository of social capital in America."[62] It is unclear whether religiosity itself generates social capital. Although some commentators argue as much, their claim is somewhat undermined by the fact that self-reported religiosity has remained relatively stable in the United States during a time period in which social capital has declined.[63] A better explanation, in our view, is that the practice of religion promotes social interactions that facilitate social capital. For example, there is evidence that religious people know more people and communicate with more people on a daily basis than nonreligious people.[64]

And, of course, since religion tends to promote prosocial norms, the social networks generated by religious institutions are likely to reinforce the kinds of norms that will suppress crime and disorder. Importantly for the present purposes, a substantial literature documents the importance of churches as stabilizing institutions in inner-city communities. As Tracey Meares has observed, not only are churches central to disadvantaged communities, but "it is not a stretch to say that churches are *the* central institution in these communities."[65] The widespread efforts of urban police forces to cultivate relationships with, and harness the social capital production function of, churches also suggest that local governments understand the importance of the religious institutions in poor communities.[66] Perhaps the centrality of churches in certain inner-city communities is denomination blind—that is, the respect accorded religious institutions among non-Catholic residents of these communities extends to the Catholic Church and its institutions. Moreover, the institutional view of social capital (as opposed to the relational view) emphasizes the social capital that can arise from affiliations with larger institutions, even absent personal relationships between members of the institutions.[67] Therefore, the enrollment of a non-Catholic student in a Catholic school may conceivably promote social capital by extending the number of individuals affiliated with the Catholic Church, a large and otherwise influential social institution. And, as Meares's work on prayer vigils in Chicago demonstrates, interdenominational networks are particularly important in poor inner-city communities, where religious leaders are both influential and unlikely to know one another well.[68]

The Catholic School Effect Explanation

While we do not doubt the explanatory value of many of the factors we have discussed thus far, we do question whether any of them (or even all of them combined) completely explain our findings. In the end, we believe that Catholic schools succeed as urban neighborhood institutions for the same reason that they succeed as urban educational institutions. That is, as we hinted previously, we suspect that there are feedback effects between the social capital generated within a Catholic school and the level of social capital in a community surrounding it. Neighborhood-level social capital is, in other words, a positive externality of within-school social capital. We know—thanks to Bryk, Coleman, and others—that Catholic schools' educational successes are at least partially attributable to an educational formula that generates within-school social capital that helps to overcome neighborhood structural impediments to learning (including low levels of social capital). We also know that the level of social capital in a community affects educational outcomes in schools—that is, that schools in communities with low levels of social capital tend to struggle academically. We therefore think it entirely plausible that the same mechanisms that generate social capital within a school may act to increase the level of social capital in the community outside it.

To be sure, we do not know the precise mechanisms by which these positive externalities are generated. They may be related to the communitarian aspects of the Catholic school program emphasized by Bryk. An emphasis on trust and respect among members of a school community might reasonably be expected to inculcate a culture of respect for the community in which a school is situated. For example, Bryk and his coauthors found that Catholic high school students were more likely to engage in community service than were their public school counterparts, a fact that they concluded "signif[ied] Catholic schools' commitment to a just social community."[69] If broadly shared across all of the constituencies—and, as Bryk repeatedly emphasizes, if a central goal of Catholic school administrators is to build a "community among faculty, students, and parents" that endorses the academic and social goals of a school—this commitment to civic engagement, service, and tolerance is likely to generate positive community externalities. Students engaged in community service activities likely help generate social capital in a community. Teachers and parents who endorse the schools' communitarian goals and enable and encourage community service also may be more likely to engage in community-building activities themselves, especially if they live in the neighborhood themselves. Students engaged in community activities are probably also less likely to act in ways that undermine existing social capital—such as, by engaging in antisocial or even criminal behavior. Catholic schools also might be more likely to sponsor community activities (including school-related activities) in after-school hours that draw adults into public spaces. Moreover, as we discuss in greater detail in chapter 8, Catholic schools appear to do a good job at the citizen-formation function of education. That is, the available evidence suggests that Catholic school students exhibit a greater understanding of democratic principles, more civic knowledge, higher levels of community engagement, and a greater tolerance for diversity than their public school counterparts—realities that, again, we would expect to generate positive community externalities.

The same might also be said for the Catholic schools' academic and behavioral expectations. Discipline inside the classroom may encourage discipline outside of it, and high academic expectations may limit neighborhood disorder for the simple reason that students who are busy with schoolwork have less time to cause trouble. This possibility is colorfully captured in Charles Payne's description of interactions with students who moved back and forth between public schools and Catholic schools in Chicago. Recounting these interactions, Payne observes that "the most memorable was a boy who told me that when he was in Catholic schools, he went to school every day just loaded down with books, but when he was back in the neighborhood public school, 'all I bring is my radio.'"[70]

Catholic schools' effects may not stop at the school house doors if for no other reason than that students, parents, and teachers embracing the communitarian aspirations of a Catholic school are likely to be good citizens. Good citizens are likely not only to avoid engaging in antisocial behavior, but they probably are also more likely to engage in prosocial behavior. As the literature on social norms suggests, communities where prosocial norms are frayed need individuals who are "norm entrepreneurs," who can shift the prevailing norms in a community and even trigger what Robert Ellickson has called a "norm cascade" that causes more community members to embrace prosocial norms. The neighborhood impact of these citizen norm entrepreneurs and their effectiveness as "change agents" likely is greatest when a Catholic school is also a neighborhood school, but we doubt that the positive neighborhood effects of Catholic schools' communitarian successes are limited to this context.[71]

We also doubt, however, that the social capital generated by Catholic schools is solely the result of the students, faculty, and parents (and other extended family members) in a Catholic school community. In some communities, we suspect that Catholic schools themselves may be norm entrepreneurs. That is, a Catholic school stands out as a model of success in the midst of failure, of order in the midst of chaos—and therefore of the possibility that demographics need not dictate destiny. Catholic schools have long exhibited faith in the ability of all children to learn regardless of circumstance and apparently have also fostered community in neighborhoods where social ties are frayed by poverty, disorder, and violence. In doing so, Catholic schools may serve, to borrow from legal theory, an expressive function: the very fact that urban Catholic schools have weathered the storms of economic and social decay in a community—and have continued to succeed in spite of these circumstances—sends a symbolic message that success and order are possible. Unfortunately, we fear that when a school that has weathered these storms closes, a community may internalize the opposite message—the message that, in keeping with neighborhood expectations, failure is inevitable. As a bishop who was ordained a priest in the Archdiocese of Chicago (and who years ago attended one of the closed schools in our study) told one of us privately, in some Chicago neighborhoods, the Catholic school was one of the last remaining functional social institutions. It is hardly surprising, he remarked, that when that institution folded, the neighborhood declined rapidly.

If we are correct about the norm-enforcement function of Catholic schools in poor neighborhoods, our findings are worrisome, but they also hint at opportunities. We suspect that other kinds of high-functioning schools, including charter and public schools, that incorporate many aspects of the Catholic schools' communitarian model might, over time, come to serve as norm entrepreneurs as well. As Michael Heise has recently observed, there is a growing convergence between the public and private school sectors, with increasing numbers of charter and public schools embracing many elements of the traditional Catholic school model. Our study suggests that these developments may have unanticipated community benefits. And, importantly, we find that Catholic schools that remain open in urban neighborhoods continue to serve the critical role of building social capital. Thus, shifts in education policy favoring school choice may help stabilize urban communities by maintaining the vitality of urban Catholic schools.

CHAPTER EIGHT

Expanding the Case for School Choice

Our findings contribute new evidence to important debates about education reform generally and about the question of school choice in particular. They also shed light on the effects of the U.S. Supreme Court's constitutional line drawing in the federal Establishment Clause context and the possible effects of the further evolution of that doctrine on permitting religious schools to participate more fully in public programs funding K–12 education, including the possibility of authentic religious charter schools. This chapter begins by canvassing the school-choice debate and outlining our contributions to it before turning to these legal questions.

THE GEOGRAPHY OF EDUCATION REFORM

The traditional system of geographically based, neighborhood public schools has been eroding, especially in major urban centers, at least since the Supreme Court decided *Brown v. Board of Education* in 1954.[1] That *Brown* would presage the unraveling of neighborhood schools was not immediately apparent. As Jim Ryan and Michael Heise have noted, "School desegregation did not always threaten the neighborhood school; in districts that were residentially integrated, school desegregation, if anything, was more consistent with the neighborhood school concept than was school segregation."[2] This was more likely to be the case in the South, where residential housing patterns have always been—and remain—less racially segregated than in northern cities. A decade after *Brown*, in fact, the Supreme Court invalidated a "freedom of choice" plan for student assignment that was quite obviously designed to get around this reality.[3]

In cities with segregated housing patterns, however, merely eliminating de jure segregation could not, standing alone, ensure integration. Moreover, school officials could (and did) avoid desegregation mandates by shifting school attendance boundaries.[4] Thus, by the early 1970s, federal courts had grown weary of state and local officials' efforts to avoid the *Brown* mandate and had become frustrated with the slow pace of integration efforts. The resulting policy innovations designed to promote integration—especially judicially mandated busing[5] and, after the Supreme Court's refusal to sanction a multidistrict desegregation remedy in *Milliken v. Bradley*,[6] magnet schools[7]—have pulled many thousands of students away from their neighborhood schools. In fact, in a follow-up case (*Milliken II*), the Supreme Court arguably encouraged the rise of magnet schools by authorizing federal courts to order state governments to help fund remedial and compensatory education programs in majority-minority school districts.[8] The extent of mandatory desegregation efforts has declined dramatically over the past few decades, as increasing numbers of school districts have been found to have achieved "unitary status"—that is, to have remedied, to the greatest extent possible, the effects of past intentional discrimination—and have been released from federal court supervision.[9] The trend toward intradistrict public school choice prompted by desegregation decrees has only intensified, however, especially in urban districts. For example, 40 percent of central city school districts operate magnet schools, compared with less than 10 percent of districts nationwide.[10] Competition for entry into magnet schools is frequently fierce, and local school officials' efforts to achieve racial diversity by racially balancing student body composition have prompted successful Equal Protection challenges.[11] In addition to magnet schools, 71 percent of central city school districts offer intradistrict school choice, permitting students to attend an in-district public school other than the one geographically assigned to them.[12] A number of districts (again, especially large urban ones) have implemented "school within a school" reforms, which feature multiple, specialized, autonomous public schools operating in a single building.[13]

During the same time that these reforms began to take hold, efforts to attack on state law grounds the traditional property tax–dependent system of funding public education also gained traction. To date, over half of state supreme courts have invalidated their state's system of funding public education. Some courts have found that the traditional property tax–based system results in unconstitutional interdistrict fiscal inequalities. Others have found unconstitutional disparities in educational quality between districts.[14] These school finance reform decisions do not require districts to dismantle neighborhood schools nor do they require wealthier districts to accept students from poorer ones.[15] By causing districts to rely more heavily on centralized (i.e., state-level) funding, school finance decisions do arguably undermine local control over public education policy.[16] And, by making more money available to poorer districts, they may also catalyze greater experimentation with educational choice and diversity—just as the influx of state money in the post-*Milliken II* era did.

Over the course of the last few decades, other choice-based reforms, motivated primarily by a desire to improve educational outcomes (rather than to desegregate public schools), have also taken hold. We discussed one of these developments—that is, the exponential rise of charter schools—previously. This chapter addresses the second significant development—namely, the increasing momentum for private school choice—that is, for permitting students to use public funds at private schools. The intellectual roots of the school-choice movement are usually traced to Nobel Laureate Milton Friedman, who authored an article in 1955 arguing that the states should permit students to allocate their public education funds as their parents see fit, including by spending these public funds in a private school. Friedman reasoned that the injection of competition would improve overall performance.[17] It was not until over three decades later, however, that Friedman's proposal gained political traction. In 1990, African American activists in Milwaukee—led by former Milwaukee school superintendent Howard Fuller and a firebrand state legislator named Polly Williams—combined forces with Republican governor Tommy Thompson to secure the passage of the nation's first school voucher program. Initially, the Milwaukee Parental Choice Program entitled poor public school children in the city of Milwaukee to spend a portion of their public education funds at a nonsectarian private school; the program was expanded to include religious schools in 1995.[18] Ohio followed suit in 1995, enacting a similar voucher program, which subsequently sustained an Establishment Clause challenge in the U.S. Supreme Court, clearing the federal constitutional path for the expansion of private school choice.[19]

As of 2013, nine states, the District of Columbia, and Douglas County, Colorado, have scholarship or voucher programs that enable targeted groups of students to spend public funds to attend a private school. For example, Indiana, Wisconsin, Ohio, and Washington, D.C., have voucher programs in place that provide resources to enable low-income children to attend private schools. Arizona, Florida, Georgia, Ohio, and Utah's programs assist children with disabilities; and Louisiana's program targets students in low-performing schools. In addition, twelve states grant tax credits for charitable donations to nonprofit organizations that provide scholarships to attend private schools—indeed, since Arizona adopted the first such "scholarship tax credit programs" in 1997, scholarship tax credits arguably have surpassed vouchers as the preferred school-choice mechanism; they certainly seem to be carrying the day politically. During the 2012-13 school year, 97,252 children enrolled in private schools through school voucher programs and 148,300 received tax credit-financed scholarships at private schools.[20]

The total number of students participating in both kinds of programs likely will grow significantly in the near future. Indiana's voucher program, which began in the 2011-12 school year, extended public funding to all eligible low- and middle-income students in the state who wish to attend qualifying private schools in the fall of 2013. The program was capped at 7,500 scholarships during its first year of operation and 15,000 scholarships during its second. And, in June 2011, the Wisconsin legislature lifted the cap on the number of participants in the Milwaukee Parental Choice Program, expanded the program geographically, and increased the family income qualification guidelines to 300 percent of the federal poverty level (about $60,000 for a family of four, or over 64 percent of Milwaukee families). It is estimated that these changes will increase the number of eligible children from 22,500 (the previously legislated cap) to over 84,000. Alabama adopted a significant new tax credit program in 2013, and a number of other states appear poised to adopt new voucher or tax credit programs. Moreover, the total amount of funding permitted in the existing school-choice programs tends to increase over time. Moreover, in many states, the scholarship organizations participating in the scholarship tax credit programs could, by law, raise more money than they currently do. For example, in 2009, Arizona's Corporate School Tuition Organization Tax Credit raised $7 million less than the $14.4 million allocated to the program; in 2010, Georgia's scholarship tax credit program attracted $25 million less in donations than the $50 million allocated by state law; Indiana's $5 million program garnered only $435,050 in donations in the first year of its operation. And, Arizona's individual tax credit program is not capped at all. In 2010, the program attracted $52 million in donations to scholarship organizations, an amount that is clearly only a fraction of the total tax dollars that might be allocated to scholarships by taxpayers.[21]

THE SCHOOL-CHOICE DEBATE(S)

The gradual evolution toward greater parental choice in elementary and secondary education, generally, and the partial privatization of education delivery characterized by school-choice programs have catalyzed intense debate.[22] Initially, school-choice advocates took their cues from the movement's intellectual godfather—Milton Friedman—and argued that school choice would subject public schools to much needed competition, thereby incentivizing reform and improving educational attainment. Early momentum for school choice, in fact, can be traced to John Chubb and Terry Moe's articulation of this argument in their influential 1990 book, *Politics, Markets and America's Schools*. Chubb and Moe argued that efforts to reform public education inevitably will fail as long as the education system remains democratically controlled and "owned" by vested interests such as teachers unions. They asserted that by exposing public schools to competition, school choice would break the grip of interest groups and enable the reforms necessary to achieve academic excellence in our schools. School choice, they argued, "has the capacity *all by itself* to bring about the kind of transformation that, for years, reformers have been seeking to engineer in myriad other ways . . . Taken seriously, choice is not a system-preserving reform. It is a revolutionary reform that introduces a new system of public education."[23]

Other proponents support private school choice on parental and religious liberty grounds, arguing that choice ought not to be valued merely instrumentally, as a means of effective systemic change, but rather as the intrinsic good of empowering parents, and especially poor parents, to control their children's education. Proponents basing their support for school choice on parental and religious liberty grounds therefore assert that choice is justifiable regardless of whether public schools respond to private competition with meaningful reform or whether choice students' academic performance improves. In an influential 1992 article, for example, John Coons challenged the free market premises of Chubb and Moe's book. "The case for choice in education," Coons asserted, "goes much deeper than market efficiency and the hope to overtake Japan. Shifting educational authority from government to parents is a policy that rests upon basic beliefs about the dignity of the person, the rights of children, and the sanctity of the family."[24]

Proponents of school choice today tend to frame their arguments in equality-of-opportunity terms, arguing that school choice is a matter of social and racial justice. These arguments flow from the dual reality that first, most Americans of any financial means choose their children's schools, either by enrolling them in private schools or by moving to suburban locales with high-quality public ones, and second, many poor and minority children are trapped by economic circumstance in failing public schools.[25] According to this view, the goal of school choice ought to be the improvement of student educational outcomes, and the best way to achieve this improvement is to enable poor students to transfer out of low-performing and into high-performing schools. As James Forman has argued, these social and racial justice arguments have roots far deeper than Milton Friedman—they arguably trace their lineage to post-Emancipation efforts to educate freed slaves.[26] It was these arguments that ultimately catalyzed state legislative action, resulting in the enactment of the first school-choice program, the Milwaukee Parental Choice Program described previously, and they have come to dominate debates about school choice. For example, the Alliance for School Choice—the largest school-choice advocacy group—asserts, "Millions of American children are trapped in schools that continue to fail, year after year. . . . [W]e believe that the best way to improve education is to put parents in charge."[27]

Opponents of school choice argue that, rather than catalyzing reform in public schools, school-choice efforts will divert needed resources away from public schools and will "cream skim" the best students, with the most motivated parents, away from public school classrooms. Both the student diversion and resource diversion effects of school choice will, they argue, harm public schools and the students whom they serve. In response to the social justice arguments framed above, choice opponents argue that the available evidence does not support the conclusion that school choice leads to gains in academic achievement among private school transfers. That is, they assert that students enrolled in charter schools and voucher/tax credit programs do not outperform their public school counterparts, as promised by choice advocates.

The empirical debate about the academic effects of school choice is an intense one. Our goal is not to enter the test-score fray, although we tend to find persuasive empirical studies suggesting that students enrolled in private schools through school-choice programs make modest academic gains over their public school peers (especially over time). But we also join those who suggest that significant gains in public school performance academic achievement should not necessarily be the sine qua non for supporting school choice. Even if test scores remain flat, school choice might be justifiable on other grounds. We turn to one such ground here, which has not previously been explored—the fact that assisting poor children financially may have the secondary effect of slowing the disappearance of the Catholic schools and their beneficial community effects from urban neighborhoods that are desperately in need of stabilizing institutions.

A NEW COMMUNITARIAN DEFENSE OF SCHOOL CHOICE

While our findings do not contribute directly to any of the standard debates about school choice—which focus on public school reform, parental and religious liberty, and academic achievement—they are relevant to what may be called the "communitarian" debate over the wisdom and efficacy of school choice. Here we situate these findings within the two different versions of these "communitarian" arguments. First, some scholars argue that government-operated schools are needed to inculcate the civic values that represent the building blocks of our diverse, democratic society. Second, other commentators, especially William Fischel, worry that the erosion of the geographically based system of locally controlled public schools will both undermine educational quality and reduce local social capital. After discussing each of these arguments, and their rejoinders, we conclude by reflecting upon what we contribute to these important education reform debates.

Private Schools and Public Values

The view that public schools are needed to inculcate democratic values, and that, therefore, the rise of parental choice threatens to undermine those values, is most closely associated with philosopher Amy Gutmann.[28] In her influential book, *Democratic Education*, Gutmann argues that public schools serve the purpose of "conscious social reproduction" of the "core value of democracy" and the "cultural orientations of our country."[29] Although she eschews articulating exactly which values and principles public schools should inculcate—reasoning that these decisions should be democratic ones[30]—Gutmann worries in particular that school-choice programs and the parental autonomy arguments undergirding them "attempt to avoid rather than settle our disagreements over how to develop democratic character through schooling."[31] School choice is dangerous, Gutmann asserts, because most parents are "unwilling to resist a strong human impulse: the desire to pass some of their particular prejudices onto their children."[32] Stephen Macedo has similarly expressed concern that private schools generally, and school-choice programs in particular, may undermine democratic values.[33] As Macedo asserts, "Because [public schools] are democratically controlled and generally locally controlled, they are unlikely to be at radical loggerheads with the views of most parents. In addition, they are public, common institutions, and so are suited to representing our broadest and most inclusive educative ambitions."[34] Unlike Gutmann, however, Macedo expresses a willingness to be open to school choice, provided that appropriate government controls over participating private schools are in place.[35]

In response to these arguments, a number of social scientists have sought to measure how well private schools in general, and private schools participating in school-choice programs in particular, perform as civic educators. Most of these studies find, *contra* Gutmann and Macedo, that private schools appear to do a better job of preparing students to be engaged members of a diverse, democratic society.[36] For example, using data from the 1996 National Household Education Survey, which conducted a large nationwide survey of parents and adolescent children enrolled in five types of schools (assigned public, magnet, Catholic, religious but not Catholic, and private secular), David Campbell compared students enrolled in each educational setting along four variables—community service, civic skills (that is, the ability of students to engage in political activities), political knowledge, and political tolerance. Campbell found that private school students were significantly more likely to engage in community service than public school students, were more likely to learn civic skills in school, were better informed about the political process, and were, on average, more politically tolerant than students in public schools. Interestingly, however, Campbell also found that the distinction between public and private schools disappeared when Catholic schools were excluded from the analysis, leading him to conclude that "students in Catholic schools drive the private school effect."[37]

These results mirror other studies comparing public and private school students. In 2007, Patrick Wolf examined twenty-one quantitative studies regarding the effects of school choice on seven civic values—political tolerance, volunteerism, political knowledge, political participation, social capital, civic skills, and patriotism—and found that the effect of private schooling and school choice was almost always neutral or positive. Wolf noted that these studies found even more positive effects of school choice (that is, a move from public to private schools enabled by school choice): twenty-one found a school-choice advantage in promoting citizenship, thirteen found no effect, and two showed benefits from traditional public schools.[38] While not all of these studies, as Wolf acknowledges, take account of selection bias—that is, the fact that civic-minded, well-educated parents might be opting into private schools—selection bias alone does not appear to drive the results. In a more recent unpublished paper, for example, Campbell found a strong school-choice effect even after controlling for selection bias. Campbell used data from the Children's Scholarship Fund, a private voucher program that awards scholarships to enable poor children to attend private schools. In 1999, 1.25 million children applied for one of 40,000 scholarships awarded by lottery. Because recipients were randomly selected, Campbell was able to measure whether there was a school-choice effect on political tolerance and political knowledge based upon surveys conducted of both successful and unsuccessful applicants. That is, since they were differentiated by lot, they should not vary on selection bias characteristics. Campbell found that spending one year in a private school led to a considerable increase in a student's political tolerance and political knowledge.[39]

The empirical evidence, in other words, runs strongly counter to the communitarian concerns propounded by Gutmann, Macedo, and others. Private schools—especially Catholic schools—do not appear to be privatizing. Indeed, there is strong evidence that these schools actually outperform their public counterparts in inculcating basic democratic values. As Patrick Wolf observes, "The statistical record shows that private schooling and school choice often enhances the realization of the civic values that are central to a well-functioning democracy. This seems to be the case particularly . . . when Catholic schools are the schools of choice."[40]

Local Public Schools, Interdistrict Competition, and Community-Specific Social Capital

A distinctive communitarian defense of public schools focuses not on the values that they inculcate but rather on the role of local public schools as community-building institutions. This populist defense of public schools as community institutions came into sharp focus during the era of forced busing. For example, in *Milliken v. Bradley*, the Supreme Court observed, "No single tradition in public education is more deeply rooted than local control over the operation of schools; local autonomy has long been thought essential both to the maintenance of community concern and support for public schools and to the quality of the educational process."[41] This argument was also captured in a 1972 televised address by President Richard Nixon, who proclaimed, "[T]he great majority of Americans—white and black—feel strongly that the busing of school children away from their own neighborhoods for the purpose of achieving racial balance is wrong."[42] Resistance to integration undoubtedly was one motivation for the rallying cry in support of neighborhood schools, although as Drew Days has observed, Nixon was right that many African American families also came to support a return to neighborhood schools, even when segregated housing patterns precluded the possibility of integration.[43]

Most wealthy families in the United States, regardless of race, express their preferences for neighborhood schools by electing to live in suburban school districts with top-flight public schools, where neighborhood schools remain the norm. In 2004, for example, almost one-quarter of parents reported having moved to their current neighborhood to enable their children to attend the local public school.[44] Both civil rights advocates championing integration and proponents of choice-based education reform voice frustration with Americans' devotion to local public schools, albeit for different reasons. Civil rights advocates worry that the persistence of segregated housing patterns means that a return to neighborhood schools represents the abandonment of a decades-old struggle for racial integration in our public schools.[45] They also worry that predominantly minority neighborhood schools will suffer from "benign neglect . . . in terms of resources allocated for facilities, materials and personnel."[46] School-choice proponents, on the other hand, assert that the one-size-fits-all model of neighborhood public school, cannot—and does not—serve the diverse needs of the young students entrusted to it. According to this view, the neighborhood school system is—for many students, and in many districts—broken, yet American attachment to the ideal of local public education remains a significant political impediment to implementing school choice on a broad scale.[47]

In contrast, academic champions of locally controlled, geographically assigned public schools, especially economist William Fischel, argue that local financing, assignment, and control of public education improve outcomes and foster social capital. Local control over public schools arguably promotes educational excellence for two related reasons. First, as economist Charles Tiebout influentially hypothesized, local governments use a variety of policies and public goods to compete with one another for "consumer voters."[48] The available evidence supports Tiebout's prediction that this competition for preferred residents tends to promote efficiency and enhance the quality of local public goods and services by subjecting local governments to some approximation of market forces.[49] There is little doubt that public school quality is one of the most important drivers of the competition: as discussed previously, most parents with the financial means to do so exercise school choice by moving to districts with high-quality public schools. The fact that this competition generated by these moves works—that is, improves school quality—is strongly suggested by studies finding that educational outcomes (measured by standardized test scores) improve as the number of school districts in a metropolitan area increases.[50] Second, because local public school quality is reflected in housing prices, homeowners have strong incentives to take steps to ensure that their local public schools perform well—including monitoring and participating in their children's schools, influencing local expenditure policies, and so on.[51] And, because local politics, especially in the suburbs, is sensitive to majoritarian preferences, homeowners—or, to borrow from Fischel, "homevoters"—frequently exert strong influence in the setting of local priorities.[52]

As we discussed in chapter 7, Fischel also has defended local public schools as engines of what he calls "community-specific social capital."[53] Fischel argues that voters consistently reject statewide school-choice proposals because neighborhood schools benefit not only the children who attend them but also, importantly, their parents. He reasons that local public schools enable residents of a neighborhood to network and build relationships with one another—and therefore hypothesizes that school choice would undermine these networks because "community-specific social capital is more difficult to form if members of the community send their children to schools in other communities." Contrary to the suggestions of those who argue, as discussed above, that private schools are privatizing, Fischel acknowledges the evidence that the parental networks in private schools are no less extensive or inclusive than public school–generated networks. This evidence, he admits, suggests that school choice would not reduce the aggregate amount of social capital but might affect the location of the social capital generated by school networks—and school-choice-generated networks are likely to be more dispersed than those of neighborhood public schools.

We have no reason to believe that local public schools cannot or do not generate community-specific social capital, although our findings about charter schools in Chicago—which Fischel also hypothesizes generate social capital and which, at least in Chicago, are primarily neighborhood schools— suggest that whatever social capital is being generated by charter schools has not yet translated into reduced crime rates. But we strongly resist the suggestion that school choice would necessarily reduce community-specific social capital by drawing students away from their neighborhood schools. In fact, at least in Chicago, our findings suggest the opposite.[54] To the extent that participation in school-choice programs would stabilize urban Catholic schools and forestall school closures, our findings suggest that expanding school choice likely would increase neighborhood social capital where it is arguably needed most—in poor urban neighborhoods. Our instincts on this point do not, in fact, run contrary to Fischel's. While Fischel expresses skepticism about statewide voucher programs, he also suggests that school choice makes the most sense — and may actually increase social capital — in large urban districts, where parents find it harder to get to know one another, where the political power of homeowners is diminished vis-à-vis other groups exerting influence on education policy (for example, teachers' unions), and where the prevalence of intradistrict public school choice diminishes the likelihood that parental networks, even in public schools, will be local ones. His conclusion, and ours, is arguably supported by evidence suggesting lower levels of social capital in states with larger school districts.[55]

We recognize that our study is not directly relevant to the distinct communitarian question of whether private schools (and school choice) may be privatizing. We are convinced by the empirical evidence strongly suggesting that the answer to those questions is *no*, but that evidence concerns what goes on inside schools, and our study focuses on the schools' external effects. (Still, as we discuss in chapter 7, we suspect that there is a connection between the social capital generated within a school and a school's effectiveness as a community institution.) While it may well be that the neighborhood effects we find are positive externalities generated by Catholic schools' success as democratic educators, we cannot make this empirical claim based upon our data. Still, our findings that Catholic schools anchor and stabilize struggling urban neighborhoods bolsters the case for school choice, especially when considered together with the empirical evidence suggesting that private schools (and especially Catholic schools) are at least as good (if not better) at democratic education as are public schools. Moreover, we think it worth noting the obvious: not only are a majority of students participating in private school-choice programs likely to enroll in Catholic schools (because they are relatively inexpensive and located in central city neighborhoods), but an expansion of school choice may help stem the tide of Catholic school closures from our urban centers. Moreover, there is evidence that, where public funding becomes available for students attending private schools, Catholic schools can and do effectively compete with charter schools for choice students. For example, a 2006 RAND Corporation study of Michigan found that "[p]rivate schools will lose one student for every three students gained in charter schools." In contrast, a more recent study comparing the competitive effects of charter schools on Catholic schools in Michigan and Arizona, which also operates two tuition tax credit programs and two voucher programs, found that charter school competition had not negatively affected Catholic school enrollment. The author concluded that the private school-choice programs in Arizona increased Catholic schools' competitiveness.[56]

RELIGIOUS CHARTER SCHOOLS AND THE COST OF (ESTABLISHMENT CLAUSE) RIGHTS

Theoretically, an alternative means of preserving Catholic schools' positive neighborhood benefits would be to permit dioceses to operate their Catholic schools as charter schools. Currently, this option is legally off the table. As discussed above, all of the states that authorize charter schools—including the handful of states that permit affiliation between charter schools and religious institutions—prohibit authentically religious charter schools. (By "authentically religious," we mean schools that teach religion as the truth of the matter rather than as a cultural or historical subject.[57]) The conversion of a Catholic school to a charter school therefore always requires that the Catholic Church secularize the school's curriculum; it usually requires that the Church relinquish operational authority over the school as well. Both requirements make charter conversions a controversial option within the Catholic Church. These requirements undoubtedly limit the number of charter conversions that will occur, since many Church leaders object to allocating scarce resources to secular education and/or view secularization of religious schools as too high a price to pay for public funds. They may also limit the ability of converted schools to continue to generate the positive externalities we observe, although we make no predictive judgments on the latter question.

The prohibition on religious charter schools results from both political and constitutional considerations. As a political matter, all state laws make clear that charter schools are privately operated public schools—rather than publicly funded private schools. And, if the Supreme Court's Establishment Clause canon establishes anything clearly, it is that public schools cannot teach religion as the truth of the matter. Thus, in order to even engage the question of whether the Establishment Clause would allow states to authorize religious charter schools, state laws would have to be amended to provide that charter schools are private, not public, ones. We leave to one side the political likelihood of these enabling legal reforms, although we acknowledge that there are significant public choice impediments to achieving them.

The remainder of this chapter asks whether such reforms could be structured so as to avoid constitutional pitfalls. In particular, we focus on the aspect of Establishment Clause doctrine—the distinction that the court has drawn between direct and indirect aid to religious institutions—that currently prohibits the states from authorizing and funding authentically religious charter schools. Our purpose of highlighting the consequence of this important distinction is not, we emphasize, to build a constitutional case for eliminating it. Rather, we merely seek to highlight what Dan Kahan has called, in the criminal procedure context, a "cost of rights" problem.[58] By forcing bishops to choose between shuttering Catholic schools or secularizing them, constitutional limitations on the ability of states to aid religious schools impose costs—costs that extend beyond classrooms walls and into the surrounding neighborhoods.

Currently, federal Establishment Clause doctrine distinguishes between government programs that provide aid directly to religious institutions and those that benefit a religious institution indirectly as a result of individual beneficiaries' private choices. As the Court observed in *Zelman v. Simmons-Harris*, "our decisions have drawn a consistent distinction between government programs that provide aid directly to religious schools and programs of true private choice, in which government aid reaches religious schools only as a result of the genuine and independent choices of private individuals."[59] In the indirect aid context, the Court has held that the Establishment Clause does not prohibit religious institutions from participating in religion-neutral government programs, including funds that provide tuition assistance to students attending authentically religious schools. The Court has reasoned, in this context, that the relevant decision maker is the private recipient of the funds (or, in the case of school-aged children, the recipients' parents), not the government. Thus, in *Zelman*, the Court rejected an Establishment Clause challenge to the Ohio Pilot Scholarship Program, which provided tuition assistance to poor children in the City of Cleveland, despite the fact that 96 percent of the participating children attended an authentically religious school. The Court reasoned that the program was formally neutral toward religion—that is, private religious schools were but one among a wide range of educational options available to Cleveland schoolchildren—and that the program was one of "true private choice."

In contrast, the Court has held that the government may not directly fund religious activities or instruction. As a result, when the government (rather than a private beneficiary) selects the beneficiary of government largess, the Court has ruled that the Establishment Clause permits the government to fund only secular aspects of a religious organization's activities. This rule extends through a long line of cases addressing the constitutionality of programs providing secular aid to religious institutions—for example, transportation for religious school students,[60] secular textbooks,[61] educational materials including computers,[62] tutors for secular remedial instruction,[63] and capital expenditures for the construction of secular buildings at religious colleges.[64] In large part because the Court has assumed that most religiously affiliated elementary and secondary schools, especially Catholic ones, are "pervasively sectarian"—that is, that religion pervades all aspects of instruction—direct financial assistance to sectarian elementary and secondary schools has long been considered a constitutional taboo.[65]

The Court, to be sure, remains divided about what constitutes a program of private choice. For example, in *Mitchell v. Helms*, the Court considered an Establishment Clause challenge to the decision of Jefferson Parish, Louisiana, to use federal funds to purchase instructional equipment[66]—for example, books, computers, software, overhead projectors, televisions, tape recorders, maps, globes, filmstrips, and lab equipment—for use in private schools (including religious schools).[67] The Court had previously rejected nearly identical expenditures, in large part because it characterized them as providing "direct" rather than "indirect" aid to religious schools.[68] In approving the expenditures at issue in *Mitchell*, a plurality of the Court rejected the direct/indirect aid distinction, instead characterizing the relevant constitutional questions as whether the program at issue was religion-neutral—that is, whether the "aid program 'define[s] its recipients by reference to religion.'"[69] Moreover, the plurality characterized the assistance provided as a program of private choice. Building upon the Court's decision in *Agostini v. Felton* two years earlier,[70] the plurality reasoned that the amount of aid was determined by private school enrollment and that, therefore, private school students benefited from the aid by virtue of their parents' decisions to enroll them in a private school. Justice Thomas, writing for the plurality, observed,

> If aid to schools, even "direct aid," is neutrally available and, before reaching or benefiting any religious schools, first passes through the hands (literally or figuratively) of numerous private citizens who are free to direct the aid elsewhere, the government has not provided any support of religion. Although the presence of private choice is easier to see when aid literally passes through the hands of individuals—which is why we have mentioned directness in the same breath with private choice—there is no reason why the Establishment Clause requires such a form.[71]

According to the *Mitchell* plurality, therefore, religious schools can benefit from government aid made available on a religion-neutral basis, at least when the level of aid is determined by the level of private school enrollment. The parents' decisions to enroll their children in the school receiving the aid—rather than the parents' decision to direct public funds to the school of their choice—supplies the private "choice" needed to satisfy the Establishment Clause.

Had the *Mitchell* plurality's rejection of the distinction between direct and indirect aid commanded a majority of the Court's votes, conversation about religious charter schools would take a very different tone. We might envision a religion-neutral charter school law, which would permit the authorization of both secular and religious charter schools as private schools surviving Establishment Clause scrutiny, with the fact that parents chose to enroll their children in charter schools serving as the required "private choice" necessary to disentangle the government from the business of religious education. After all, as the Court emphasized in *Zelman*, charter schools are schools of choice. Public funds flow to a charter school only as a result of parents' decisions to enroll their children in it. The plurality's interpretation of "private choice," however, did not command a majority. Justice O'Connor, joined by Justice Breyer, refused to join the opinion and instead wrote separately to express her concern about the "unprecedented breadth" of the plurality's opinion, especially its rejection of the direct-indirect aid distinction and its treatment of the neutrality principle, which "comes close to assigning that factor singular importance in the future adjudication of Establishment Clause challenges to government school aid programs."[72] Justice O'Connor also expressed discomfort with the plurality's "approval of actual diversion of government aid to religious indoctrination."[73] It is possible that, with Justice O'Connor's retirement, these aspects of the plurality opinion might command a majority in a future case. Until that time, however, her *Mitchell* concurrence makes clear that the constitutional door to authentically religious schools is, at least at this point, likely closed.

Even if the *Mitchell* plurality's interpretation of the Establishment Clause—the elevation of the neutrality principle, rejection of the direct-indirect aid distinction, and broad understanding of private choice—were endorsed by the Court, other constitutional obstacles to authentically religious charter schools would persist. Indeed, the primary obstacle to state funding of such schools would, as discussed above, undoubtedly be the widely accepted view that charter schools are public schools, not private ones. To be sure, in states where charter schools enjoy substantial operational autonomy, the line between charter and private schools is not sharply demarcated. Most charter schools are, like private schools that might participate in a voucher or tax credit program, privately operated. And, like charter schools, all states regulate private schools to some extent. Many also place conditions on the "approval" to operate, usually in the form of private accreditation. Moreover, the Supreme Court's "state action" doctrine makes clear that neither comprehensive regulation (including licensing) nor public funding has the effect of transforming a private entity into a public one. For example, in *Rendall-Baker v. Kohn*, the Supreme Court held that a heavily regulated private school for special-needs high school students that received more than 90 percent of its funds from the state was not a state actor. "The school," the Court observed, "is not fundamentally different from many private corporations whose business depends on [government] contracts. Acts of such private contractors do not become acts of the government by reason of their significant or even total engagement in performing public contracts."[74]

That said, charter schools arguably differ from government-regulated or -funded private schools in at least two significant respects. First, a majority of charter school laws cap the number of charters available.[75] The details of these caps vary dramatically—some states cap the number of new charters per year, others limit the total number of charter schools in the state (with the caps ranging from forty-two to 850 schools), still others limit charter schools' geographic location. The fact that participation in a government program is limited does not, standing alone, undermine religious neutrality. Federal courts have consistently rejected Establishment Clause challenges to the inclusion of religious providers of social services in governmental programs, even when the government participation in these programs is limited. The relevant question, courts have held, is whether the government has accepted both religious and secular providers, not whether it accepts all possible providers. For example, in a case of particular relevance to the instant question, the D.C. Circuit ruled that the Establishment Clause did not bar the University of Notre Dame's Alliance for Catholic Education—a volunteer-teacher program similar to Teach for America that places recent college graduates in underserved Catholic schools—from participating in the AmeriCorps program, despite the fact that the program includes explicitly religious content and the volunteers teach in authentically religious schools. AmeriCorps provides volunteers with a sizeable education grant for participating and covers a small portion of the operational costs of participating programs. The Court rejected the argument that the extension of these benefits to the Alliance for Catholic Education program and participants undermined AmeriCorps' religion neutrality. In commenting on the benefits received by the Catholic school teachers, the Court observed:

The relevant question is whether participants . . . possess a genuine independent choice between religious and non-religious organizations in which to perform their national service. Of course the number of such opportunities is . . .
limited. It could hardly be unlimited. The important points are (1) that there are
numerous AmeriCorps teaching positions in public and private secular schools;
and (2) that there is no evidence of any participant who wanted to teach in a
secular school, but was impermissibly channeled to a religious school.[76]

In other words, it is not the fact of government discretion that undermines
religion-neutrality, but rather the lack of neutrality in the application of
that discretion. Still, it is reasonable to assume that caps inevitably raise
concerns about the exercise of discretion.

Second, and more significantly, almost all charter schools are created by
a government act. That is, unlike private schools, charter schools do not
exist before they are chartered. And, in most states, the power to approve
a charter application — thereby creating a charter school — is reserved for
a government entity (most frequently state boards of education and local
school boards and, in some states, public universities). The distinction is,
in some ways a semantic one, since private schools, at least in some states,
may not operate without government approval. But in this case, semantics
arguably establish a real, formal distinction with significant constitutional
implications: charter schools are not private schools; they are, by virtue of
a government act, privately operated public schools. And while the Court
made clear in *Zelman* that the government may provide financial assistance
to students attending private schools, it has also made clear in numerous
cases that public schools' curricula must be secular. Therefore, as long as
charter schools remain public schools, they cannot — at least according to
current Establishment Clause doctrine — be authentically religious schools.

But what if they were not public schools? Because a consequence of current Establishment Clause doctrine is to force dioceses to choose between
secularizing their schools and closing them, we think it appropriate to comment on the possibility of restructuring state laws to both comport with current doctrine and open up the possibility of authentically religious schools.
Indeed, Minnesota law already provides a model for such a reform. Minnesota law authorizes nongovernmental entities — including private universities and nonprofit organizations — to authorize the creation of charter
schools, subject to ratification by the state's department of education. Minnesota also does not cap the number of charters available. And, during the
2009–2010 school year, 109 out of Minnesota's 149 charter schools were
authorized by private entities, including twenty-six authorized by religious

institutions (primarily religiously affiliated colleges). Put differently, nearly 75 percent of the state's charter schools were not, in fact, created by the government but instead by a private entity that is not bound by the Establishment Clause at all. In other words, Minnesota's charter schools arguably are public only because the state law says that they are. And, while formalism matters in the law, if Minnesota were to change the law—from the Public Charter School Law to the Private Charter School Law, it would be plausible, we believe, to analogize the funding flowing to students in those schools, all of which are today secular (as required by state law), to the funding flowing to private schools participating in voucher or tax credit programs. That is, the government is funding the private educational choices of parents choosing to send their children to schools that are privately operated, and privately created.

In the end, however, the goal of preserving the benefits authentic to educational pluralism—including the positive community effects of urban Catholic schools—likely is best advanced through expanded opportunities for parental choice rather than through permitting the creation of religious charter schools. As we previously observed with respect to the conversion of Catholic schools to charter schools, we cannot know whether "Catholic" charter schools (whatever their institutional form) will behave in the same way, as either educational or community institutions, as the Catholic schools that they replace. The same might be said of religious charter schools. Thus, even if religious charter schools were constitutionally permissible, and we have grave doubts that they will be, we see no reason to take the policy risk of forcing an evolution in the form of educational institutions that serve the common good as they are currently structured. Finally, it is safe to say that any doctrinal evolution that might permit authentic religious charter schools will come too late to many of the fragile Catholic schools in cities like Chicago. School choice is constitutionally permissible today, and we therefore see no need to wait for such an evolution.

In May 2010, the Archdiocese of Indianapolis announced its decision to close two inner-city Catholic schools (Saint Anthony Academy and Saint Andrew/Saint Rita Academy) and to reopen them as charter schools (Padua Academy and Andrew Academy). As we discuss in chapter 2, the Archdiocese justified the decision as a way to "save" the schools, explaining, "Many urban Catholic schools are closing across the nation, and we did not want to leave the students or communities we currently serve. Through this transformation, an urgent and unmet need within urban Indianapolis will be filled."[77] A year after the Archdiocese announced its decision to close Saint Anthony and Saint Andrew/Saint Rita, the governor of Indiana signed legislation enacting the most comprehensive school-choice program in the United States. The legislation enables low-income children to spend up to $4,500 of public funds at a private school of their choice. During the first year of the program, over 4,000 students transferred to a private school as a result of the program, and more than thirty Catholic schools in the Archdiocese of Indianapolis are currently participating in the program.

In a speech to the National Catholic Education Association in 1991, Father Andrew Greeley—a renowned sociologist and author of some of the most important studies of Catholic schools' academic performance—predicted that the first voucher would arrive on the day that the last Catholic school closed. As Diane Ravitch recently observed, Greeley knew that, despite their educational successes, Catholic schools were struggling, and he "knew that help was not on the way." What he did not—and indeed, could not—have known was that charter schools would soon explode onto the educational scene, offering a free alternative to failing public schools to poor students and the promise of public funding to Catholic leaders willing to secularize their schools.[78] Padua and Andrew Academies are cases in point: had the state legislature acted a year earlier, or had the Archdiocese known that help was, in fact, on the way, Saint Anthony and Saint Andrew/Saint Rita likely would have been among them. That they were not is a result of public education policy choices, the implications of which will take years to unfold.

CHAPTER NINE

Imagining Cities without Catholic Schools

In contrast to previous scholarship, this book has focused primarily on Catholic schools as community institutions—on the consequences, beyond classroom walls, of their disappearance from urban neighborhoods. These community effects, of course, are not the only consequences of Catholic school closures. In closing, we therefore think it appropriate to restate, in an abbreviated manner, the implications of losing Catholic schools as educational institutions. These implications are twofold. First, Catholic schools' departure from cities will have the direct effect of reducing the number of quality educational options available to the students who need them the most—disadvantaged urban residents. This alone is a sobering fact given these schools' demonstrated record of educating at-risk children. Second, the reduction in educational options also may affect the residential choices of middle-class parents who frequently opt to leave urban communities for suburban ones precisely to search for good schools for their children. The educational consequences of Catholic school closures therefore are not only related to the community effects of Catholic school closures but are likely to be felt most acutely in the very neighborhoods that will suffer most from the loss of social capital that appears to be triggered when Catholic schools close.

THE URBAN EDUCATION DEFICIT AND THE POOR

Since we do not conceive of this book as primarily focusing on Catholic schools as educational institutions, we are not primarily concerned with the academic performance of Catholic schools. That said, it is important not to ignore the fact that one consequence of Catholic school closures is the gradual disappearance of high-performing, relatively affordable, educational options from urban neighborhoods. By any measure, our cities need high-quality educational options. In 2010, for example, the *Chicago Tribune* secured access to the Chicago Public Schools'(CPS) internal evaluation of its schools. The evaluation assigned each school a letter grade (A–F) based on academic performance. The district's own internal evaluation concluded that nearly one-quarter of CPS elementary schools and more than 40 percent of CPS high schools were failing. In 2011, the district placed about half of its schools on probation—meaning that they were in danger of losing autonomy over staffing and even of being closed.[1] Unfortunately, things are hardly better in the other two cities we study here. The State of Pennsylvania assumed control over the public schools of Philadelphia in 2002, after years of frustration with low performance and financial mismanagement.[2] More recently, the *Philadelphia Inquirer* published a seven-part exposé detailing how the chronic violence plaguing the troubled school system impeded learning and left hundreds of students seriously injured, traumatized, or both. The schools have yet to be returned to local control.[3] Meanwhile, the Los Angeles Unified School District has one of the lowest high school graduation rates in the country (only 40.6 percent), although Philadelphia's (48.4 percent) and Chicago's (55.4 percent) are hardly cause for celebration.[4]

We do not underestimate the challenges faced by large urban public school districts in general, and by public schools in poor neighborhoods in particular. As we discuss in chapter7, educational outcomes are undeniably linked to student and neighborhood demographics. They are also linked to the level of social capital in the neighborhood where a school is situated, and many urban public schools are situated in neighborhoods with extremely low levels of social capital.[5] That said, some schools—including especially urban Catholic schools—have a strong track record of surmounting these challenges. As public school reformer Charles Payne has observed, "[T]he Catholic school . . . is probably the closest thing we have to an answer to the question about how one scales up effective education in the inner city."[6] In fact, decades of social science research suggests that Catholic schools excel at the task of educating disadvantaged children who do not, generally, fare well in public schools. Beginning with the groundbreaking research of James Coleman and Andrew Greeley, numerous scholars have found that Catholic school students—especially poor minority students—tend to outperform their public school counterparts. Greeley found, for example, that the achievement of minority students in Catholic schools not only surpassed that of students in public schools but, moreover, that the differences were the greatest for the poorest, most disadvantaged, students.[7] More recently, Derek Neal confirmed Greeley's Catholic school effect by demonstrating that Catholic school attendance increased the likelihood that a minority student would graduate from high school from 62 percent to 88 percent and more than doubled the likelihood that a similar student would graduate from college.[8]

Catholic schools' success is often attributed to selection effects—that is, to the fact that better educated and motivated parents select Catholic schools for their children. We do not doubt the difficulty of overcoming selection effects when comparing Catholic and public school performance. Since Catholic schools charge tuition and exercise veto rights over students, and public schools cannot, there is a real risk that any comparisons between the two are of apples to oranges. Still, there remains a substantial body of social science evidence suggesting that selection effects are not the primary driver of the so-called Catholic school effect on student performance—at least insofar as that performance is reflected in high graduation rates. As Payne concludes, "I would not go so far as to say that selection effects make no difference, but my experience is that kids themselves describe dramatic changes in their own behavior" when they migrate between public and Catholic schools. "I am very much affected by my own experience of talking with kids in Chicago who moved back and forth between Catholic and public schools, depending on fluctuations in family income, and having them tell me, without exception that I can recall, that they worked harder and took school more seriously when they were in Catholic school."[9]

To be sure, Catholic schools are not the only high-performing urban schools. Most urban districts feature outstanding magnet schools, as well as some neighborhood schools that succeed against the odds and overcome neighborhood structural factors predicting low school performance. Increasingly, high-performing charter schools also are working educational miracles in disadvantaged urban neighborhoods. As we discuss in chapter 2, some dioceses are opting to convert their Catholic schools to charter schools—that is, to relinquish control over and secularize them—in order to avoid closing them altogether. Conceivably, these converted schools may excel as educational institutions, performing at or above the level of the Catholic schools that they replace. While we hope that they will, we see little reason to assume that the academic records of charter schools resulting from private school conversions will mimic that of their private school predecessors. After all, these converted schools are, and are required by law to be, entirely new schools. And, in most states, these new schools cannot be operated, even as secular schools, by the institutions that operated them as academically successful private schools (that is, by Catholic churches). In any event, there is every reason to believe that high-quality urban educational options will remain, for the foreseeable future, in short supply. Thus, any diminishment in that supply—including the diminishment resulting from Catholic school closures—raises concerns about the educational prospects of the urban poor.

THE URBAN EDUCATION DEFICIT AND THE MIDDLE CLASS

Quality educational options are not only important for poor urban residents; they are important for all urban residents. As urban officials well understand, many families with the financial means to do so migrate away from cities to suburbs with high-performing public schools. Thus, the urban education deficit seriously affects the future prospects not just of the disadvantaged but also of cities themselves, because the dearth of affordable, high-quality schools in urban areas makes it difficult for cities to attract and retain residents with the financial means to move elsewhere. For this reason, Catholic schools—since they tend to be both high quality and affordable, relative to other private schools—also serve to help cities compete with surrounding suburbs for middle-class residents.

Not long ago, most major cities' prospects seemed dim. Our cities were slowly dying. They were so mired in poverty, crime, and disorder as to appear unredeemable—and an urban rebound seemed an unrealistic pipedream. Nevertheless, in recent years, many urban centers have experienced an unexpected comeback.[10] While the so-called urban rebound is complex, and its causes somewhat mysterious,[11] Edward Glaeser and Joshua Gottlieb provide a plausible explanatory summary of the phenomenon. They argue that large cities rebounded because elites increasingly developed an affinity for urban life, especially the social interactions and consumer amenities enabled by dense, mixed land use urban environments. The reasons for the shift in lifestyle preferences, Glaeser and Gottlieb posit, include rising incomes and educational attainment and, importantly, a dramatic decline in central city crime rates. Glaeser and Gottlieb argue that as crime rates declined and urban officials began to focus on improving the quality of life in public places, city dwellers (and would-be city dwellers) found it easier to enjoy the advantages of urban life.[12]

Glaeser and Gottlieb's hypothesis provides some support for what social critic Joel Kotkin derisively refers to as "the cool city strategy."[13] Many cities now pin urban development hopes on promoting a "hip" image in order to compete for young, childless professionals. The logic of this strategy is obvious: seek out residents who can "risk moving to neighborhoods with subpar school systems, fixer-upper housing stock or a little street crime."[14] The cool-city strategy draws intellectual heft from Richard Florida's influential 2002 book *The Rise of the Creative Class*. Florida argues that cities are benefiting from the energy provided by creative young professionals, who stay single longer than in previous generations and who prefer to live in diverse, urban neighborhoods.[15]

Even assuming that this creative class is disproportionately attracted to urban life—a questionable proposition, since many of its members have spent their entire lives in suburbs[16]—there are limits to the cool city strategy. In an influential article, Kotkin demonstrates that the most successful cities focus on important, but decidedly "uncool," issues like housing, public safety, and—importantly—education. There are obvious reasons why. No matter how creative or cool, all young professionals grow up. Most do not remain unattached and childless forever but eventually face the same pressures and demands that all parents face—including the need for good schools for their children. These life-cycle pressures inevitably lead many of them to move to the suburbs. Creativity may be a key to modern economic success, but, as Kotkin quips, "It turns out that many of the most prized members of the 'creative class' are not 25-year-old hip cools but forty something adults who, particularly if they have children, end up gravitating to the suburbs and more economically dynamic cities like Phoenix, Boise, Charlotte or Orlando."[17]

Retaining families with children is not important just for cities' long-term economic prospects, it also is important for the long-term stability of urban neighborhoods. We leave to one side the most obvious reasons why this is so—including the uncontested benefits of breaking up pockets of concentrated poverty and the connections between residents' wealth and educational attainment and neighborhood stability—and focus instead on the link between rooted middle-class families and collective efficacy. As we discuss throughout this book, collective efficacy is the term used by sociologists and social psychologists to describe the "ability of neighborhoods to realize the common values of residents and maintain effective social controls."[18] In this sense, collective efficacy is perhaps best understood as a kind of applied social capital—or, put slightly differently, as an output of the social networks that generate social capital. Not surprisingly, neighborhoods with high levels of collective efficacy are healthier than those with lower levels. Numerous studies demonstrate that neighborhoods with low levels of collective efficacy exhibit more signs of social distress—for example, they are more dangerous and disorderly and residents are more fearful—than those with higher levels.[19]

There are a number of ways that cities can bolster collective efficacy, including taking steps to attract and retain residents who are likely to purchase homes and put down roots in their neighborhoods. This is because collective efficacy increases with increased residential tenure and homeownership. For example, in a major study of 343 Chicago neighborhoods, Robert Sampson, Stephen Raudenbush, and Felton Earls, using the Project on Human Development in Chicago Neighborhoods data we employ in chapter 3, found that residential stability, measured by average residential tenure and levels of homeownership, was one of three major factors explaining neighborhood variation in collective efficacy. They found that residential stability, in turn, mitigated the negative effects of the other two factors—economic disadvantage and immigration—enough to reduce violent victimization in a community.[20] These findings are consistent with other social science research linking residential tenure and homeownership, especially of single-family homes, with high levels of collective efficacy.[21] This connection between homeownership and residential tenure is easily explained. Not only do homeowners have economic incentives to organize in order to address neighborhood problems, but social integration into a neighborhood naturally increases over time, providing opportunities to build trust relationships.[22] These realities suggest that the most successful, safest, city neighborhoods ultimately will be the kinds of places where people choose to make their lives long term—to live, work, and raise families.

City officials also should not ignore the historical connection between middle-class rootedness and urban health. Historians date the origins of the urban crisis differently. Conventional wisdom blames the postwar urban crisis on white flight from integrating city neighborhoods.[23] But a plausible case can be made that the roots of urban woes date from far earlier and that postwar suburbanizers were the last strands of a well-frayed urban fabric.[24] Our cities began decanting before the turn of the twentieth century, and middle-class "flight" from urban centers was well underway by the 1920s.[25] As Gerald Gamm argues in his fascinating study of Boston's Dorchester neighborhood, a majority of Protestant and Jewish families exited urban neighborhoods well before the Second World War. The white urban enclaves that remained intact well into the 1960s tended to be Catholic, where allegiance to parishes and their schools rooted residents to their neighborhoods. Postwar suburbanization, Gamm argues, occurred when Catholics' attachments to their neighborhoods and parishes finally gave way.[26]

Whatever the cause, no one disputes that the disappearance of stable middle-class urban enclaves was a disaster for cities. And, unfortunately, cities have failed, in the intervening years, to reverse this trend. Each year, fewer and fewer families—especially middle-class families—choose to build their lives in urban neighborhoods. While a handful of central cities are gaining wealthy residents, almost all cities continue to lose families in general and middle-class families in particular. A 2006 Brookings Institution study of twelve large metropolitan areas found that only 23 percent of central city neighborhoods had middle-income profiles (that is, incomes between 80 and 120 percent of the median metropolitan income), compared with 45 percent in 1970.[27] As a result, even "successful" cities find themselves home to a growing upper class and a large, although slightly shrinking, lower class.[28]

There are many reasons why middle-class families shun cities. Race undoubtedly remains a factor for some,[29] although the fact that minorities accounted for the bulk of suburban population gains during the 1990s strongly suggests that the pull of the suburbs is race blind.[30] Crime and the fear of crime also play a major role,[31] as do the American preference for single family homes, concerns about local tax levels, local government responsiveness, and public service quality. Still, cities arguably should be doing a better job at reversing middle-class losses. After all, many cities have begun to overcome some of the obstacles described above: urban governments have become more responsive and efficient, thanks in part to innovations in local government, including tax increment financing, business improvement districts, and enterprise and empowerment zones.[32] Crime rates have declined dramatically, and urban police forces now focus intensely on curbing disorder and increasing residents' sense of security.[33] City densities have been declining for much of the past century; infill projects and teardowns offer a greater range of housing options,[34] and tax incentives frequently are made available to middle-class homebuyers.[35] And, importantly, as Glaeser and Gottlieb argue, demand for the consumer amenities and social interactions provided by urban life appears to be on the rise.

Unfortunately, efforts to reform perhaps the most important governmental function for families—public education—have proceeded in fits and starts. Despite decades of prodding from state and federal officials as well as courts, the records of most urban public schools remain abysmal, especially when compared with the records of most suburban public schools. Furthermore, for obvious reasons, most parents prioritize the quality of public education available for their children. In other words, an important—perhaps the most important—reason cities find it so hard to attract and retain middle-class families is that most middle-class parents do not trust urban public schools to educate their children. Charles Tiebout was right. Local governments do compete for consumer voters. And, without question, the quality of public schools drives the competition for parents.[36] In 2004, almost one-quarter of parents reported having moved to their current neighborhood primarily to enable their children to attend the local public school. Moreover, this kind of residential sorting increases as parents' educational attainment rises.[37]

These statistics are suggestive of the critical importance of education reform to the goal of rebuilding middle-class cities. Public education reforms—including public school choice, magnet schools, and charter schools—undoubtedly help cities retain some middle-class families who prefer city life. As noted previously, 40 percent of central city school districts operate magnet schools, compared with less than 10 percent of districts nationwide.[38] Competition to enter magnet schools frequently is fierce, and local school officials' efforts to achieve racial diversity in these schools suggests that middle-class white families are among the most successful competitors for scarce spaces.[39] Intradistrict public school choice (an option in 71 percent of central cities)[40] and an explosion in the number and diversity of urban charter schools[41] also offer valuable educational options for parents.[42] Without discounting the importance of public education reform, however, it is also important to recognize that, for many parents, a decision to live in a major city also entails a decision to send their children to private schools. The evidence is difficult to contest: 31 percent of students living in Seattle, 25 percent of students in San Francisco, and close to 20 percent of students in Chicago, Denver, and New York are enrolled in private schools.[43] For the nation as a whole, private school enrollment approximates 10 percent.

Undoubtedly, one reason why many center cities are gaining wealthy residents but losing middle-class ones is that the wealthy can afford educational options that those of modest means cannot. Sticker shock over private school tuition likely tips the balance in favor of suburban life for many families. According to the National Center for Education Statistics, in 2007 (the most recent year for which data is available), the average private school tuition in the United States was $8,549–$6,733 for elementary schools and $10,549 for secondary schools. These figures would have been much higher if not for the fact that about half of private school students attended Catholic schools, which charged, on average, less than $5,000 for elementary schools and less than $8,000 for secondary schools. The average tuition at nonsectarian private schools was $15,945 for elementary schools and $27,302 for high schools, respectively, 30 and 51 percent of the real median household income in the United States.[44]

In other words, the disappearance of Catholic schools from urban neighborhoods eliminates from the urban scene schools that are both relatively affordable and relatively high performing—raising the real possibility that some families that might otherwise choose to remain in urban neighborhoods will exit for suburbia. In making this observation, we do not suggest by any means that Catholic schools are the lynchpin of urban development hopes. Catholic schools obviously are more attractive to some parents than others, for a variety of religious and philosophical reasons. Moreover, absent a dramatic change in education policy, those that remain open are likely to become increasingly expensive and out of reach financially for many middle-class parents. Still, it remains the case that some Catholic schools likely continue to serve a function similar to that which Gamm demonstrates they served in postwar Boston: they anchor and preserve city neighborhoods by providing an alternative to struggling urban public schools and elite private schools.

Throughout this book, we have presented evidence suggesting that Catholic schools are not just important educational institutions but important community institutions as well—that is, that Catholic schools foster not only human but also social capital in urban communities. In closing, we think it important to emphasize that the human capital and social capital production functions of Catholic schools intersect, that is, that Catholic schools' educational benefits and community benefits likely have feedback effects on one another. To begin, Catholic schools' educational successes likely affect neighborhood stability since educational successes are closely linked to economic ones, and it is well understood that there is an inverse relationship between income on the one hand and social cohesion, disorder, and crime on the other. Second, the disorder and crime that we link, in a direct way, with Catholic school closures also influences—like the availability of good schools—residential decision making. That is, residents with financial means often choose to move away from dangerous and disorderly neighborhoods. After all, as city leaders understand well, safe and socially cohesive neighborhoods are attractive places to raise families. Thus, Catholic school closures may increase the probability of families migrating to the suburbs, both because their disappearance limits the diversity of educational options in our cities and because their disappearance appears to make urban neighborhoods more dangerous. Finally, there is ample evidence, which we discussed in more detail in chapter 7, that schools perform better in stable neighborhoods characterized by high levels of social capital—the very thing we find that Catholic school closures suppress.

We write this book at an uncertain time for American cities. The economic downturn has not only slowed the pace of urban development, but many urban centers are facing nearly unprecedented fiscal crises that hamper prospects of recovery. As we acknowledge in the Introduction, Catholic schools alone cannot save our cities. But for a host of reasons, it is reasonable to assume that Catholic school closures portend a decline in social capital in urban communities. Our cities may well survive (indeed, they may have to survive) without Catholic schools, but our evidence suggests strongly that they would be better off if they did not have to do so.

Notes

PREFACE

1. "48 Philadelphia Catholic Schools to Close or Consolidate as Enrollments Fall, Costs Increase," *Washington Post*, January 6, 2012.

2. B. A. Birch, "Roman Catholic Diocese to Shut Schools in Philadelphia," *Education News*, January 12, 2012.

3. Greg Toppo, "Catholic School Enrollment Dwindling," *USA Today*, April 11, 2008; National Catholic Educational Association, "Catholic Education Questions," http://ncea.org/FAQ/CatholicEducationFAQ.asp, accessed January 23, 2012.

INTRODUCTION

1. An in depth ethnographic study of one or more Catholic schools also might provide insight into their role as community institutions. While we would be delighted if our book spurs further research by scholars trained in these qualitative research methods (which we are not), the PHCDN data (despite their limitations) enable us to measure the effects of school closures across all Chicago neighborhoods, rather than merely capturing a snapshot of the effects of a few in a handful of neighborhoods.

CHAPTER ONE

1. The Council, which met from 1962 to 1965, promulgated significant changes for the Catholic Church. Proceedings of the Second Vatican Council can be found at http://www.christusrex.org/www1/CDHN/v1.html, accessed November 25, 2010. For a discussion of the connection between the Council and Catholics' increasingly attenuated attachments to their parishes, see John T. McGreevy, "Religious Roots," *American History* 28 (2000): 418–21.

2. John T. McGreevy, *Parish Boundaries: The Catholic Encounter with Race in the 20th Century Urban North* (Chicago: University of Chicago Press, 1996), 15. See also Jay P. Dolan, *In Search of an American Catholicism* (New York: Oxford University Press, 2002), 130 (observing that "the local parish became the center of people's lives, it ordered their universe").

3. Eileen M. McMahon, *What Parish Are You From? A Chicago Irish Community and Race Relations* (Lexington, KY: University Press of Kentucky, 1995), 18; McGreevy, *Parish Boundaries*, 10.

4. Parish boundaries are rarely enforced today. As a result, Catholics have become church shoppers with the blessings of church leaders in most dioceses—a reality that has profound implications for Catholic parishes and their schools. See McGreevy, "Religious Roots," *American History* 28 (2000): 416.

5. McGreevy, *Parish Boundaries*, 15.

6. McGreevy, *Parish Boundaries*, 10–22.

7. McGreevy, *Parish Boundaries*, 21. *See also* Steven M. Avella, *This Confident Church: Catholic Leadership and Life in Chicago 1940–1965* (South Bend, IN: University of Notre Dame Press 1993), 187 ("Chicagoans more so than other urban dwellers associated themselves with their neighborhoods as a kind of 'social skin' and often identified their home turf by responding to the question: what parish do you belong to?"); McMahon, *What Parish Are You From?* 19 ("Irish identification with parish was so strong that Philadelphians referred to their parishes rather than their street addresses or city neighborhoods to explain where they lived"); McMahon, *What Parish Are You From?* 25 ("Chicago Catholics began to respond to the question 'Where are you from?' with the name of a parish instead of a street address").

8. McMahon, *What Parish Are You From?* 114.

9. Archdiocese of Philadelphia, *A Brief History of the Archdiocese of Philadelphia*, http://www .archdiocese-phl.org/history.htm.

10. James F. Connelly, *The History of the Archdiocese of Philadelphia* (Philadelphia: Archdiocese of Philadelphia, 1976), 67.

11. Francis X. McGowan, *A Historical Sketch of St. Augustine's Church* (Philadelphia: Augustinian Fathers, 1896), 15.

12. Connelly, *The History of the Archdiocese*, 197.

13. Timothy Walch, *Parish Schools: American Catholic Parochial Education from Colonial Times to the Present* (Arlington, VA: National Catholic Education Association, 2003), 24–25.

14. Philip Hamburger, *Separation of Church and State* (Cambridge: Harvard University Press, 2002), 216.

15. Harold A. Buetow, *Of Singular Benefit: The Story of Catholic Education in the United States* (New York: MacMillan Publishers, 1970), 89.

16. Lloyd P. Jorgenson, *The State and the Non-Public School* (Columbia: University of Missouri Press, 1987), 77.

17. Jorgenson, *The State and the Non-Public School*, 37.

18. Breckenridge served as the first state superintendent of public instruction (1847–1853).

19. Jorgenson, *The State and the Non-Public School*, 43–44.

20. This dispute may strike modern readers as odd since the substance of the Ten Commandments is (and was) the same in both the Protestant and Catholic Bibles. By the 1840s, however, the mandatory Bible recitation in public schools had become emblematic of a very real Catholic concern about ubiquitous Protestant indoctrination in public schools, including textbooks that combined celebrations of the efforts of Luther and Calvin with warnings about the dangers of "popery." In addition, there were practical differences between Protestant and Catholic Bibles, including the fact that the Catholic Bible (as well as the Orthodox Church's version) contains several Old Testament books that Protestant reformers removed and the fact that, at the time, all Catholic Bibles included officially approved annotations to guide readers' interpretation of the text. John T. McGreevy, *Catholicism and American Freedom: A History* (New York: W. W. Norton and Company, 2003), 39.

21. McGreevy, *Catholicism and American Freedom*, 31–54.

22. McGreevy, *Catholicism and American Freedom*, 7–11.

23. *Donahoe v. Richards*, 38 Me. 379 (1854).

24. Jorgenson, *The State and the Non-Public School*, 172.

25. Jorgenson, *The State and the Non-Public School*, 76–83; Connelly, *The History of the Archdiocese of Philadelphia*, 178–86.

26. Hamburger, *Separation of Church and State*, 216-17.

27. Hamburger, *Separation of Church and State*, 217.

28. Joseph P. Viteritti, "Framing the Issue: Liberty, Equality, and Opportunity in Historical Perspective." In *White House Summit on Inner-City Children and Faith Based Schools: Proceedings* (2008), 76.

29. Jorgenson, *The State and the Non-Public School*, 84.

30. Jorgenson, *The State and the Non-Public School*, 84.

31. Walch, *Parish Schools*, 61.

32. Walch, *Parish Schools*, 68-71.

33. Jorgenson, *The State and the Non-Public School*, 75; Hamburger, *Separation of Church and State*, 219-29.

34. On the nineteenth-century "school wars," see generally Jorgenson, *The State and the Non-Public School*, 69-146; Joseph P. Viteritti, *Choosing Equality: School Choice, The Constitution, and Civil Society* (Washington: Brookings Institute Press, 1999); Richard W. Garnett, "The Theology of the Blaine Amendments," *First Amendment Law Review*, 2 (2004): 45.

35. President Ulysses S. Grant, Address to the Army of Tennessee at Des Moines, Iowa, quoted in Douglas Laycock, "The Underlying Unity of Separation and Neutrality," *Emory Law Journal* 46 (1997): 51; John Higham, *Strangers in the Land: Patterns of American Nativism 1860-1925* (Chapel Hill: Rutgers University Press, 1955), 29.

36. Jorgenson, *The State and the Non-Public School*, 139.

37. Hamburger, *Separation of Church and State*, 335.

38. Peter Meyer, "Can Catholic Schools Be Saved?" *Education Next* (Spring 2007): 13.

39. Connelly, *The History of the Archdiocese of Philadelphia*, 227.

40. Walch, *Parish Schools*, 60.

41. National Catholic Educational Association, *A Brief Overview of Catholic Schools in America*, http://www.ncea.org/about/historicaloverviewofcatholicschoolsinamerica.asp.

42. Archdiocese of Philadelphia, *A Brief History*.

43. Edward R. Kantowicz, *The Archdiocese of Chicago: A Journey of Faith* (Brooklyn: BookLinks Publishers, 2006) 23.

44. Higham, *Strangers in the Land*, 260; *Meyer v. Nebraska*, 262 U.S. 390 (1923); *Pierce v. Society of Sisters*, 268 U.S. 510 (1925).

45. Jay P. Dolan, *The American Catholic Experience* (South Bend, IN: University of Notre Dame Press, 1992), 278-83; Walch, *Parish Schools*, 73-77.

46. McGreevy, *Parish Boundaries*, 34.

47. Walch, *Parish Schools*, 77-83.

48. Kantowicz, *The Archdiocese of Chicago*, 23-24.

49. To understand the magnitude of this growth, consider the following: in 1850, there were 1,300 sisters in the United States (compared with 1,100 priests), by 1900, the number of religious sisters had risen to over 40,000 (compared with 11,636 priests).

50. Dolan, *The American Catholic Experience*, 277.

51. See, e.g., Arnold R. Hirsch, *Making the Second Ghetto: Race and Housing in Chicago, 1940-1960* (Chicago: University of Chicago Press, 1983), 18-35; Adam Cohen and Elizabeth Taylor, *American Pharaoh: Mayor Richard J. Daley, His Battle for Chicago and the Nation* (Boston: Bay Back Books, 2000), 67-68, 76; Alexander Polikoff, *Waiting for Gautreaux: A Story of Segregation, Housing, and the Black Ghetto* (Chicago: Northwestern University Press, 2006), 27-29.

52. See Cohen and Taylor, *American Pharaoh*, 184-89.

53. Hirsch, *Making the Second Ghetto*; McGreevy, *Parish Boundaries*; Thomas J. Sugrue, *The Origins of the Urban Crisis: Race and Inequality in Postwar Detroit* (Princeton: Princeton University Press, 1996).

54. Gerald Gamm, *Urban Exodus: Why the Jews Left Boston and the Catholics Stayed* (Cam-

bridge: Harvard University Press, 1999); Robert Bruegmann, *Sprawl: A Compact History* (Chicago: University of Chicago Press, 2006).

55. Gamm, *Urban Exodus*, 237–47.

56. Gamm, *Urban Exodus*, 27.

57. Avella, *This Confident Church*, 79; Gamm, *Urban Exodus*, 276–78.

58. See McGreevy, *Catholicism and American Freedom*, 79–90; (asserting that economic factors, especially the increasing wealth of Catholics, was most significant) and 94–101 (describing clashes over African American migration to Catholic neighborhoods). See also Avella, *This Confident Church*, 276–78 (discussing suburbanization of Chicago Catholics); Gamm, *Urban Exodus*, 276–78 (discussing Catholic suburbanization more generally).

59. McGreevy, *Parish Boundaries*, 33–35

60. McGreevy, *Parish Boundaries*, 62–63

61. McMahon, *What Parish Are You From?* 8–26.

62. McMahon, *What Parish Are You From?* 47.

63. McMahon, *What Parish Are You From?* 160.

64. McMahon, *What Parish Are You From?* 174–75.

65. McMahon, *What Parish Are You From?* 181–84. See http://www.saintsabina.org and http://www.stsabinaacademy.org/. Saint Sabina is today perhaps best known for its controversial pastor, Father Michael Pfleger, who has drawn attention for, among other things, publicly defying the local bishop by adopting a child, defacing billboards advertising alcohol and cigarettes, and, most recently, rallying to the defense of Reverend Jeremiah Wright by preaching a sermon in Wright's church that ridiculed Hillary Clinton. See, e.g., Cathleen Falsani, "Priest Promised to Obey, but Has Long Habit of Rebellion," *Chicago Sun-Times* (Feb. 13, 2002): 3; Margaret Ramirez and Manya A. Brachear, "Trinity's Life Renewed: Caught in a Storm of Unwanted Attention, Worshipers Look to Thrive Once Again," *Chicago Tribune* (Jan. 4, 2009): C1.

66. Walch, *Parish Schools*, 170–75.

67. Walch, *Parish Schools*, 176.

68. Gamm, *Urban Exodus*, 237–38.

69. Gamm, *Urban Exodus*, 239.

70. McGreevy, *Parish Boundaries*, 236 (observing that, well into the 1960s, most Catholic schools continued to charge only a nominal fee).

71. McGreevy, *Parish Boundaries*, 10, 236.

72. Dolan, *The American Catholic Experience*, 424–28.

73. The transformation of the Catholic school labor force is illustrated by the Archdiocese of Chicago, which indicates that only 3 percent of Catholic school teachers and 20 percent of Catholic school administrators are "religious" (a term encompassing priests and nuns). The administration numbers are inflated by the fact that many of the Catholic high schools in the Archdiocese are operated by religious orders; they also likely mask the reality that many religious administrators are approaching retirement age. See "Office of Catholic Schools 'Fact Sheet,'" http://schools.archchicago.org/public/factsheet.shtm#teacher_profile.

74. Overall enrollment in Catholic schools also plummeted during this time, from more than 5.2 million students in 1960 to 2.3 million students in 2006. See Meyer, "Can Catholic Schools Be Saved?," 14.

75. McGreevy, *Parish Boundaries*, 235–40.

76. The church was completed in 1801, and, apparently, President George Washington contributed $50 to its construction fund.

77. Francis E. Tourscher, *Old St. Augustine's* (1937), 17.

78. Tourscher, *Old St. Augustine's*, 85; Buetow, *Of Singular Benefit*, 134–35; Archdiocese of Philadelphia Catholic Schools Annual Report 1899–1900.

79. In 1993, Saint Columba was consolidated with two other parishes to create Saint Martin

de Porres Parish. The school at the consolidated parish now enrolls 290 students, all of whom are African American.

80. McGreevy, *Parish Boundaries*, 214–15.

81. McGreevy, *Parish Boundaries*, 242.

82. Andrew Greeley, *Catholic High Schools and Minority Students* (Piscataway, NJ: Transaction Publishers, 1982); James Coleman, et al. *High School Achievement* (New York: Basic Books, 1982).

83. Nicholas Lemann, "The Origins of the Underclass," *Atlantic Monthly* (July 1986): 54.

84. David M. Herzenhorn, "3 Financially Troubled Schools Will Be Closed by Archdiocese," *New York Times* (May 2, 2001).

85. Frank Bruni, "Giuliani Backs Catholic Offer of School Slots," *New York Times* (Sept. 9, 1996).

86. Sol Stern, "The Invisible Miracle of Catholic Schools," *City Journal* (Summer 1996).

87. Anemona Hartocollis, "School Voucher Experiment Will Be Extended and Expanded," *New York Times* (Nov. 26, 1997).

88. McGreevy, *Parish Boundaries*, 224; Avella, *This Confident Church*, 254–61.

89. Avella, *This Confident Church*, 260–61.

90. The Robert Taylor Homes comprised the largest public housing project in the world when they were completed in 1962—with twenty-eight identical sixteen-story towers that originally housed 27,000 residents. Hirsch, *Making the Second Ghetto*, 262–63. The Robert Taylor Homes were demolished as part of the federal HOPE VI public housing reform program between 1996 and 2007.

91. Teresa Puente and Dionne Searcey, "Southside Priest, 65, Found Slain in Home, Holy Angels Mourns Ex-Principal," *Chicago Tribune* (Nov. 26, 1996): C1; Jan Crawford, "Athlete, Teen Role Model, Murder Victim," *Chicago Tribune* (Nov. 2, 1993): N1; Sonya C. Vann, "More Patrols Sought Near School; Parents Seek Patrols Against Violence at Holy Angels," *Chicago Tribune* (Nov. 22, 1993): N2; Herbert H. Denton, "Tuition Tax Credit Plan Is Outlined; Reagan Urges Cut as 'Equity' for Working Families," *Washington Post* (Apr. 15, 1982): A1; Henri E. Cauvin, "Summer Studies: Holy Angels Teachers, Students Say All-Year Classes Heavenly," *Chicago Tribune* (July 27, 1994): N1; Jim Spencer, "Preaching by Doing: This Inner City Priest Adopts Unwanted Children, Reaches Out to Street Gangs and Demands the Utmost from Both Old and Young," *Chicago Tribune* (July 19, 1987): C8.

92. Remarks of Mary McDonald in *Preserving a Critical National Asset: America's Disadvantaged Students and the Crisis in Urban Faith Based Schools* 117 (White House Domestic Policy Council, 2008).

93. For example, since 1997, the "Big Shoulders Fund" has funded scholarships, special education programs, equipment and facilities improvements, faculty support, and operating grants for struggling urban Chicago schools. In 2007, Big Shoulders supported ninety-three schools in Chicago. See http://www.bigshouldersfund.org. On archdiocesan support in Chicago, see http://www.archchicago.org/stewardship/supporting_CS/Default.aspx (describing various philanthropic initiatives targeting Catholic schools). See also, e.g., Mary Ann Zehr, "Outside Donations Keep Five Catholic Schools off Closure List," *Education Week* (May 25, 2005): 9 (mentioning a Chicago school receiving about 25 percent of its budget from the Archdiocese and the Big Shoulders Fund); Patrick McCloskey, *The Street Stops Here: A Year at a Catholic High School in Harlem* (Berkeley: University of California Press, 2009), 251-52 (describing the "Patrons' Program" at Rice High School, a predominantly African American Catholic high school in Harlem).

94. Paul Vitello, "Plan to Cut Back Catholic Schools Severs Parish Links," *New York Times* (Sept. 20, 2010).

95. Peter Meyer, "Can Catholic Schools Be Saved?" *Education Next* (Spring 2007).

96. Nationwide, 15 percent of Catholic children were enrolled in Catholic schools in 2007, compared with 50 percent in 1964. Sol Stern, "Save the Catholic Schools!" *City Journal* (Spring 2007). A survey of Catholic parents conducted in 2005 found that 23 percent of those with elementary school–age children had enrolled at least one child in a Catholic school in the previous five years. An additional 4 percent had attempted to enroll a child in Catholic school but could not, either because they could not afford tuition or because the school had a waiting list. *Primary Trends, Challenges, and Outlook: A Special Report on U.S. Catholic Elementary Schools, 2000–2005* 2 (Center for Applied Research in the Apostolate: 2006).

97. Timothy M. Dolan, "The Catholic Schools We Need," *America: The National Catholic Weekly* (September 13, 2010): 10; Robert Costa, "Reviving the Catholic Schools," *National Review Online* (May 12, 2010).

98. Reconfiguration Committee of the Archdiocese of New York Announces Preliminary Determinations of 'At-Risk' Schools," *Archdiocese of New York* (Nov. 9, 2010), http://www.archny .org/news-events/news-press-releases/index.cfm?i=18153.

CHAPTER TWO

1. Samuel G. Freedman, "Lessons from Catholic Schools for Public Educators," *New York Times*, April 30, 2010; Mitchell Landsberg, Doug Smith, and Howard Blume, "LA. Charter Schools Flex Their Educational Muscles," *Los Angeles Times*, Jan. 10, 2010.

2. Matthew Ladner, "The Impact of Charter Schools on Catholic Schools: A Comparison of Programs in Arizona and Michigan," *Catholic Education: A Journal of Inquiry and Practice*, Summer 2007: 102.

3. "Promises and Facts on Charter Schools," Editorial, *New York Times*, Jan. 10, 2010.

4. Chester E. Finn, Jr., Bruno V. Manno, Gregg Vanourek, *Charter Schools in Action: Renewing Public Education* (Princeton, NJ: Princeton University Press, 2000), 221.

5. "Public Charter Schools Dashboard: Charter School Age," National Alliance for Public Charter Schools, http://dashboard.publiccharters.org/dashboard/schools/page/age/year/2012.

6. The Center for Education Reform, *National Charter School and Enrollment Statistics*, December 2011, http://www.edreform.com/2011/12/national-charter-school-enrollment-statistics-2011–12; Dale McDonald and Margaret M. Schultz, "United States Catholic Elementary and Secondary Schools 2012–2013: The Annual Statistical Report on Schools, Enrollment and Staffing," *The National Catholic Educational Association*, http://www.ncea.org/news/annualdatareport.asp.

7. Finn, Manno, and Vanourek, *Charter Schools in Action*.

8. Finn, Manno, and Vanourek, *Charter Schools in Action*, 134–38.

9. "Obama's Charter Stimulus," *Wall Street Journal*, June 12, 2009.

10. Jack Buckley and Mark Schneider, *Charter Schools: Hope or Hype?* (Princeton, NJ: Princeton University Press, 2007), 3.

11. Democratic National Committee, *Strong at Home, Respected in the World: The 2004 Democratic National Platform for America*, 34, http://www.democrats.org/pdfs/2004platform.pdf; "Key Issues," American Federation of Teachers, http://www.aft.org/issues/, accessed October 13, 2010.

12. Finn, Manno, and Vanourek, *Charter Schools in Action*, 18; Diane Ravitch, *The Death and Life of the Great American School System: How Testing and Choice Are Undermining Education* (New York: Basic Books, 2010), 122–24.

13. Shanker reversed his position and became a vociferous opponent of charter schools in 1993, when he became convinced the charter movement was dominated by private and corporate interests and, therefore, had become a threat to public education. Ravitch, *The Death and Life of the Great American School System*, 122–24.

14. John Tierney, "The Coming Revolution in Public Education," *Atlantic Monthly*, April 25, 2013.

15. Kara Finnigan et al., *Evaluation of the Public Charter Schools Program: Final Report* (2004), http://www.ed.gov/rschstat/eval/choice/pcspfinal/index.html; Center for Research on Educational Outcomes, *Multiple Choice: Charter School Performance in 16 States* (2009), http://credo .stanford.edu/reports/MULTIPLE_CHOICE_CREDO.pdf.

16. Caroline M. Hoxby, Sonali Murarka, and Jenny Kang, "How New York City's Charter Schools Affect Achievement," *New York City Charter Schools Evaluation Project*, 2009; Julian R. Betts and Y. Emily Tang, "Value-Added and Experimental Studies of the Effect of Charter Schools on Student Achievement," *National Charter School Research Project*, 2008.

17. Buckley and Schneider, *Charter Schools*; Caroline Minter Hoxby and Jonah E. Rockoff, *The Impact of Charter Schools on Student Achievement* (working paper, Department of Economics, Harvard University, 2004). http://www.rand.org/content/dam/rand/www/external/labor/ seminars/adp/pdfs/2005hoxby.pdf.

18. "Knowledge is Power Program," KIPP, accessed November 2, 2011, http://www.kipp .org/; "Work Hard, Be Nice: A New Breed of Schools for Some of the Poorest Kids," *Economist*, July 9, 2009; Greg Toppo, "Knowledge Is Power Program Shown as Urban Triumph," *USA Today*, Feb. 11, 2009; Jay Mathews, "Ivy League Aspirations: Getting Fifth Graders to Think about College Seems a Little Goofy. But It's Key to the Prospects of the Next Generation," *Newsweek*, Jan. 17, 2009. The story of KIPP schools is told in Jay Mathews, *Work Hard, Be Nice: How Two Inspired Teachers Created the Most Promising Schools in America* (Chapel Hill, NC: Algonquin Books of Chapel Hill, 2009).

19. Finn, Manno, and Vanourek, *Charter Schools in Action*, 136–37.

20. "The State of Charter Schools," Center for Education Reform, http://www.edreform .com/2011/12/charter-school-closure-report/.

21. "Charter School Law Ranking and Scorecard 2011," Center for Education Reform, http:// www.charterschoolresearch.com/laws/minnesota.htm.

22. "Charter School Laws across the States 2012," Center for Education Reform, http:// www.edreform.com/wp-content/uploads/2012/04/CER_2012_Charter_Laws.pdf.

23. "Public Charter School Dashboard," National Alliance for Public Charter Schools, http:// dashboard.publiccharters.org/dashboard/schools/year/2012.

24. "Public Charter School Dashboard," National Alliance for Public Charter Schools, http:// www.publiccharters.org/dashboard/home; "Catholic School Data: United States Catholic Elementary and Secondary Schools 2012–2013," National Catholic Educational Association, http://www.ncea.org/news/annualdatareport.asp.

25. "Public Charter School Dashboard: Charter School Market Share 2011–2012 National," National Alliance for Public Charter Schools, http://dashboard.publiccharters.org/dashboard/ students/page/mkt/year/2012.

26. "Church, Choice, and Charters: A New Wrinkle for Public Education," *Harvard Law Review* 122 (2009): 1750.

27. *Daugherty v. Vanguard Charter Sch. Acad.*, 116 F. Supp. 2d 897 (W.D. Mich. 2000).

28. "At a Glance," National Heritage Academies, accessed March 25, 2013, http://www .nhaschools.com/About-Us/Pages/At-a-Glance.aspx. "FAQs," National Heritage Academies, accessed March 25, 2013, http://www.nhaschools.com/About-Us/Pages/Frequently-Asked -Questions.aspx.

29. Nathaniel Popper, "Chartering a New Course," *Wall Street Journal*, August 31, 2007, http://online.wsj.com/article/SB118852754540714337.html?mod=googlenews_wsj.

30. Popper, "Chartering a New Course."

31. For example, the Yoder Charter School in Reno City, Kansas, where about half of the students are Amish, is exempt from the state sex-ed requirement and promises parents that it will

practice and reinforce "the values taught at home, including responsibility, compassion, honesty and a strong work ethic."

32. Katherine Kersten, "Storm Brewing between State Officials and TIZA School," *Star Tribune*, September 11, 2008, http://www.startribune.com/local/south/28117969. html?page=1&c=y.

33. Katherine Kersten, a writer with the *Center of the American Experience*, has been writing about the school for several years, leading to a state investigation of the school and instigating the ACLU lawsuit. http://www.amexp.org/author/katherine-kersten. Sarah Lemagie, "State Orders Charter School to Correct Two Areas Tied to Islam," *Star Tribune*, May 28, 2008; Sarah Lemagie, "ACLU Settles with School, Sponsor," *Star Tribune*, Feb. 7, 2008.

34. Benjamin Siracusa Hillman, "Is There a Place for Religious Charter Schools?" *Yale Law Journal* 118 (2008): 568-71.

35. Abby Goodnough, "Hebrew Charter School Spurs Dispute in Florida," *New York Times*, August 24, 2007.

36. Goodnough, "Hebrew Charter School."

37. "School Can Resume Lessons in Hebrew," *Associated Press*, September 12, 2007.

38. Elissa Gootman, "State Weighs Approval of School Dedicated to Hebrew," *New York Times*, Jan. 11, 2009.

39. Finn, Manno, and Vanourek, *Charter Schools in Action*, 220.

40. Finn, Manno, and Vanourek, *Charter Schools in Action*, 162.

41. NativityMiguel website, accessed October 25, 2011, http://www.nativitymiguelschools .org.

42. "Public Charter Schools Dashboard: Catalyst Elementary Charter School—Howland," National Alliance for Public Charter Schools, http://dashboard.publiccharters.org/dashboard/ select/school/catalyst_elementary_howland/year/2012. "2011 Year End Report," San Miguel Schools, http://sanmiguelchicago.org/images/stories/events/2011EndYearReport.pdf.

43. "History and Mission," San Miguel Schools Chicago, accessed October 25, 2011, http:// www.sanmiguelchicago.org/about-san-miguel/mission-history.html.

44. "Public Charter Schools Dashboard: Catalyst Elementary Charter School—Circle Rock," National Alliance for Public Charter Schools, http://dashboard.publiccharters.org/dashboard/ select/school/catalyst_elementary_circle_rock/year/2012.

45. Catalyst Schools, http://www.catalystschools.org/, accessed October 20, 2010; Catalyst Charter School Blog, http://catalystcharterschool.wordpress.com/about/, accessed October 20, 2010.

46. Erica L. Green, "Charters Emerge as Threat to Catholic Schools," *Baltimore Sun*, Mar. 16, 2011.

47. "Charter Schools," National Education Association, http://www.nea.org/home/16332 .htm, accessed October 21, 2010.

48. Mother Theodore Catholic Academies, *Press Release: Indianapolis City-County Council Votes to Transform Two Catholic Schools into Mayor-Supported Charters*, April 8, 2010.

49. Mother Theodore Catholic Academies, *Press Release*.

50. Andy Smarick, "Can Catholic Schools Be Saved?" *National Affairs*, Spring 2011, http:// www.nationalaffairs.com/publications/detail/can-catholic-schools-be-saved.

51. Andy Smarick, "Catholic Schools Become Charter Schools: Lessons from the Washington Experience," *Seton Education Partners*, 17, http://www.setonpartners.org/Seton_DC_Case_ Study_FINAL.pdf.; District of Columbia Public Charter Schools Board, 2009 School Performance Reports, http://www.dcpubliccharter.com/data/images/pcsb_spr_2009_webfinal.pdf.

52. Smarick, "Catholic Schools Become Charter Schools," 16. Michael Birnbaum, "Former D.C. Catholic Schools seeking Identity as Charter Schools," *Washington Post*, January 28, 2010.

53. Smarick, "Catholic Schools become Charter Schools," 16.

54. Dana Brinson, "Turning Loss into Renewal: Catholic Schools, Charter Schools, and the Miami Experience," *Seton Education Partners*, 15, http://setonpartners.org//userfiles/file/Seton _Miami_Case_Study_Web.pdf.

55. Catholics will immediately notice the connection between the names of the charter school and its Catholic antecedent. Both were named for Saint Anthony of Padua—a thirteenth-century priest renowned for his preaching, who is popularly revered as the patron saint of lost things. Anthony of Padua was canonized in 1232, less than a year after his death, and, in 1946, named a "doctor of the church."

56. "Archdiocese Gets OK to Create Two New Charter Schools," *The Criterion Online Edition*, http://www.archindy.org/criterion/local/2010/04-16/charter.html, accessed August 17, 2011).

57. Named for Mother Theodore Guerin, a French nun who established Catholic schools throughout Indiana during the mid-nineteenth century, the Mother Theodore Catholic Academies have the explicit mission of providing a Catholic education in inner-city Indianapolis. http://www.archindy.org/criterion/local/2010/04-16/charter.html. Mother Guerin was canonized Saint Theodora by Pope Benedict the XVI in 2006. http://www.spsmw.org/sisters-of -providence/saint-mother-theodore/about-saint-mother-theodore-guerin.aspx.

58. Interview with Ken Ogorek, Director of Catechesis for the Archdiocese of Indianapolis (May 11, 2011).

CHAPTER THREE

1. "Office of Catholic Schools, about US: Fact Sheet," Archdiocese of Chicago, accessed December 21, 2011, http://schools.archchicago.org/public/factsheet.shtm.

2. "Office of Catholic Schools of Cook and Lake Counties, Report 2009," Archdiocese of Chicago, accessed December 21, 2011, http://schools.archchicago.org/pdf/annual_reports/ annual_report.pdf.

3. "What We Do," Big Shoulders Fund, accessed December 21, 2011, http://www .bigshouldersfund.org/content/index.asp?s=489&t=What-We-Do.

4. "Office of Catholic Schools of Cook and Lake Counties, Report 2009," Archdiocese of Chicago, accessed December 21, 2011, http://schools.archchicago.org/pdf/annual_reports/ annual_report.pdf.

5. Eighteen Catholic high schools also closed during this time. An additional fifty-eight of the elementary schools in the City of Chicago closed before 1984. All told, 35 percent of the Archdiocese's schools closed before 1994. Paul Simons, "Closed School History: 1984–2004," accessed December 21, 2011, http://www.illinoisloop.org/cath_closed_school_84_04.pdf.

6. The median family income in neighborhoods with closed schools was $20,000 in 1994, while for the city as a whole it was about $24,000.

7. Most of the schools in the Archdiocese, especially urban schools, operate in the red. For schools remaining open in 1994, the average operating deficit was $120,369, resulting in a net loss for parishes operating schools of $8,316.93.

8. "Office of Catholic Schools, Catholic Schools Viability Assessment," Archdiocese of Chicago (internal document on file with authors).

9. Ronald James Nuzzi, James M. Frabutt, and Anthony C. Holter, *Faith, Finances, and the Future: The Notre Dame Study of U.S. Pastors* (South Bend: Alliance for Catholic Education Press, 2008), 45. Nuzzi notes the importance of school finances in a nationwide survey of pastors serving parishes with schools.

10. Chicago Public Schools, Office of New Schools, *Office of New Schools, 2007–08 Charter School Performance Report* (Chicago 2008), 5, http://www.cps.edu/NewSchools/

Documents/2007-2008_PerformanceReport.pdf. During the 2007–2008 school year, there were sixty-four charter schools operating in Chicago.

11. Sol Stern, "Save the Catholic Schools!," *City Journal* (Spring 2007).

12. "Private School Universe Survey, Number and Percentage Distribution of Students in Private Schools, by Religious Orientation, Community Type, and Race/Ethnicity," National Center for Education Statistics, last accessed December 21, 2011,http://nces.ed.gov/surveys/pss/tables/table_whs_05.asp.

13. Information on clergy abuse comes both from the official archdiocesan website, "Archdiocesan Priests with Substantiated Allegations of Sexual Misconduct with Minors," Archdiocese of Chicago, last accessed December 21, 2011, http://www.archchicago.org/c_s_abuse/report_032006/list.pdf, and from a larger collection (including some unsubstantiated reports), "Accused Priests Who Worked in the Archdiocese of Chicago," BishopAccountability.org, last accessed December 21, 2011, http://www.bishop-accountability.org/il_chicago/.

14. For the relationships described in the text between upscale restaurants and lounges and subsequent school closing, the correlation coefficient was .108, with significance at $p<.01$.

15. There were three during the period 1984–2004; two from outside the United States.

16. The mean years of service for pastors with closed schools was 3.88 years, compared with 5.05 years for those with schools that remained open.

17. "Years since ordination" and "age" are not perfectly correlated, since men may be ordained to the priesthood at any time in their life. We do not, however, have data on the age of the pastor, only the year of ordination.

18. In Table 3.1, irregularity in the parish was significant at $p<.000$, meaning that it is nearly completely certain that this was not obtained by chance (that is, there is less than a 1/1,000 chance that it would occur randomly).

19. Simons, "Closed School History," note 5.

20. For this we used software provided by Geolytics. The data is also available from www.census.gov.

21. For example, in one case, only one person from a neighborhood in which a school closed answered the survey questions about social cohesion, while in another neighborhood there were more than thirty respondents for the same question.

22. Robert J. Sampson and Stephen W. Raudenbush, "Seeing Disorder: Neighborhood Stigma and the Social Construction of "Broken Windows," *Social Psychology Quarterly* 67 (2004): 319. The authors compared PHDCN systematic and perceived disorder variables and find that residents, regardless of race, perceived more disorder in African American neighborhoods.

23. An alternative method is to use two-stage least squares. Some literature suggests that estimating the two equations simultaneously is appropriate even where there are dummy (binomial) endogenous variables like whether or not the school closed. Joshua D. Angrist, "Estimation of Limited-Dependent Variable Models with Dummy Endogenous Regressors: Simple Strategies for Empirical Practice," *Journal of Business and Economic Statistics* 19 (2001): 2.

24. Sampson and Raudenbush, "Seeing Disorder," 324, n.4.

25. In the study itself, this variable was called ebcohesi (while the individual scaled observation was cohesion). Similar regressions can be performed using the individual data, as was done in the disorder regression above, but they are less reliable statistically because sometimes only one person answered the cohesion questions and sometimes more than twenty answered within a neighborhood. Because the school and demographic variables are the same for each person in a neighborhood, the neighborhood-level aggregate two-stage least squares is more reflective of actual neighborhood conditions.

26. Tracey L. Meares, "Praying for Community Policing," *California Law Review* 90 (2002): 1604–10. Meares discusses the literature on both collective efficacy and social capital.

27. Robert Putnam, *Bowling Alone: The Collapse and Revival of American Community* (New

York: Simon & Schuster, 2000). On social capital generally, see David Halpern, *Social Capital* (Cambridge: Polity Publishers, 2004), 1–45.

28. Robert J. Sampson, Stephen W. Raudenbush, and Felton Earls, "Neighborhoods and Violent Crime: A Multivariate Study of Collective Efficacy," *Science* 277 (1997): 919.

29. Sampson, Raudenbush, and Earls, "Neighborhoods and Violent Crime": 923; Robert J. Sampson and Stephen W. Raudenbush, "Systematic Social Observation in Public Spaces: A New Look at Disorder in Urban Neighborhoods," *American Journal of Sociology* 105 (1999): 610; Edmund F. McGarrell, Andrew L. Giacomazzi, and Quint C. Thurman, "Neighborhood Disorder, Integration, and the Fear of Violent Crime," *Justice Quarterly* 14 (1997): 484; Chris L. Gibson et al., "Social Integration, Individual Perceptions of Collective Efficacy, and Fear of Crime in Three Cities," *Justice Quarterly* 19 (2002): 552; Julie Berry Cullen and Steven D. Levitt, "Crime, Urban Flight, and the Consequences for Cities," *Review of Economics and Statistics* 81 (1999): 159–69.

30. Sampson and Raudenbush, "Systematic Social Observation," 624–26. Gibson et al., "Social Integration," 542, 552; Albert Hunter and Terry L. Baumer, "Street Traffic, Social Integration and Fear of Crime," *Social Inquiry* 52 (1982): 123–31; Pamela Wilcox Rountree and Kenneth C. Land, "Burglary Victimization, Perceptions of Crime Risk, and Routine Activities: A Multilevel Analysis across Seattle Neighborhoods and Census Tracts," *Journal of Research in Crime and Delinquency* 33 (1996): 147–80.

31. Willam A. Fischel, "Why Voters Veto Vouchers: Public Schools and Community-Specific Social Capital," *Economics of Governance* 7, 109 (2006): 113. Fischel argues, "When bottom up collective action is necessary, having established a network of personal relationships makes it much easier to organize and get the job done."

32. Sampson and Raudenbush, "Systematic Social Observation," 638.

33. Sampson and Raudenbush, "Systematic Social Observation," 637–38.

34. Randy L. LaGrange, Kenneth F. Ferraro, and Michael Supancic, "Perceived Risk and Fear of Crime: Role of Social and Physical Incivilities," *Journal of Research in Crime and Delinquency* 29 (1992): 311–34. McGarrell Giacomazzi, and Thurman, "Neighborhood Disorder," 493. Gibson et al., "Social Integration," 541; Jeanette Covington and Ralph Taylor, "Fear of Crime in Urban Residential Neighborhoods: Implications of between- and within-Neighborhoods for Current Models," *Sociology Quarterly* 32 (1991): 241–43.

35. Police Foundation, *The Newark Foot Patrol Experiment* (Washington, D.C.: Police Foundation, 1981); Robert Trojanowicz, *An Evaluation of the Neighborhood Foot Patrol Program in Flint, Michigan* (Flint, MI: Mott Foundation, 1982), 15, 19–20; David Weisburd and John E. Eck, "What Can Police Do to Reduce Crime, Disorder, and Fear?" *Annals of the American Academy of Politics and Sociology* 593 (May 2004): 42–65; G.W. Cordner, "Fear of Crime and the Police: An Evaluation of a Fear-Reduction Strategy," *Policing Science and Administration* 14 (1986): 223; J. Solomon Zhao, "The Effect of Police Presence on Public Fear Reduction and Satisfaction: A Review of the Literature," *Justice Professional* 15 (2002): 273; Brian C. Renauer, "Reducing Fear of Crime: Citizen, Police, or Government Responsibility?" *Police Quarterly* 10 (2007): 41, 47.

36. Wesley G. Skogan, "Measuring What Matters: Crime, Disorder, and Fear." In *Measuring What Matters: Proceedings from the Policing Institute Meetings*, ed. Robert H. Langworthy (Washington, DC: Department of Justice, 1999), 37, 47–48.

37. Robert A. Mikos, "'Eggshell' Victims, Private Precautions, and the Societal Benefits of Shifting Crime," *Michigan Law Review* 105 (2006): 308.

38. "Redistribution of Crime Has No Net Social Benefit." Robert Cooter and Thomas Ulen, *Law and Economics*, 4th ed. (Reading: Addison-Wesley, 2004), 276; Ian Ayres and Steven D. Levitt, "Measuring Positive Externalities from Unobservable Victim Precaution: An Empirical Analysis of LoJack," *Quarter Journal of Economics* 113 (1998): 76; Omri Ben-Shahar and Alon

Harel, "The Economics of the Law of Criminal Attempts: A Victim-Centered Perspective," *University of Pennsylvania Law Review* 145 (1996): 299; Steven Shavell, "Individual Precautions to Prevent Theft: Private v. Socially Optimal Behavior," *International Review of Law and Economics* 11 (1991): 123. Cf. Mikos, "'Eggshell' Victims," 339–49.

39. Dan M. Kahan, "Social Influence, Social Meaning, and Deterrence," *Virginia Law Review* 83 (1997): 350. On social influence theory, see generally Elliot Aronson, *The Social Animal*, 7th ed. (New York: Worth Publishers, 1995); Lawrence Lessig, "The Regulation of Social Meaning," *University of Chicago Law Review* 62 (1996): 943; Cass R. Sunstein, "Social Norms and Social Roles," *Columbia Law Review* 96 (1996): 903.

40. Not surprisingly, therefore, many "community policing" efforts seek to help neighbors overcome their fears by catalyzing new forms of collective efficacy. Chicago Community Policing Evaluation Consortium, *Community Policing in Chicago, Year Ten: An Evaluation of Chicago's Alternative Policing Strategy* (New York: Oxford University Press, 2004).

CHAPTER FOUR

1. Wesley G. Skogan, et al., *Taking Stock: Community Policing in Chicago*, National Institute for Justice (July 2002), http://www.ncjrs.gov/pdffiles1/nij/189909.pdf.; Chicago Community Policing Evaluation Consortium, *Community Policing in Chicago, Year 10* (January 2004) http://www.northwestern.edu/ipr/publications/policing_papers/Yr10-CAPSeval.pdf.

2. Margaret F. Brinig and Nicole Stelle Garnett, "Catholic Schools and Broken Windows," *Journal of Empirical Legal Studies* 9, no. 2 (2012): 347–67.

3. Robert J. Sampson and Stephen W. Raudenbush, "Systematic Social Observation of Public Spaces: A New Look at Disorder in Public Spaces," *American Journal of Sociology* 105, no. 3 (1999): 603.

Andrew Papachristos, Tracey L. Meares, and Jeffrey Fagan. "Attention Felons: Evaluating Project Safe Neighborhoods in Chicago," *Journal of Empirical Legal Studies* 4 no. 2 (2007): 246.

4. The supporting calculations first appeared in Brinig and Garnett, supra note 2.

5. James Q. Wilson and George L. Kelling, "Broken Windows: The Police and Neighborhood Safety," *Atlantic Monthly* (March 1982): 29.

6. Robert C. Ellickson, "Controlling Chronic Misconduct in City Spaces: Of Panhandlers, Skid Rows, and Public Space Zoning," *Yale Law Journal* 105, no. 5 (1996): 1165–248; Debra Livingston, "Police Discretion and the Quality of Life in Public Places," *Columbia Law Review* 97, no.3 (1997): 551.

7. Livingston, "Police Discretion"; Herman Goldstein, *Problem Oriented Policing* (Philadelphia: Temple University Press, 1990); George L. Kelling and Catherine M. Coles, *Fixing Broken Windows: Restoring Order and Reducing Crime in Our Communities* (New York: Martin Kessler Books, 1996).

8. Jerome H. Skolnick and David H. Bayley, *The New Blue Line: Police Innovation in Six American Cities* (New York: Free Press, 1986); Dan M. Kahan, "Reciprocity, Collective Action, and Community Policing," *California Law Review* 90, no. 5 (2002): 1527–38.

9. Wesley G. Skogan, *Disorder and Decline: Crime and the Spiral of Decay in American Neighborhoods* (Berkeley: University of California Press, 1981), 65–84. Skogan purports to demonstrate a connection between disorder and robbery rates. Hope Corman and Naci Mocan, "Carrots, Sticks, and Broken Windows," *Journal of Law and Economics* 48 (2005): 251–63. The authors find that New York City's order-maintenance policy of aggressive misdemeanor arrests reduced motor vehicle theft, robbery, and grand larceny. George L. Kelling and William H. Sousa, Jr., "Do Police Matter? An Analysis of the Impact of New York City's Police Reforms," *Civic Report* (December 2001): 22. The report found that misdemeanor arrests in New York City prevented over 60,000 crimes between 1989 and 1999. But see Bernard E. Harcourt, *Illusion*

of Order: The False Promise of Broken Windows Policing (Cambridge: Harvard University Press, 2002), 67–75. Harcourt replicates Skogan's study and challenges his results. Bernard E. Harcourt and Jens Ludwig, "Broken Windows: New Evidence from New York City and a Five-City Social Experiment," *University of Chicago Law Review* 73 (2006): 271. Harcourt and Ludwig challenge Kelling and Sousa's study. Steven D. Levitt, "Understanding Why Crime Fell in the 1990s: Four Factors That Explain the Decline and Six That Do Not," *Journal of Economic Perspectives* 18 (2004): 163. Levitt rejects the argument that changing police tactics contributed to reduced rates of violent crime.

10. Dan M. Kahan, "Social Influence, Social Meaning, and Deterrence," *Virginia Law Review* 83, no. 2 (1997): 387.

11. Kahan, "Social Influence," 367–73; Dan M. Kahan, "Reciprocity, Collective Action, and Community Policing," *California Law Review* 90, no. 5 (2002): 1527–38.

12. Skogan, *Disorder and Decline.*

13. George L. Kelling and William H. Sousa, Jr., "Do Police Matter?"; Corman and Mocan, "Carrots, Sticks, and Broken Windows."

14. Bernard E. Harcourt and Jens Ludwig, "Broken Windows," 271.

15. Jeffrey Fagan and Garth Davies, "Street Stops and Broken Windows: *Terry,* Race and Disorder in New York City," *Fordham Urban Law Journal* 28 (2000): 457–504.

16. Sampson and Raudenbush, "Systematic Social Observation of Public Spaces."

17. We note that our analysis also differs from Sampson and Raudenbush's in terms of the number of years of crime studied (in our case, seven, in theirs, one, allowing us to examine trends) and in the number of crimes included (in our case, six, rather than three). Sampson and Raudenbush studied homicide, robbery, and burglary. We also include aggravated sexual assault and aggravated assault and aggravated battery, the latter two of which might fairly be characterized as serious versions of conduct traditionally included in many definitions of social disorder. Again, these questions are somewhat beyond the scope of our current investigation, which seeks to explore school closure effects rather than disorder effects on their own. We note, however, that our findings do hint that future research along these lines might prove fruitful.

18. Tracey L. Meares, "Praying for Community Policing," *California Law Review* 90, no. 5 (2002): 1593–1634.

19. James Q. Wilson, "The Urban Unease: Community vs. City," *National Affairs* 12 (Summer 1968): 25–39.

CHAPTER FIVE

1. See "Search Map: Find a school in Chicago," Illinois Network of Charter Schools, http://incschools.org/charters/find_a_charter_school/search_map, accessed March 26, 2013.

2. See 105 ILL. COMP. STAT. 5/27A-4(b) (2012), http://www.ilga.gov/legislation/ilcs/ilcs4.asp?DocName=010500050HArt.+27A&ActID=1005&ChapterID=17&SeqStart=164500000&SeqEnd=166400000.

3. See "Charter Sector Overview," Illinois Network of Charter Schools, http://incschools.org/charters/charter-school-data-finder/data-illinois-charter-overview, accessed March 26, 2013; "What you Should Know," Illinois Network of Charter Schools, http://www.incschools.org/docs/INCS_Backgrounder_2012.pdf; "Stats and Facts," Chicago Public Schools, http://cps.edu/About_CPS/At-a-glance/Pages/Stats_and_facts.aspx, accessed March 26, 2013; Chicago Public Schools, Office of New Schools, 2008–09 Charter and Contract Schools Performance Report 5 (2009), available at http://www.cps.edu/NewSchools/Documents/2008-2009_PerformanceReport.pdf .

4. See Chicago Public Schools: Office of New Schools, http://www.cps.edu/newschools/Pages/ONS.aspx, accessed January 9, 2011. Because of the geographical area covered by our crime data, we were interested only in those schools located in the City of Chicago and only

in schools open by 2004. This information was obtained by clicking on the various links to individual schools found at Illinois Network of Charter Schools, http://incschools.org/charters/find_a_charter_school/full_list, accessed January 9, 2011.

5. United States Department of Commerce, Bureau of the Census, http://www.census.gov/. The data was downloaded using software provided by Geolytics.

6. See, e.g., Catalyst Schools, About Catalyst, http://www.catalystschools.org/about_catalyst/, accessed January 9, 2011.

7. This ESRI program matches shape files, and the intersection function generates a table of the matches. The number of census tracts in each beat varied from three to twenty-three, with an average of more than ten per beat. Visual inspection of the census tract/police beat matches revealed that it would be nearly impossible to choose a majority or typical tract for many beats, so we decided to include them all to eliminate subjectivity. One beat (3100) had no people living in it, so the data was simply excluded, leaving us with 2902 beat/tract observations for which there was both crime and census information. Beat 1611 had two Catholic schools but was entered only once for each tract. Beat 922 had two charters located in one closed school and was also entered only once for each tract.

8. To keep the logarithms positive, this quotient was multiplied by 100. Andrew V. Papachristos, Tracey L. Meares, and Jeffrey Fagan. "Attention Felons: Evaluating Project Safe Neighborhoods in Chicago," *Journal of Empirical Legal Studies* 4 no. 2 (2007): 245–46; Margaret F. Brinig and Nicole Stelle Garnett, "Catholic Schools and Broken Windows," *Journal of Empirical Legal Studies* 9 no. 2 (2012): 347–67; Robert J. Sampson and Stephen W. Raudenbush, "Systematic Social Observation of Public Spaces: A New Look at Disorder in Public Spaces," *American Journal of Sociology*, 105, no. 3 (1999): 621.

9. See, e.g., Papachristos, Meares, and Fagan, "Attention Felons," 240.

10. The same technique has been used on Chicago crime data (there called alpha-scoring factor analysis and also accounting for mixed land use) in the earlier Sampson and Raudenbush, "Systematic Social Observation," 621–23 (citing other sources).

11. We would be happy to supply the corresponding results using Model 2. They are nearly identical. For example, for 1999, the gray line's value would be at 2.3442, while the darker line would be at 1.8161; for 2000, the gray value would be at 2.3836 and the darker at 1.6494, and so forth. Not surprisingly, the equation's R^2 (or the amount of variance predicted) improves considerably when the individual characteristics are used.

12. Share nonwhite is used to determine the PCAs of Model 1 and appears as well in Papachristos, Meares, and Fagan, "Attention Felons."

13. In the simplest model of all, looking at the correlation between open Catholic elementary schools and the logged crime rate, the coefficient is $-.086$ at $p < .001$. A model that simply considers race and income generates an adjusted R^2 of .141 ($F = 119.934$), with the coefficients as follows in table 5.1. The effect of the Catholic school being open, standardized, is almost exactly the same as the effect of income.

TABLE 5.1. Regression results: Log crime rate and open Catholic school

	B	Beta (standardized)
(Constant)	3.603 (.100)***	
Open Catholic school (as of 2004)	−.371 (.113)***	−.058
Percent black in census tract, 2000	.987 (.074)***	.399
Percent Hispanic in census tract, 2000	.591 (.097)***	.156
Median income, 2000	−3.749E−6 (.000)***	−.059

Note: Dependent variable: log crime rate. $P < .001$ for all coefficients.

CHAPTER SIX

1. For example, a well-executed random study of the effects of mandatory arrest on domestic violence in Milwaukee could not be replicated in other cities. Lawrence W. Sherman, Douglas A. Smith, Janell D. Schmidt, and Dennis P. Rogan, "Crime, Punishment, and Stake in Conformity: Legal and Informal Control of Domestic Violence," *American Sociological Review* 57 (1992): 680–90; Lawrence W. Sherman et al., "The Variable Effects of Arrest on Criminal Careers: The Milwaukee Domestic Violence Experiment," *Journal of Criminal Law and Criminology* 83, no. 1 (1992): 137–69.

2. Philadelphia Health Management Corporation, 2004 *Household Health Survey, Adult Respondent Questionnaire* at 31–32, available at http://www.chdbdata.org/. The documentation is available from the Philadelphia Health Management Corporation. A publication using the questions from 2002 and finding statistically significant relationships between social capital and health is Philadelphia Health Management Corporation Community Health Data Base, *Social Capital and Health: Does a Relationship Exist?* (2003), available at http://www.chdbdata.org/uploads/datareports/APHA%20Presentation.pdf.

3. The four principal components extracted roughly measure poverty (47 percent of the variance, more mobile youthful foreign population [16 percent], older foreign population [13 percent], population generally [8.6 percent]).

4. In addition to the crime rate's profile not showing a steady decline, the smaller population tracts in Philadelphia (i.e., population of less than five hundred), did not demonstrate regular effects (see Fig. 8.2, showing tracts at top and bottom with huge variations among years). This complicated use of a latent growth model is like the one employed in chapter 4. The results reported are for a mixed effects maximum-likelihood regression model only. The Wald chi-square was 278.32; $p<.0000$, log likelihood $= -102.6736$. The logged crime rate was used as in Chicago.

5. The first three components accounted for roughly 71 percent of the variance in the demographic variables, while the first accounts for about 42 percent. This first component seems indicative of a general poverty level, with high positive loadings seen with poverty, public assistance, single motherhood, nonwhite, foreign born, and linguistic isolation. Strong negative loadings were seen with median income, high school graduation, and employment. The estimated coefficient on this variable was 8.677, $p<.000$.

6. While in a random effects model including poverty, the coefficient for closed school loses statistical significance, that of social capital remains significant at $p<.001$. Repeated tests did not show the indirect effect of Catholic school closing working through social capital.

7. We obtained restricted crime data from the Los Angeles Police Department (with addresses, as in Philadelphia), the Los Angeles Sheriff's Department (historic crime statistics by year at http://www.lasdhq.org/sites/yir9600/index.html after mapping through http://projects.latimes.com/mapping-la/neighborhoods), and various independent cities in Los Angeles County (using http://projects.latimes.com/mapping-la/neighborhoods for some after pinpointing the locations using Google Maps) for eighty-six tracts identified through data obtained from the Los Angeles Family and Neighborhood Study, http://dx.doi.org/10.3886/ICPSR22940.v4. We also obtained scattered data from ten cities after numerous phone calls and emails to their police departments. The City of Downey collects data for its six police beats only at the city level, so we divided historic levels by 6 and obtained actual data for 2008–2009 from their online mapping program. Similarly, we obtained data for Whittier from the total crime numbers reported on the Rand California statistics website, dividing by 4. We were never able to obtain data from the City of Whittier directly.

8. Los Angeles Family and Neighborhood Study Database, http://dx.doi.org/10.3886/ICPSR22940.v4.

9. For example, for 2009, the year in which our crime data is the most complete, the R^2 of a regression with the dependent variable being the log of the crime rate = .285. For the log of crime rates 2005–2009, R^2 was .286.

10. The principal component for poverty included measures of income (logged), linguistic isolation, nonwhite, share of foreign born, poverty ratio, welfare receipt, and renters.

11. In the 2009 regression, for public schools the significance was $p<.980$; for Catholic schools, $p<.560$. For the 2005–2009 equation, for public schools the significance was $p<.958$; for Catholic schools, $p<.801$).

12. California Community Foundation, *Social Capital Community Benchmark Survey: Data Highlights from the Los Angeles Sample*: 3, accessed January 10, 2012, http://www.cfsv.org/communitysurvey/docs/cala_sh.pdf.

13. Edward L. Glaeser, David Laibson, and Bruce Sacerdote, "An Economic Approach to Social Capital," *Economic Journal* 112 (November): F437–F458.

14. California Community Foundation, *Social Capital Community*, 3.

15. Robert D. Putnam, "E Pluribus Unum: Diversity and Community in the Twenty-First Century, The 2006 Johan Skytte Prize Lecture," *Scandinavian Political Studies* 30 (2007): 137–74. Putnam's Figure 4, "Racial Homogeneity and Trust of Neighbors" shows an inverse relationship between diversity and trust, with Los Angeles and San Francisco among the two most diverse and least trusting cities. Putnam, "E Pluribus Unum," 148.

16. California Community Foundation, *Social Capital Community*, 3.

17. California Community Foundation, *Social Capital Community*, 3.

18. Fifty percent of religious individuals in Los Angeles were members of a religious congregation, compared with 65 percent who claim a religious identity nationwide, while only 39 percent report being involved with members of their congregation in an activity outside regular services, contrasted with 46 percent nationwide. California Community Foundation, *Social Capital Community*, 4.

19. Hyunsun Choi, in his doctoral dissertation on urban planning that focuses on Korean immigrants to Los Angeles, includes table 6.7:

TABLE 6.7. Survey results: Trust of others

How much you trust different groups of people	*Total*	*Average*	*Standard deviation*
1. People in your race or ethnic group	134	2.9	1.0
2. Same religion	192	3.6	0.8
3. People in your village/neighborhood	176	2.2	1.1
4. People who belong to the same clubs, organizations, or groups	189	4.1	0.9
5. People in your church or other religious organizations	189	4.1	0.9
6. Business owners and traders you do business with	123	2.7	0.5
7. Family	216	4.7	0.5
8. Korean community leaders	107	1.7	1.0
9. Politicians	97	2.1	1.1
10. Government service providers	123	2.7	0.7

Note: N = 46.

Hyunsun Choi, *Social Capital and Community Economic Development in Los Angeles Koreatown: Faith-Based-Organizations in Transitional Ethnic Community* (Los Angeles: University of Southern California, 2004), 121.

20. Glaeser, Laibson, and Sacerdote, "An Economic Approach," F437–F458.

21. Jane Jacobs, *Death and Life of Great American Cities* (New York: Vintage Books, 1961).

22. Putnam, "E Pluribus Unum," 22–24.

23. See, e.g., Ralph B. Taylor et al., "Street Blocks with More Nonresidential Land Uses Have More Physical Deterioration," *Urban Affairs Review* 31 (1995): 120–36; Stephanie W. Greenberg, William M. Rohe, and Jay R. Williams, "Safety in Urban Neighborhoods: A Comparison of Physical Characteristics and Informal Control in High and Low Crime Neighborhoods," *Population and Environment* 5 (1982): 141–65. See Robert J. Sampson and Stephen W. Raudenbush, "Systematic Social Observation of Public Spaces: A New Look at Disorder in Public Spaces," *American Journal of Sociology* 105, no. 3 (1999): 624 ("Neighborhoods with mixed residential and commercial development exhibit higher levels of both physical and social disorder, regardless of sociodemographic characteristics").

24. Glaeser, Laibson, and Sacerdote, "An Economic Approach," F437–F458.

25. "History of the Schools in the Archdiocese of Los Angeles," Archdiocese of Los Angeles, http://www.archdiocese.la/learning/schools/about/history.html, accessed January 10, 2012. Schools were located among the Los Angeles parishes less often than in the other cities (with 210 elementary schools in 287 parishes in what is now the region) and were deliberately spaced. Msgr. Francis J. Weber, *His Eminence of Los Angeles: James Francis Cardinal McIntyre* (Mission Hills, California: Saint Francis Historical Society, 1997): 249–53.

CHAPTER SEVEN

1. See, e.g., Theodore W. Schultz, *Investment in Human Capital: The Role of Education and of Research* (New York: Free Press, 1971).

2. Gary S. Becker, *Human Capital: A Theoretical and Empirical Analysis, with Special Reference to Education*. 3d ed. (Chicago: University of Chicago Press, 1994).

3. James Coleman, *Foundations of Social Theory* (Cambridge, MA: Belknap Press,1990), 302–4.

4. Robert D. Putnam, *Bowling Alone: The Collapse and Revival of American Community* (New York: Touchstone, 2000), 18.

5. James S. Coleman, "Social Capital in the Creation of Human Capital," *American Journal of Sociology* 94 (1988): S95–S120.

6. Putnam, *Bowling Alone*, 67.

7. See, e.g., Frank F. Furstenberg Jr. and Mary Elizabeth Hughes, "Social Capital and Successful Development among At-Risk Youth," *Journal of Marriage and Family* 57, no. 3 (1995): 580–92 (mothers' social capital positively affects their children, and relative lack of it causes them to do less well).

8. Partha Dasgupta, "Economics of Social Capital," *Economic Record* 81, no. S1 (2005): S3–S6.

9. Coleman, "Social Capital in the Creation of Human Capital."

10. Robert D. Putnam and David E. Campbell, *American Grace: How Religion Divides and Unites Us* (New York: Simon & Schuster, 2010).

11. James M. Buchanan, "An Economic Theory of Clubs," *Economica*, New Series 32, no. 125 (Feb. 1965): 1–14.

12. For example, mobility will lower social capital. See, e.g., Luke Dauter and Bruce Fuller, *How Diverse Schools Affect Students' Mobility: Charter, Magnet and Newly Built Campuses in Los Angeles* (Policy Analysis for California Education, July 2011), http://www.edpolicyinca.org/. Compare Robert K. Ream and Ricardo D. Stanton-Salazar, "The Mobility/Social Capital Dynamic: Understanding Mexican American Families and Students," in *Narrowing the Achievement Gap: Strategies for Educating Latino, Black, and Asian Students*, ed. Susan J. Paik and Herbert J.

Walberg (New York: Springer, 2007): 67, 69 (rapid assimilation undermines utility of social capital among Latino youth).

13. Dasgupta, "Economics of Social Capital," S14, n. 14; and others "may inhibit the flow of resources such as physical capital from one place to another." Dasgupta, "Economics of Social Capital," S17.

14. See, e.g., Dasgupta, "Economics of Social Capital," S2–S21. See also Francis Fukuyama, *Trust: The Social Virtues and the Creation of Prosperity* (New York: Free Press Paperbacks, 1995).

15. In the case of the neighborhood parishes in the Midwest studied by John McGreevy in his *Parish Boundaries* (Chicago: University of Chicago Press, 1996), the churches first acted to keep minorities out of the neighborhood. Only later did they become agents for positive social change. The Korean networks studied by Hyunsun Choi in his doctoral dissertation, *Social Capital and Community Economic Development in Los Angeles Koreatown: Faith-Based Organizations in Transitional Ethnic Community* (University of Southern California, August 2004), exhibited both traits. Strong faith-based bonds developed throughout the Korean community that not only facilitated individual families' and the community's economic success (and greater safety) but also harmed integration into the broader community. Choi, *Social Capital and Community Economic Development*, 29.

16. Dasgupta, "Economics of Social Capital," S17–18. Similarly, Elijah Anderson reports that strong male-mother ties may inhibit lasting bonds with adult sexual partners in the inner city. Elijah Anderson, "Sex Codes and Family Life among Poor Inner City Youths," *Annals of the American Academy of Political and Social Science* 501 (Jan. 1989): 69.

17. Coleman, "Social Capital in the Creation of Human Capital," S98.

18. Coleman, "Social Capital in the Creation of Human Capital," S106–7.

19. Coleman, "Social Capital in the Creation of Human Capital," S106–7.

20. Coleman, "Social Capital in the Creation of Human Capital," S114–15.

21. Anthony S. Bryk, Valerie E. Lee, and Peter B. Holland, *Catholic Schools and the Common Good* (Cambridge, MA: Harvard University Press 1993), 276.

22. Bryk, Lee, and Holland, *Catholic Schools and the Common Good*, 305.

23. Stephen L. Morgan and Aage B. Sorensen, "Parental Networks, Social Closure, and Mathematics Learning: A Test of Coleman's Social Capital Explanation of School Effects," *American Sociological Review* 64, no. 5 (1991): 644–81.

24. Anthony S. Bryk et al., *Organizing Schools for Improvement: Lessons from Chicago* (Chicago: University of Chicago Press, 2010). See also Anthony S. Bryk and Barbara Schneider, *Trust: A Core Resource for Improvement* (New York: Russell Sage Foundation, 2002).

25. Bryk et al., *Organizing Schools for Improvement*.

26. Charles M Payne, *So Much Reform, So Little Change* (Cambridge, MA: Harvard Education Press, 2008).

27. Matthew P. Steinberg, Elaine Allensworth, and David W. Johnson, *Student and Teacher Safety in Chicago Public Schools: The Roles of Community Context and Social Organization* (Consortium on Chicago School Research at the University of Chicago, May 2011).

28. Patrick J. Wolf, "Civics Exam," *Education Next*, Summer 2007.

29. Wolf, "Civics Exam," (reviewing literature); David E. Campbell, "The Civic Side of School Choice: An Empirical Analysis of Civic Education in Public and Private Schools," *B.Y.U. Law Review* 2008 (2008): 501–10. See also David E. Campbell, "Bowling Together: Private Schools, Public Ends," *Education Next*, Fall 2001.

30. Richard H. Chused, "Euclid's Historical Imagery," *Case Western Reserve Law Review* 51 (2001): 601.

31. Jane Jacobs, *Death and Life of Great American Cities* (New York: Random House 1961).

32. Putnam, *Bowling Alone*, 22–24.

33. See, e.g., Robert Bruegmann, *Sprawl: A Compact History* (Chicago: University of Chicago

Press, 2005): 151–53 (describing new urbanism's influence on suburban design); "Hope VI Funds New Urban Neighborhoods," *New Urban News*, Jan./Feb. 2002 (asserting that the Congress for the New Urbanism shaped many HOPE VI projects and trains participating developers); Nicole Stelle Garnett, "Ordering (and Order in) the City," *Stanford Law Review* 57 (2004): 58.

34. See Robert J. Sampson and Stephen W. Raudenbush, "Systematic Social Observation of Public Spaces: A New Look at Disorder in Public Places," *American Journal of Sociology* 105 (1999): 624 ("Neighborhoods with mixed residential and commercial development exhibit higher levels of both physical and social disorder, regardless of sociodemographic characteristics.").

35. See, e.g., Ralph Taylor et al., "Street Blocks with More Nonresidential Land Uses Have More Physical Deterioration," *Urban Affairs Review* 31, no.1 (1995): 120; Stephanie W. Greenberg, William M. Rohe, and Jay R. Williams, "Safety in Urban Neighborhoods: A Comparison of Physical Characteristics and Informal Control in High and Low Crime Neighborhoods," *Population and Environment* 5, no. 3 (Fall 1982): 141; Pamela Wilcox, Neil Quisenberry, Debra T. Cabrera, and Shayne Jones, "Busy Places and Broken Windows? Toward Defining the Role of Physical Structure and Process in Community Crime Models," *Sociological Quarterly* 45 (2004): 191.

36. Sampson and Raudenbush, "Systematic Social Observation," 610.

37. Ralph Taylor et al., "Street Blocks"; Greenberg, Rohe, and Williams, "Safety in Urban Neighborhoods," 162; Wilcox et al., "Busy Places and Broken Windows"; Sampson and Raudenbush, "Systematic Social Observation," 610.

38. See generally Oscar Newman, *Defensible Space: Crime Prevention through Urban Design* (1972); Neal Kumar Katyal, "Architecture as Crime Control," *Yale Law Journal* 111 (2002): 1039.

39. Taylor et al., "Street Blocks," 122.

40. Ellen M. Kurtz, Barbara A. Koons, and Ralph B. Taylor, "Land Use, Physical Deterioration, Resident-Based Control, and Calls for Service on Urban Streetblocks," *Justice Quarterly* 15 (1998): 135.

41. William A. Fischel, "Education Reforms and Social Capital in School Districts," in *Making the Grade: The Economic Evolution of American School Districts* (Chicago: University of Chicago Press, 2009).

42. Caterina Gouvis Roman, *Schools as Generators of Crime: Routine Activities and the Sociology of Place* (Villanova, PA: American University 2002); Dennis W. Roncek and Donald Faggiani, "High Schools and Crime: A Replication," *Sociological Quarterly* 26 (1985): 491; Dennis W. Roncek and Antoinette LoBosco, "The Effect of High Schools on Crime in Their Neighborhoods," *Social Science Quarterly* 64 (1983): 598.

43. Roncek and Faggiani, "High Schools and Crime," 491; Roncek and LoBosco, "The Effect of High Schools on Crime," 598. None has shown an increase for private elementary schools.

44. Jon Hurdle, "Philadelphia Officials Vote to Close 23 Schools," *New York Times*, March 7, 2013; Kim Geiger, "People Protesting Planned School Closings Arrested at City Hall," *Chicago Tribune*, May 20, 2013.

45. Douglas Belkin, "School Crisis Rattles Missouri: Kansas City Board Approves Plan to Shutter Nearly Half of District's Buildings," *Wall Street Journal*, March 11, 2010.

46. "HBS Cases: Reforming New Orleans Schools after Katrina," Harvard Business School, http://hbswk.hbs.edu/item/5826.html .

47. Nick Anderson, "Most Schools Could Face 'Failing' Label under No Child Left Behind, Duncan Says," *Washington Post*, March 10, 2011.

48. See, e.g., Jonah E. Rockoff and Benjamin B. Lockwood, "Stuck in the Middle," *Education Next*.

49. Payne, *So Much Reform*, 117.

50. See "Charter School Law, Policy, and Agreements Requirements for Enrollment Lottery,"

Chicago Public Schools, http://www.ren2010.cps.k12.il.us/docs/Enrollment_Lottery_Guide lines_for_Charter_Schools.pdf, accessed February 1, 2010.

51. In 2007–2008, the average tuition at a Catholic elementary school was $4,944; the average tuition at a nonsectarian elementary school was $15,945, "Facts and Studies," Council for American Private Education 2010, http://www.capenet.org/facts.html.

52. Bryk et al., *Organizing Schools for Improvement*, 272.

53. See Payne, *So Much Reform*, 117 (discussing literature).

54. See Andrew M. Greeley, *Catholic High Schools and Minority Students* (New Brunswick, NJ: Transaction Publishers, 1982), 107–8; see also James S. Coleman et al., *High School Achievement* (1982), 143–46 ; Darlene Eleanor York, "The Academic Achievement of African-American Students in Catholic Schools: A Review of the Literature," in *Growing Up African American in Catholic Schools*, ed. J.J. Irving and M. Foster (New York: Teachers College Press, 1996), 44; Jeffrey Grogger and Derek Neal, *Further Evidence on the Effects of Catholic Secondary Schooling* (Washington, DC: Brookings Wharton Papers on Urban Affairs 2000); Payne, *So Much Reform*, 117.

55. Jack Buckley and Mark Schneider, "School Choices, Parental Information, and Tiebout Sorting: Evidence from Washington, D.C.," in *The Tiebout Model at Fifty*, ed. William A. Fischel (Cambridge, MA: Lincoln Institute of Land Policy , 2006), 101, 104.

56. While this is a reasonable assumption in many cases, we also recognize that other factors—for example, school quality/reputation, church affiliation, and family/social connections with other students—may draw students to a less proximate school.

57. William A. Fischel, *Why Voters Veto Vouchers*, 117.

58. See Julie Berry Cullen and Brian A. Jacob, "Is Gaining Access to Selective Elementary Schools Gaining Ground: Evidence from Randomized Lotteries," in *An Economics Perspective on the Problems of Disadvantaged Youth*, ed. Jonathan Gruber (Chicago: University of Chicago Press, 2009).

59. Chicago Public Schools, Office of New Schools, 2008–09 *Charter and Contract Schools Performance Report* (2009), 5, http://www.cps.edu/NewSchools/Documents/2008-2009 _PerformanceReport.pdf .

60. Mildred Warner, "Building Social Capital: The Role of Local Government," *Journal of Socio-Economics* 30 (2001): 187; Robert D. Putnam, "Bowling Alone: America's Declining Social Capital," *Journal of Democracy* 6 (1995): 65. Sheila Foster, "The City as Ecological Space: Social Capital and Urban Land Use," *Notre Dame Law Review* 82 (2006): 534–38.

61. Nicole Stelle Garnett, *Ordering the City: Land Use, Policing, and the Restoration of Urban America*, ch. 6 (New Haven, CT: Yale University Press 2010).

62. Putnam, *Bowling Alone*, 66.

63. See generally Corwin Smidt, ed., *Religion as Social Capital* (Waco, TX: Baylor University Press, 2003).

64. Putnam, *Bowling Alone*, 66.

65. Tracey L. Meares and Kelsi Brown Corkran, "When 2 or 3 Come Together," *William and Mary Law Review* 48 (2007): 1335.

66. Wesley G. Skogan and Susan M. Hartnett, *Community Policing, Chicago Style* (Oxford, 1997), 144–46 (noting that the importance of inner-city churches made them a "separate analytic focus" of policing policy in Chicago); Tracey Meares, "Praying for Community Policing," *California Law Review* 90 (2002): 1593.

67. Robert Wuthnow, "Can Religion Revitalize Society?" in *Religion as Social Capital*, 191, 193.

68. Meares, "Praying for Community Policing."

69. Bryk, Lee, and Holland, *Catholic Schools and the Common Good*, 139.

70. Payne, *So Much Reform*, 117

71. Robert C. Ellickson, *Order without Law: How Neighbors Settle Disputes* (Cambridge, MA:

Harvard University Press 1991), 26–29; Richard H. McAdams, "The Origin, Development, and Regulation of Norms," *Michigan Law Review* 96 (1997): 365–72.

CHAPTER EIGHT

1. *Brown v. Board of Education*, 347 U.S. 483 (1954).

2. James E. Ryan and Michael Heise, "The Political Economy of School Choice," *Yale Law Journal* 111 (2002): 2051, n. 21.

3. *Greene v. County Sch. Bd.*, 391 U.S. 430 (1968).

4. See *Keyes v. Sch. Dist. No. 1*, 413 U.S. 189 (1969) (finding that the Denver public school district "by use of various techniques such as the manipulation of student attendance zones, school site selection and a neighborhood school policy, created . . . segregated schools").

5. See *Swann v. Charlotte-Mecklenburg Bd. of Ed.*, 402 U.S. 1 (1971) (approving court-ordered busing of students).

6. 402 U.S. 1 (1971) (invalidating a desegregation plan that would have required the integration of the predominantly black Detroit public schools with the predominantly white surrounding suburban public schools).

7. Generally speaking, magnet schools are specialized, often competitive, public schools. Magnet schools seek to aid desegregation efforts by attracting families to urban public schools who would otherwise attend private schools or suburban public schools. They respond to the reality that, without attracting white students back to urban districts, integration is impossible because, as Jim Ryan observes, in many districts "there [are] not enough white students to go around." James. E. Ryan, "Schools, Race, and Money," *Yale Law Journal* 109 (1999): 312. On magnet schools, see also, e.g., Ryan and Heise, "The Political Economy of School Choice," 2064–65.

8. See *Milliken v. Bradley (Milliken II)*, 433 U.S. 267 (1977).

9. See, e.g., Ryan, "Schools, Race, and Money," 265; Wendy Parker, "The Future of School Desegregation," *Northwestern University Law Review* 94 (2000): 1175–76, 1189; Gary Orfield and Susan E. Eaton, *Dismantling Desegregation: The Quiet Reversal of Brown v. Board of Education* (New York: New Press, 1996), 341.

10. See Ryan, "Schools, Race, and Money," 104.

11. See, e.g., *Parents Involved in Comm. Sch. v. Seattle Sch. Dist.*, 551 U.S. 701 (2007); *Wessmann v. Gittens*, 160 F.3d 790 (1st Cir. 1998). For information about competition for magnet schools on Chicago, see Julie Berry Cullen et al., "Is Gaining Access to Selective Elementary Schools Gaining Ground: Evidence from Randomized Lotteries," in *The Problems of Disadvantaged Youth: An Economic Perspective*, ed. Jonathan Gruber (Chicago: University of Chicago Press, 2009), 14.

12. Between 1993 and 2003, the percentage of students attending a "chosen" public school increased from 11 to 15 percent. "Fast Facts," National Center for Education Statistics, accessed January 13, 2012,http://nces.ed.gov/FastFacts/display.asp?id=6.

13. See, e.g., Education Resources Information Center, "The School-within-a-School Model," *ERIC Digest* (Dec. 1999), available at http://www.education.com/reference/article/Ref_School _within_School/. For a moving account of one successful school-within-a-school effort, see Seymour Fliegel, *Miracle in East Harlem: The Fight for Choice in Public Education* (New York: Random House, 1990).

14. See, e.g., Ryan and Heise, "The Political Economy of School Choice," 2058–59 (describing trends in school finance reform litigation); Peter Enrich, "Leaving Equality Behind: New Directions in School Finance Reform," *Vanderbilt Law Review* 48 (1995): 121–40.

15. Ryan and Heise, "The Political Economy of School Choice," 2059–62.

16. See William A. Fischel, *Homevoter Hypothesis* (Cambridge: Harvard University Press, 2005): 145–61.

17. See "What Is School Choice," Friedman Foundation for School Choice, accessed January 13, 2012, http://www.friedmanfoundation.org/schoolchoice/ ("In 1955, Dr. Milton Friedman proposed the idea of school vouchers, which would separate the financing and administration of schools, effectively jumpstarting the modern school choice movement."); Milton Friedman, "The Role of Government in Education," in *Economics and the Public Interest*, ed. Robert A. Solo (New Jersey: Rutgers University Press, 1955).

18. See *State ex rel Jackson v. Benson*, 578 N.W.2d 602, 608–10 (1998) (summarizing the history of the Milwaukee Parental Choice Program).

19. *Zelman v. Simmons-Harris*, 536 U.S. 639 (2002).

20. See Alliance for School Choice, *School Choice Yearbook—2012–13* (2013): 12–13.

21. Nicole Stelle Garnett, "A *Winn* for Educational Pluralism," *Yale Law Journal Online* 121 (2011): 31.

22. For a compilation of perspectives on school choice, see Alan Wolfe, ed., *School Choice: The Moral Debate* (Princeton, N.J.: Princeton University Press, 2003).

23. John E. Chubb and Terry M. Moe, *Politics, Markets and American Schools* (Washington, D.C.: Brookings Institution, 1990): 217.

24. See, e.g., Joseph P. Viteritti, *Choosing Equality: School Choice, the Constitution and Civil Society* (Washington, D.C.: Brookings Institution, 1999); John E. Coons and Stephen D. Sugarman, *Education by Choice: The Case for Family Control* (Los Angeles: University of California Press, 1978); Richard W. Garnett, "The Right Questions about School Choice: Education, Religious Freedom, and the Common Good," *Cardozo. Law Review* 23 (2002): 1281.

25. Viteritti, *Choosing Equality*.

26. James Forman, Jr., "The Secret History of School Choice: How Progressives Got There First," *Georgetown Law Journal* 93 (2005): 1288 (situating the roots of the school-choice movement in the postemancipation period).

27. http://www.allianceforschoolchoice.org/SchoolChoice/#TOP.

28. See Amy Gutmann, *Democratic Education* (New Jersey: Princeton University Press, 2000); Stephen Macedo, *Diversity and Distrust* (Cambridge: First Harvard University Press, 2000). See also William A. Galston, "Political Knowledge, Political Engagement, and Civic Education," *Annotated Review of Political Science* 4 (2001): 231 ("Public schools have been regarded as the most appropriate sites for forming citizens, while private schools have been regarded with suspicion as sources of separatism, elitism, and antidemocratic principles.").

29. Gutmann, *Democratic Nation*, 39–42.

30. Gutmann, *Democratic Nation*, 42 (articulating a theory of education that involves the sharing of educational authority among parents, citizens, and professional educators with no set guiding principles).

31. Gutmann, *Democratic Nation*, 68.

32. Gutmann, *Democratic Nation*, 34.

33. Macedo, *Diversity and Distrust*, 250–65.

34. Macedo, *Diversity and Distrust*, 238.

35. Macedo, *Diversity and Distrust*, 270–74. He also praises Catholic schools for inculcating civic values, although he expresses concern about other kinds of religious schools and criticizes pre-Vatican II Catholics (and their schools) as illiberal. Macedo, *Diversity and Distrust*, 61–62.

36. See, e.g., Terry M. Moe, *Schools, Vouchers, and the American Public* (Washington, D.C.: Brookings Institution, 2001) (arguing that private schools are, because of their independence from bureaucracy, better suited to serve as models for democratic education than public schools); Patrick J. Wolf et al., "Private Schooling and Political Tolerance," in *Charters, Vouchers, and*

Public Education, ed. Paul E. Peterson and David E. Campbell (Washington, D.C.: Brookings Institution, 2001) (finding that college students who attended private schools score higher on measures of political tolerance); Jay P. Greene, "Civic Values in Public and Private Schools," in *Learning from School Choice*, ed. Paul E. Peterson (Washington, D.C.: Brookings Institute, 1998) (finding that students in private schools are more likely to participate in public service than public school students); Richard G. Niemi, "Community Service by High School Students: A Cure for Civic Ills?" *Political Behavior* 22 (2000): 45 (same for religiously affiliated schools); Kenneth R. Godwin et al., "Teaching Tolerance in Public and Private Schools," *Phi Delta Kappan* 82 (2001): 524 (finding that private schools do a slightly better job than public schools of encouraging interethnic friendships and developing support for democratic norms). But see Kent L. Tedin and Gregory R. Weiher, "General Social Capital, Education-Related Social Capital, and Choosing Charter Schools," *Policy Studies Journal* 39, no. 2 (2011): 609.

37. See David E. Campbell, "The Civic Side of School Choice: An Empirical Analysis of Civic Education in Public and Private Schools," *B.Y.U. Law Review* 2008 (2008): 501–10. See also David E. Campbell, "Bowling Together: Private Schools, Public Ends," *Education Next*, Fall 2001.

38. Patrick J. Wolf, "Civics Exam," *Education Next*, Summer 2007.

39. David E. Campbell, *The Civic Side of School Reform: Private Schools, School Vouchers, and Civic Education*, 23–26 (unpublished manuscript on file with authors). Although Campbell was not able to differentiate between the kinds of schools any given student attended, most of the Children's Scholarship Fund scholarship recipients attended a religiously affiliated school (53 percent attended a Catholic school, 39 percent attended a religious/non-Catholic school), and 8 percent attended a secular private school).

40. Wolf, "Civics Exam."

41. 418 U.S. 717 (1974).

42. "Transcript of Nixon's Statement on School Busing," *NY Times*, March 17, 1972.

43. Drew S. Days III, "Brown Blues: Rethinking the Integrative Ideal," *William & Mary Law Review* 34 (1992): 53. See also, e.g., Robert Woodson, Jr., "Ironically, Busing Denies Quality Education to Black Students," *Headway* 8 (1996): 7 (citing survey evidence suggesting that black parents reject busing and prefer neighborhood schools).

44. Jack Buckley and Mark Schneider, "School Choice, Parental Information, and Tiebout Sorting: Evidence from Washington, D.C.," in *The Tiebout Model at Fifty: Essays in Honor of Wallace Oats*, ed. William A. Fischel (Cambridge: Lincoln Institute of Land Policy, 2006): 101, 104.

45. See, e.g., Kevin Brown, *Race, Law and Education in the Post-Desegregation Era* (Durham, N.C.: Carolina Academic Press, 2005), 1–20 (summarizing concerns); James Ryan, "The Influence of Race in School Finance Reform," *Michigan Law Review* 98 (1999): 432.

46. Days, "Brown Blues," 58.

47. See, e.g., Ryan and Heise, "The Political Economy of School Choice," 2085–91 (discussing the political impediments to unconstrained choice); William A. Fischel, "Why Voters Veto Vouchers: Public Schools and Community-Specific Social Capital," *Economics of Governance* 7 (2006): 109, 111 (arguing that support for local public schools leads voters to reject voucher programs).

48. See Charles M. Tiebout, "A Pure Theory of Local Expenditures," *Journal of Political Economics* 64 (1956): 416. See generally Fischel, ed., *The Tiebout Model at Fifty*.

49. See, e.g., Fischel, *Homevoter Hypothesis*, 207–8; John D. Donahue, "Tiebout? Or Not Tiebout? The Market Metaphor and America's Devolution Debate," *Journal of Economic Perspectives* 11 (1997): 73, 74 ("Diverse policy regimes can cater to heterogeneous preferences."); Robert P. Inman and Daniel L. Rubinfeld, "The Political Economy of Federalism" (arguing that interlocal competition will increase efficiency in production of public goods), in *Perspectives on Public Choice: A Handbook*, ed. Dennis C. Mueller (Cambridge: Cambridge University Press, 1997): 73, 83–85; Richard E. Wagner and Warren E. Weber, "Competition, Monopoly, and the Organiza-

tion of Government in Metropolitan Areas," *Journal of Law and Economics* 18 (1975): 661, 684 ("[A]n increase in the number of competing and overlapping governments will lead the public economy more closely to perform as a competitive industry."); see also, e.g., Mark Schneider, *The Competitive City: The Political Economy of Suburbia* (Pittsburgh: University of Pittsburgh Press, 1989): 63–69 (purporting to find that tax rates and government expenditures are lower in more fragmented metropolitan areas).

50. Fischel, *Homevoter Hypothesis*, 144–45 (discussing literature); Caroline M. Hoxby, "Does Competition among Public Schools Benefit Students and Taxpayers," *American Economic Review* 90 (2000): 1209 (nationwide); Michael L. Marlow, "Public Education Supply and Student Performance," *Applied Economics* 29 (1997): 617 (same); Blair R. Zanzig, "Measuring the Impact of Competition in Local Government Education Markets," *Economics of Education Review* 16 (1997): 431 (California); John P. Blair and Sam Stanley, "Quality Competition and Public Schools: Further Evidence," *Economics of Education Review* 14 (1995): 193 (Ohio); Melvin V. Borland and Roy M. Howsen, "On the Determination of the Critical Level of Market Concentration in Education," *Economics of Education Review* 12 (1993): 165 (Kentucky).

51. Fischel, *Homevoter Hypothesis*, 154–55; Sandra E. Black, "Do Better Schools Matter? Parental Valuation of Elementary Education," *Quarterly Journal of Economics* 114 (1999): 577; Donald R. Haurin and David Brasington, "School Quality and Real Housing Prices: Inter-and Intrametropolitan Effects," *Journal of Housing Economics* 5 (1996): 351.

52. See, e.g., Robert C. Ellickson, "Suburban Growth Controls: An Economic and Legal Analysis," *Yale Law Journal* 86 (1977): 385, 408–10; Fischel, *Homevoter Hypothesis*, 72–97.

53. See Willam A. Fischel, "Why Voters Veto Vouchers: Public Schools and Community-Specific Social Capital," *Economics of Governance* 7 (2006): 109, 113 ("The social capital I am concerned with is what I call 'community specific social capital.' It is not just the people that you know, but the people you know within a given social community.").

54. Our instincts about the benefits of school choice outside the urban context run contrary to Fischel's. For example, we suspect that, all told, the benefits of competition between public and private schools may well outweigh any reduction of interdistrict competition. And we suspect that Fischel may underestimate the extent to which private schools, charter schools, and nontraditional public schools also generate community-specific social capital. Since our research does not yield any empirical insights into whether other kinds of schools, in other kinds of neighborhoods, serve the community-building and neighborhood-stabilizing functions that Chicago's urban Catholic schools apparently serve, we withhold our final judgment on these questions until further research can be conducted.

55. William A. Fischel, *Making the Grade* (Chicago: University of Chicago Press, 2009): chap. 6.

56. Eugenia F. Toma et al., "Beyond Achievement: Enrollment Consequences of Charter Schools in Michigan," *Advances in Applied Microeconomics* 14 (2006): 241; Matthew Ladner, "The Impact of Charter Schools on Catholic Schools: A Comparison of Programs in Arizona and Michigan," *Catholic Education* 11 (2007): 102.

57. Current Establishment Clause doctrine does not prohibit states from funding secular schools that happen to be operated by religious institutions. See *Bowen v. Kendrick*, 487 U.S. 589, 619 (1988) (asserting that, in the Establishment Clause context, "it is not enough to show that the recipient of a challenged grant is affiliated with a religious institution or that it is 'religiously inspired'"). Indeed, many states do fund such schools in various contexts.

58. Dan M. Kahan, "Social Influence, Social Meaning, and Deterrence," *Virginia Law Review* 83 (1997): 389–91.

59. 536 U.S. 639 (2002).

60. *Everson v. Bd. of Educ.*, 330 U.S. 1 (1947)

61. *Bd. of Educ. v. Allen*, 392 U.S. 236 (1968).

62. *Mitchell v. Helms*, 530 U.S. 793 (2000) (plurality). *Mitchell v. Helms* overruled two

previous cases suggesting that the Establishment Clause prohibited direct aid—in both cases, instructional materials—that might be adapted for religious purposes. See *Meek v. Pittenger*, 421 U.S. 349 (1975); *Wolman v. Walter*, 433 U.S. 229 (1977).

63. *Agostini v. Felton*, 521 U.S. 203 (1997) (overruling *Aguilar v. Felton*, 473 U.S. 402 (1997)).

64. *Tilton v. Richardson*, 403 U.S. 1672 (1971).

65. *Lemon v. Kurtzman*, 403 U.S. 602, 636-37 (1971) ("A school which operates to commingle religion with other instruction plainly cannot completely secularize its instruction. Parochial schools, in large measure, do not accept the assumption that secular subjects should be unrelated to religious teaching."); *Bowen v. Kenrick*, 487 U.S. 589, 621-22 (1988) (observing that the Court has held "parochial schools" to be "pervasively sectarian"); *Meek v. Pittenger*, 421 U.S. 349, 363 (1975) ("[I]t would simply ignore reality to attempt to separate secular education functions from the predominantly religious role performed by many of Pennsylvania's church-related elementary and secondary schools.")

66. Chapter 2 of the Education Consolidation and Improvement Act of 1981, Pub. L. 97-35, 95 Stat. 469, as amended, 20 U.S.C. §§ 7301-7373, provides funds to state and local agencies to purchase educational materials and equipment. These recipients are required to lend the materials and equipment purchased with the funds to public and private schools on a per-student basis and must "assure equitable participation" of the students in private schools.

67. *Mitchell v. Helms*, 530 U.S. 793 (2000) (plurality).

68. *Meek*, 421 U.S. at 362-63; *Wolman*, 433 U.S. at 250.

69. *Mitchell*, 530 U.S. at 813 (quoting *Agostini*).

70. 521 U.S. 203 (1997). *Agostini* held that the Establishment Clause did not bar public school teachers from providing secular remedial education services in religious schools. In so doing, the Court overruled *Aguilar v. Felton*, 473 U.S. 401 (1985).

71. *Mitchell*, 530 U.S. at 816-17.

72. *Mitchell*, 530 U.S. at 837-38.

73. *Mitchell*, 530 U.S. at 837-38.

74. *Rendell-Baker v. Kuhn*, 457 U.S. 830 (1982); *Moose Lodge Number 107 v. Irvis*, 407 U.S. 163 (holding that state grant of a liquor license to a private club was not sufficient entanglement to make the club a state actor); *Jackson v. Metropolitan Edison Co.*, 419 U.S. 345 (1974) (holding that government regulation of a utility that possessed a state-granted monopoly did not make the utility a state actor).

75. "State Comparisons—State Policies for Charter Schools," The Education Commission of the States, http://www.ecs.org/html/offsite.asp?document=educationIssues/CharterSchools/CHDB_intro.asp.

76. *American Jewish Congress v. Corporation for National and Community Service*, 399 F.3d 351, 358 (2005).

77. "Archdiocese Gets OK to Create Two New Charter Schools," *The Criterion Online Edition*, http://www.archindy.org/criterion/local/2010/04-16/charter.html, accessed August 17, 2011.

78. Diane Ravitch, *The Death and Life of the Great American School System* (New York: Basic Books, 2010, 206.

CHAPTER NINE

1. Meribah Knight, "School on Probation Faces a Struggle," *New York Times*, April 21, 2011; Azam S. Ahmed, "Chicago Report Card Shows Many Schools Struggling," *Chicago Tribune*, September 9, 2010.

2. Brian Gill, Ron Zimmer, Jolley Christman, and Suzanne Blanc, *State Takeover, School Restructuring, Private Management, and Student Achievement in Philadelphia* (Rand Corp. 2007).

3. Susan Snyder and Kristen A. Graham, "Report Confirms Shortcomings in City Schools," *Philadelphia Inquirer*, Sept. 7, 2011.

4. Gregg Toppo, "Big-City Schools Struggle with Graduation Rates," *USA Today*, June 6, 2006.

5. Matthew P. Steinberg, Elaine Allensworth, and David W. Johnson, *Student and Teacher Safety in Chicago Public Schools: The Roles of Community Context and School Social Organization* (Consortium on Chicago School Research, 2011), 22–31.

6. Charles M. Payne, *So Much Reform, So Little Change* (Cambridge, MA: Harvard Education Press, 2008), 117.

7. Andrew M. Greeley, *Catholic High Schools and Minority Students* (Piscataway, NJ: Transaction Pubs., 1982), 108. See also James S. Coleman, Thomas Hoffer, and Sally Kilgore, *High School Achievement* (New York: Basic Books 1982). For a very thoroughly researched historical view, see Timothy Walch, *Parish School: A History of American Catholic Parochial Education from Colonial Times to the Present* (New York: Crossroad Publishing Co. 2003).

8. Derek Neal, "The Effect of Catholic Secondary Schooling on Educational Attainment," *Journal of Labor Economics* 15 (1997): 98. For a recent examination of one such school, and its success, see Patrick J. McCloskey, *The Street Stops Here: A Year at a Catholic High School in Harlem* (Berkeley: University of California Press, 2009).

9. Payne, *So Much Reform*, 117.

10. Rebecca R. Sohmer and Robert E. Lang, "Downtown Rebound," in 1 *Redefining Urban and Suburban America*, ed. Alan Berube, Bruce Katz, and Robert E. Lang (Washington, D.C: Brookings Institute, 2006), 51, 63, 65.

11. Richard C. Schragger, "Rethinking the Theory and Practice of Local Economic Development," *University of Chicago Law Review* 77 (2010): 311.

12. Edward L. Glaeser and Joshua D. Gottlieb, "Urban Resurgence and the Consumer City," *Urban Studies* 43, no. 8 (2006): 1275.

13. Joel Kotkin, "Uncool Cities," *Prospect Magazine*, October, 2005.

14. John Leland, "On a Hunt for Ways to Put Sex in the City," *New York Times*, December 11, 2003."

15. Richard Florida, *The Rise of the Creative Class* (New York, N.Y.: Basic Books 2002), 67–89, 287.

16. See Nicole Stelle Garnett, "Suburbs as Exit, Suburbs as Entrance," *Michigan Law Review* 106 (2007): 277, 290–92, 301.

17. Kotkin, "Uncool Cities."

18. See generally Robert J. Sampson, Stephen W. Raudenbush, and Felton Earls, "Neighborhoods and Violent Crime: A Multilevel Study of Collective Efficacy," *Science* 277 (1997): 918; Tracey L. Meares, *"Praying* for Community Policing," *California Law Review* 90 (2002): 1604.

19. See, e.g., Chris L. Gibson, Jihong Zhao, Nicholas P. Lovrich, and Michael J. Gaffney, "Social Integration, Individual Perceptions of Collective Efficacy and the Fear of Crime in Three Cities," *Justice Quarterly* 19 (2002): 540–42 (collecting literature); Matthew R. Lee and Terri L. Earnest, "Perceived Community Cohesion and Perceived Risk of Victimization," *Justice Quarterly* 20 (2003): 138; Pamela Wilcox, Neil Quisenberry, Debra T. Cabrera, and Shayne Jones, "Busy Places and Broken Windows? Toward Defining the Role of Physical Structure and Process in Community Crime Models" *Sociological Quarterly* 45 (2004): 185.

20. Sampson, Raudenbush, and Earls, "Neighborhoods and Violent Crime," 923. This is particularly important because crime and the fear of crime tend to undermine residential stability. See Julie Berry Cullen and Steven D. Levitt, "Crime, Urban Flight, and the Consequences for Cities," *Review of Economics and Statistics* 81 (1999); 159–69; Robert J. Sampson and John D. Wooldredge, "Evidence that High Crime Rates Encourage Migration away from Central Cities," *Sociology and Social Research* 70, no. 4 (July 1986): 310–14.

21. See, e.g., Robert J. Sampson and Stephen W. Raudenbush, "Systematic Social Observation of Public Spaces: A New Look at Disorder in Public Places," *American Journal of Sociology* 105 (1999): 610.

22. Gibson et al., "Social Integration," 552.

23. See generally Arnold R. Hirsch, *Making the Second Ghetto: Race and Housing in Chicago, 1940–1960* (Chicago: University of Chicago Press, 1983); Thomas J. Sugrue, *The Origins of the Urban Crisis: Race and Inequality in Postwar Detroit* (Princeton, NJ: Princeton University Press 1996); John T. McGreevy, *Parish Boundaries: The Catholic Encounter with Race in the Twentieth-Century Urban North* (Chicago: University of Chicago Press, 1996).

24. See Gerald Gamm, *Urban Exodus: Why the Jews Left Boston and the Catholics Stayed* (Cambridge, MA: Harvard University Press,1999), 25–29; Robert Bruegmann, *Sprawl: A Compact History* (Chicago: University of Chicago Press, 2005), 24–50.

25. See generally Kenneth T. Jackson, *Crabgrass Frontier: The Suburbanization of the United States* (Oxford University Press, 1985), 73–133.

26. See Gamm, *Urban Exodus*, 24–27. For similar evidence in the Midwest, see McGreevy, *Parish Boundaries*.

27. See George Galster, Jackie Cutsinger, and Jason C. Booza, *Where Did They Go?: The Decline of Middle-Income Neighborhoods in Metropolitan America* 1, 4, 9–11 (Washington, D.C.: Brookings Institution, 2006), http://www.brook.edu/metro/pubs/20060622_middleclass .htm.

28. While concentrated urban poverty declined dramatically during the 1990s, central cities continue to contain a disproportionate number of poor families. See Paul A. Jargowsky, "Stunning Progress, Hidden Problems: The Dramatic Decline of Concentrated Poverty in the 1990s," in 2 *Redefining Urban and Suburban America* ((Washington, D.C: Brookings Institution, 2005), 137; Alan Berube and William H. Frey, "A Decade of Mixed Blessings: Urban and Suburban Poverty in the 1990s," in 2 *Redefining Urban and Suburban America*, 111.

29. For disheartening evidence that racial and ethnic diversity reduces social capital, see Robert D. Putnam, *"E Pluribus Unum*: Diversity and Community in the Twenty-first Century," *Scandinavian Political Studies* 30 (2007): 137.

30. See William H. Frey, "Melting Pot Suburbs: A 'Census 2000' Study of Suburban Diversity," in 1 *Redefining Urban and Suburban America*, 159–65.

31. See, e.g., Cullen and Levitt, "Crime, Urban Flight, and the Consequences for Cities," 159–69; Sampson and Wooldredge, "Evidence That High Crime Rates Encourage Migration."

32. See, e.g., Richard Briffault, "The Rise of Sublocal Structures in Urban Governance," *Minnesota Law Review* 82 (1997): 503.

33. See, e.g., Debra Livingston, "Police Discretion and the Quality of Life in Public Places: Courts, Communities and the New Policing," *Columbia Law Review* 97 (1997): 551; George L. Kelling and Catherine M. Coles, *Fixing Broken Windows: Restoring Order and Reducing Crime in Our Communities* (New York: Free Press 1996).

34. See, e.g., Bruegmann, *Sprawl*, 69–70.

35. See, e.g., David P. Varady and Jeffrey A. Raffel, *Selling Cities: Attracting Home-Buyers through Schools and Housing Programs* (SUNY 1995), 138–73.

36. See, e.g., William A. Fischel, "Why Voters Veto Vouchers: Public Schools and Community-Specific Social Capital," *Economics of Governance* 7 (2006): 117–18.

37. Jack Buckley and Mark Schneider, "School Choice, Parental Information, and Tiebout Sorting: Evidence from Washington, D.C.," in *The Tiebout Model at Fifty: Essays in Honor of Wallace Oats*, ed. William A. Fischel (Cambridge, MA: Lincoln Institute 2006), 101, 104.

38. Buckley and Schneider, "School Choice."

39. See, e.g., *Parents Involved in Community Schools v. Seattle School District*, 551 U.S. 701 (2007); *Wessmann v. Gittens*, 160 F.3d 790 (1st Cir. 1998).

40. Between 1993 and 2003, the percentage of students attending a "chosen" public school increased from 11 to 15 percent. "Fast Facts," National Center for Education Statistics, http://nces.ed.gov/FastFacts/display.asp?id=6.

41. In fall 2008, 1.4 million children were enrolled in more than 4,600 charter schools. "Public Charter School Dashboard," National Alliance for Public Charter Schools, http://www.publiccharters.org/dashboard/home. President Obama has made charter schools a centerpiece of his educational agenda and has urged states to lift caps on the number of available charters. See David Stout, "Obama Outlines Plan for Education Overhaul," *New York Times*, March 11, 2009.

42. Buckley and Schneider, "School Choice," 103–20 (presenting evidence that school choice/charter schools transform the traditional "move for schools" dynamic to a "move schools" paradigm).

43. See, e.g., Gerald E. Frug and David J. Barron, *City Bound: How States Stifle Urban Innovation* (Ithaca, NY: Cornell University Press, 2008), 128–29 (providing statistics on private school enrollment in several major cities); Ingrid Gould Ellen, Amy Ellen Schwartz, and Leanna Stiefel," Can Economically Integrated Neighborhoods Improve Children's Educational Outcomes?" in *Urban and Regional Policy and Its Effects*, ed. Margery Austin Turner, Howard Wial, and Harold Wolman (Washington, D.C.: Brookings Institution, 2008), 200 (noting that, in 2000, 18.4 percent of elementary and secondary students in New York City were enrolled in private schools and that the probability of private school attendance increases as income levels rise).

44. U.S. Census Bureau News, *Household Income Rises, Poverty Rate Unchanged*, Aug. 26, 2008, http://www.census.gov/Press-Release/www/releases/archives/income_wealth/012528.html (reporting that the real median income in 2007 was $50,233).

Index